# THE BIBLE BELIEVER'S HANDBOOK

THE BIBLE BELIEVER'S

# Handbook

LARRY VAUGHN

HighWay
A Division of Anomalos Publishing House
Crane

HighWay
A division of Anomalos Publishing House, Crane 65633
 Published 2008
Printed in the United States of America
08 1
ISBN-10: 0981495788 (paper)

EAN-13: 9780981495781 (paper)

Karen Ruff, Editor

Cover illustration and design by Steve Warner

All Bible quotations are from the King James Version unless otherwise noted.

A CIP catalog record for this book is available from the Library of Congress.

To Marie

# TABLE OF CONTENTS



## Part One: The Things of God



## Part Two: Things God Expects You To Do

## Part Three: Good Things

## Part Four: Evil Things



## Part Five: Life's Losers

# INTRODUCTION

The Bible Believer's Handbook is for everyone who believes that the Bible is the word of God. It is intended to help the Bible believer live a life that is pleasing to God. It contains many great passages from the Bible, verses that every believer needs to know. It is a feast of spiritual food for those who hunger for the knowledge of God, for ideas that originated in the mind of God. Taste God's word for yourself and see how excellent it is. Nothing can compare to the beauty of God's word.

When ordinary people could read the Bible on their own, they turned the world upside down. The first American settlers were Bible believers. They left behind the people who persecuted them and founded their own nation. They based it on God's word, and granted freedom of religion to everyone. Liberty and freedom are God's ideas and they are his gifts to you. The Founding Fathers were Bible believers. Because of this, they gave you the freedom of religion, speech and free assembly that you enjoy today. John Adams said, "Our Constitution was made only for a moral and religious people. It is wholly inadequate to the government of any other."[1]

The Founding Fathers also understood these words by William Penn, "Men must be governed by God, or they will be ruled by tyrants." This same principle applies to you in your personal life. You are either being governed by God, or dominated by Satan. There is no middle ground. In the Old Testament, God called his people "Israel." That name literally means "governed by God." Today, God's people are those who submit themselves to him. The Bible Believer's Handbook will tell you how to be governed by God.

---

1. John Adams, *The Works of John Adams, Second President of the United States,* Charles Francis Adams, editor (Boston: Little, Brown, and Co. 1854), Vol. IX, p. 229, October 11, 1798.

My father-in-law was a farmer in Mississippi in the Thirties. He told me what it was like to live back then. Nobody had insurance. But they didn't need it. They had something better. If a man's house burned down, his neighbors would come over and help him build a new one. And he would do the same for them. They weren't expecting anything in return. They did it because they loved their neighbor, like the Bible says. They knew the Bible. They believed it and they lived it.

I went to public school in the 1950s. In those days, a man's word was his bond. Most people were honest. Merchants and tradesmen "treated you right." Most of the people you met were Christians, or claimed to be. Schoolteachers were held to a high moral standard. Most of them were Bible believers. The Bible was part of their teaching because it was part of their everyday lives. Some of them had us answer the roll call by quoting a Bible verse. They taught us the Golden Rule. Those teachers were free to express their belief in God and in the Bible. They weren't ashamed for people to know they were Christians. They prayed with us. We were the last generation to be treated so well. We have witnessed the destruction of the unique American culture. "E pluribus Unum," the concept of unity arising from diversity has been discarded. Now we get to celebrate our diversity while we disagree on everything. The world considers worshipping a pagan idol to be the moral equivalent of worshipping the God of the Bible. But Americans have always believed in the living God. It was generally accepted that the Bible defines what is right and what is wrong. Now we have conflicting ideas embedded in our society. The secularists continue to teach our children lies instead of the truth, such as the idea that God does not exist and that nothing is either right or wrong. These lies have replaced the truth. Because America has heard these ideas so many times, she has accepted them as true. Without her foundation of Biblical morality, America is becoming just like all the other nations.

The Bible is the most influential book in history. In the recent past, people who had no knowledge of the Bible were considered uneducated. Early schools focused on teaching children to read so they could read the Bible. Our most prestigious universities, Harvard, Yale, and

Princeton were founded for the specific purpose of training ministers of the Gospel. The Bible is the foundation on which America stands. The marvelous word of God has permeated our society. It affects everything we say and do, and everything we think. God's word lives in our hearts and minds. It is the word of God that has made our American culture wonderful and unique.

The secularists seized control of our culture in the 1960s. It was in 1962, that the Supreme Court banned prayer in public schools. They prohibited Bible reading in the classroom in June of 1963. Before that year had ended, the President of the United States was brutally murdered. When our government officially rejected God, he withdrew his protection from it. Since that time our nation has spiraled in a moral decline.

Now students are killing other students in atrocities that baffle authorities and horrify even the most seasoned journalists Maybe it is because teachers are not allowed to teach them, "Thou shalt not kill." That is one of the Ten Commandments. Since 1980, it has been illegal to post a copy of the Ten Commandments in schools. Educators are afraid that these ideas might offend those students who are not a part of our Christian culture. Have you ever noticed that the only ideas that are actually censored are God's ideas? And that the only voice that is being silenced is God's voice. The same court system that tells the Bible believers of America to be silent upholds the rights of pornographers to "freedom of speech." That is how crazy and inconsistent the world is.

If you want to make a difference in this world, devote yourself to the cause of Christ. Instead of trying to change everyone else, change yourself. Learn God's word. Teach it to others, especially your children. Teach them to do right, to respect authority, and to speak evil of no one. You can help save the world, one person at a time.

Many people spend their lives looking for something to believe in, something beautiful and true. They have no idea that they're looking for Jesus. He's real. He's alive and he loves you. The Bible is all about him.

People who are successful in life have these things in common.

They're people of integrity. They know the Bible. They believe it, and they live it. It comes to life in them. It affects all of their decisions and their relationships.

When a man rejects God, it shows. He'll find something else to be his god, something he considers worthy of his devotion. Idealists choose gods such as art, science, journalism, or liberalism. The less noble prefer alcohol, drugs, money, sex, and power. They love these things so much that they make them their gods. They allow these idols to take God's place in their hearts. By worshipping false gods, they guarantee their own destruction.

The world hates you for believing the Bible. It hates you because you belong to Jesus. When you express your faith, you will be persecuted. The Lord is your protector. But you must stay in fellowship with him in order to survive and prosper. And you must teach your children to do the same.

You have to learn the Bible for yourself before you can teach it to anyone else.

> Study to show yourself approved unto God, a workman that need not be ashamed, rightly dividing the word of truth. (2 Timothy 2:15)

> And these words, which I command thee this day, shall be in thine heart: And thou shalt teach them diligently unto thy children, and shalt talk of them when thou sittest in thine house, and when thou walkest by the way, and when thou liest down, and when thou risest up. (Deuteronomy 6:6–7)

If you will follow these instructions from the Lord, you will be successful and prosper in everything you do.

> This book of the law shall not depart out of thy mouth; but thou shalt meditate therein day and night, that thou mayest observe to do according to all that is written therein: for

**then thou shalt make thy way prosperous, and then thou shalt have good success. (Joshua 1:8)**

This is what Jesus commanded you to do in Matthew 28:19–20. It's called the Great Commission. "Go ye therefore, and teach all nations… Teaching them to observe all things whatsoever I have commanded you." What are the rest of the things he commanded you to do? They can all be found within the pages of the Bible Believer's Handbook.

Your spirit is the part of you that comes from God. Your flesh is your humanity. In your mind there's a war between your flesh and your spirit. The one who's winning the war gets to run your life. Your flesh is the most dangerous opponent that you'll ever face. It has two allies, the world and the devil. Your spirit has much more powerful allies, God the Father, Jesus, and the Holy Spirit. When you obey God, he makes his power available to you. The Holy Spirit will assist you in overcoming every obstacle the enemy throws against you.

While I was working on this book, something happened to me. I spent a great deal of time with these words expressed by the Author of life. They changed the way I think. I feel as though I know God personally. I have a strong desire to please him by doing everything he says. My prayer for you, dear Reader, is that you will have the same experience.

# HOW TO USE THIS BOOK

The Bible Believer's Handbook is a study guide and a reference book. It contains essential Bible verses that you need to know. They're the most important part of the book. They're like precious stones, and my words are just a showcase for them. After you have read a topic, familiarize yourself with every Bible verse contained in it. Some parts of God's word will jump out at you and capture your attention. The Holy Spirit will cause you to remember some parts of it later. Whenever you find yourself thinking of a Bible verse, look it up in the Bible. Read the entire chapter where it appears. There will be something in those scriptures that applies to your own personal life. This is one way God reveals to you the things he wants you to know.

The Bible Believer's Handbook is divided into five parts. Part One explains some of the things that God has provided for you. Part Two is a list of things he expects you to do. Part Three describes some good things that result from obeying God's word. Part Four contains some of the evil things that are consequences of disobeying it. Part Five is a list of people who never receive the things God had in store for them.

Here, the Bible speaks for itself, or, rather God speaks for himself. The topics were derived from the ideas expressed within each batch of verses. These are subjects that God has addressed in the Bible. He's the true Author of this book, just as he's the Author of the Bible and the Author of life. I cannot take any credit for any of it. All of the glory, honor, and praise properly belong to the Lord Jesus Christ.

Repeated exposure to the word of God causes people to change. Read this book aloud to the people you love—your wife, your husband, and your children. They will love you for it. Even more importantly, they will fall in love with the Lord. He is irresistible.

PART ONE

# The Things of God

**Now we have received, not the spirit of the world, but the spirit which is of God; that we might know the things that are freely given to us of God. (1 Corinthians 2:12)**

Consider what the Bible says in Romans 8:32. "He that spareth not his own Son, but delivered him up for us all, how shall he not with him also freely give us all things?" God gave you his best gift first. Jesus is more valuable than everything on earth.

Second Peter 1:3 says that, through Jesus, God has given us "all things that pertain to life and godliness." Part One lists some of the things that God has provided for you.

## THE BLESSING OF THE LORD

The people mentioned in the Bible are not fictional characters. They actually lived. The things that happened to them represent spiritual challenges that you will encounter in your life. When God met his people at Mount Sinai, he promised that if they would obey him, he would bless them. This was a renewal of the blessing that he had bestowed on Abraham. This same blessing is available to you today. If you obey God's commandments, you will receive the blessing of the Lord.

This is God's original promise to his people.

> The Lord shall command the blessing upon thee in thy storehouses, and in all that thou settest thine hand unto; and he shall bless thee in the land which the Lord thy God giveth thee. The Lord shall establish thee an holy people unto himself, and he hath sworn unto thee, if thou shalt keep the commandments of the Lord thy God, and walk in his ways. (Deuteronomy 28:8–9)

The Bible goes into great detail in describing everything that is included in this blessing. It also mentions there is a curse that comes from disobeying God. The curse is the reverse or the opposite of the blessing. You must choose whether you will receive the blessing or the curse.

> I have set before you life and death, blessing and cursing: therefore choose life, that both thou and thy seed may live. (Deuteronomy 30:19)

This Psalm tells you what God expects from you. These are the requirements for receiving the blessing of the Lord.

> He that hath clean hands, and a pure heart; who hath not lifted up his soul unto vanity, nor sworn deceitfully. He shall

> **receive the blessing from the Lord, and righteousness from the God of his salvation. (Psalm 24:4–5)**

The blessing of the Lord extends to your children.

> **He will bless them that fear the Lord, both small and great. The Lord shall increase you more and more, you and your children. Ye are blessed of the Lord which made heaven and earth. The heaven, even the heavens, are the Lord's: but the earth hath he given to the children of men. (Psalm 115:13–16)**

The blessing of the Lord will make you rich. There will be no sorrow connected with the riches you receive from God.

> **The blessing of the Lord, it maketh rich, and he addeth no sorrow with it. (Proverbs 10:22)**

## THE BLOOD

Jesus was born of a virgin for a reason. The curse of sin and death is passed on to the children through the blood of the father, not the mother. Because Jesus did not have a human father, he did not inherit Adam's curse of sin and death. Jesus is the Son of God, and the Second Adam. He is the seed of the woman who has bruised the head of Satan.

Jesus' blood is the most valuable substance in the universe. How does it affect you personally? His blood is the evidence of the sacrifice he made for you. In Egypt, the death angel "passed over" the house to which the blood of an innocent sacrifice was applied. The Last Supper was a celebration of the Passover. Jesus explained that the wine symbolizes his blood. "For this is my blood of the new testament, which is shed for many for the remission of sins." (Matthew 26:28) "…Ye are not your own…but are bought with a price." (1 Corinthians 6:19–20) Jesus' blood is that price. He died so that you can live. You receive the benefit of his shed blood. It atones for your soul, and it covers all your sins.

"Atonement" is payment for a debt that is owed.

> For the life of the flesh is in the blood: and I have given it to you upon the altar to make an atonement for your souls: for it is the blood that maketh an atonement for the soul. (Leviticus 17:11)

Here Paul was speaking to a Gentile audience. They had no access to God, but Jesus made a way to save them. This is the same situation you were in before Jesus came into your life.

> That at that time ye were without Christ, being aliens from the commonwealth of Israel, and strangers from the covenants of promise, having no hope, and without God in the world: But now, in Christ Jesus ye who sometime were far off are made nigh by the blood of Christ. (Ephesians 2:12–13)

Innocent animals were sacrificed to God under the Old Covenant. Their blood was a symbol of the blood of Jesus that was to come. His sacrifice of blood changed your eternal destiny. It is a perfect sacrifice that he has already offered on behalf of everyone who believes in him.

> How much more shall the blood of Christ, who through the eternal Spirit offered himself without spot to God, purge your own conscience from dead works to serve the living God? And for this cause he is the mediator of the new testament, that by means of death, for the redemption of the transgressions that were under the first testament, they which are called might receive the promise of eternal inheritance. (Hebrews 9:14–15)

When you realize how much sin costs, you will avoid it. When you realize how much God loves you, you will stay close to him, and stay in touch with other believers.

> **This then is the message which we have heard of him, and declare unto you, that God is light, and in him is no darkness at all. If we say that we have fellowship with him, and walk in darkness, we lie, and do not the truth: But if we walk in the light, as he is in the light, we have fellowship one with another, and the blood of Jesus Christ his son cleanseth us from all sin. (1 John 1:5–7)**

## CHILDREN

I was raising and lowering my grandson Jack in the air when I heard him laugh out loud for the first time. His expression of joy and delight caused me great joy and delight. That is the way it is with you and God. He loves you the same way you love your children. When you express your joy, you bring him joy. God wanted so many children that they would be innumerable. He sent Jesus, to fulfill this vision. Now you are one of his children. He loves you as much as he loves Jesus.

I am a happy man. I have the greatest wife in the world. Her name is Marie, and God gave her to me. We have been married for more than forty years. God blessed us with three lovely daughters, Donna, Shawna, and Jennifer. He has further blessed us with ten grandchildren —Michael, Jason, Sarah, Haley, Jacob, Beverly, Katie, Adam, Jack, and Connor.

I know from my own life experience that these verses are true. My children and grandchildren have certainly made me happy.

> **As arrows are in the hand of a mighty man; so are children of the youth. Happy is the man that hath his quiver full of them: they shall not be ashamed, but they shall speak with the enemies in the gate. (Psalm 127:3–5)**

Loving and being loved by my grandchildren is my greatest pleasure in life.

> **Children's children are the crown of old men; and the glory of children are their fathers. (Proverbs 17:6)**

The best thing you will ever do for your children is to teach them God's concepts. When they learn God's word as children, they will never forget it. As the twig is bent, so grows the tree.

> **Train up a child in the way he should go: and when he is old, he will not depart from it. (Proverbs 22:6)**

Your children will have peace because they are doing things God's way.

> **And all thy children shall be taught of the Lord; and great shall be the peace of thy children. (Isaiah 54:13)**

When you become a parent, you have to stop acting like a child.

> **When I was a child, I spake as a child, I understood as a child, I thought as a child: but when I became a man, I put away childish things. (1 Corinthians 13:11)**

Do not have an emotional response to everything that happens. If you react to every situation with anger, your children will too. When they become parents, they will teach their children to do the same thing.

> **And, ye fathers, provoke not your children to wrath: but bring them up in the nurture and admonition of the Lord. (Ephesians 6:4)**

## COMMANDMENTS

If you had gone to public school in the 1950s, you would have been taught the Golden Rule. "Do unto others as you would have them do unto you." That is actually a paraphrase of Matthew 7:12, "Therefore all things whatsoever ye would that men should do to you, do ye even so to them: for this is the law and the prophets."

The Golden Rule is a practical way of loving your neighbor as much as you love yourself. The Lord empowers you to keep this rule. He provides you with the love you need. Loving others mostly consists of being nice to people, and overlooking their shortcomings.

The Golden Rule is the secret of success in every area of life, from business to marriage. Most people only care about themselves. They spend their time talking about themselves and looking out for their own interests. They like you when you pay attention to them.

The Golden Rule works both ways. It can help you or it can hurt you, because you are going to get back what you give out. Most people are going to treat you the same way you have treated them. Show them some respect and they will respect you back in return. When you love other people, they will usually reciprocate.

Do you want to live a long life that is filled with peace? Are you willing to pay the price to enjoy this kind of life?

> **My son, forget not my law; but let thine heart keep my commandments: For length of days, and long life, and peace, shall they add to thee. (Proverbs 3:1–2)**

Jesus said, keep these two commandments and everything else will take care of itself. All the law is based on them. You love God by loving your neighbor. When you love your neighbor, you are not going to murder him. You're not going to steal from him, cheat him, or do anything else to hurt him.

> **Master, which is the great commandment in the law? Jesus said unto him, Thou shalt love the Lord thy God with all thy**

> heart, and with all thou soul, and with all thy mind. This is the first and great commandment. And the second is like unto it, Thou shalt love thy neighbor as thyself. On these two commandments hang all the law and the prophets. (Matthew 22:36–40)

Jesus simplified commandment-keeping. He really gave you just one commandment to keep. If you are able to accomplish that, it shows you are a disciple of Jesus.

> A new commandment I give unto you, That ye love one another; as I have loved you, that ye also love one another. By this shall all men know that ye are my disciples, if ye have love one to another. (John 13:34–35)

Jesus did not do away with the law. He fulfilled it. When you are keeping the Love Commandment, you are fulfilling the law just like Jesus.

> Owe no man anything, but to love one another: for he that loveth another hath fulfilled the law. For this, Thou shalt not commit adultery, Thou shalt not kill, Thou shalt not steal, Thou shalt not bear false witness, Thou shalt not covet; and if there be any other commandment, it is briefly comprehended in this saying, namely, Thou shalt love thy neighbor as thyself. Love worketh no ill to his neighbor: therefore love is the fulfilling of the law. (Romans 13:8–10)

Focus your attention on keeping the Lord's commandment. You have the ability to fulfill the word of God.

> And this is his commandment, That we should believe on the name of his Son Jesus Christ, and love one another, as he gave us commandment. (1 John 3:23)

## CORRECTION

You discipline your child until he learns to discipline himself. God does the same thing for you. He treats you like a son, and teaches you by correcting you. You have the freedom to do whatever you want. You can things God's way and show him that you love him. He wants you to control your own thoughts, your words and your actions. That is what makes you a disciple, a "disciplined one."

Because he loves you, God treats you like his own dear child.

> **Thou shalt also consider in thine heart, that, as a man chasteneth his son, so the Lord thy God chasteneth thee. (Deuteronomy 8:5)**

This is God's promise to you.

> **I will instruct thee and teach thee in the way which thou shalt go: I will guide thee with mine eye. Be ye not as the horse, or as the mule, which have no understanding; whose mouth must be held in with bit and bridle. (Psalm 32:8–9)**

God also promises that he will correct you if you rebel against him.

> **If his children forsake my law, and walk not in my judgments; if they break my statutes, and keep not my commandments; then will I visit their transgression with the rod, and their iniquity with stripes. Nevertheless my loving—kindness will I not utterly take from him, nor suffer my faithfulness to fail. My covenant will I not break, nor alter the thing that is gone out of my lips. (Psalm 89:30–33)**

God is your Father. He disciplines you because he loves you.

> **My son, despise not the chastening of the Lord; neither be weary of his correction: For whom the Lord loveth he**

> correcteth; even as a father the son in whom he delighteth. (Proverbs 3:11–12)

Disciplining children is part of loving them. Swatting a child on the rear is not child abuse. It's the proper response to willful rebellion. The "rod" of correction is more figurative than literal. Children try you to see if you will consistently enforce your rules. When they learn that disobedience always causes pain, they will do what is right.

> He that spareth his rod hateth his son: but he that loveth him chasteneth him betimes. (Proverbs 13:24)

God's correction is not harsh, but gentle. He guides you in the right direction.

> And thine ears shall hear a word behind thee, saying, This is the way, walk ye in it, when ye turn to the right hand, and when ye turn to the left. (Isaiah 30:21)

There's always a penalty for doing things your way instead of God's.

> Thine own wickedness shall correct thee, and thy backslidings shall reprove thee: know therefore and see that it is an evil thing and bitter, that thou hast forsaken the Lord thy God, and that my fear is not in thee, saith the Lord God of hosts. (Jeremiah 2:19)

You are God's child, and he loves you. Do not be surprised when he corrects you for being disobedient.

> And ye have forgotten the exhortation which speaketh unto you as unto children, My son, despise not thou the chastening of the Lord, nor faint when thou art rebuked of him: For whom the Lord loveth he chasteneth, and scourgeth every son whom he receiveth. If ye endure

> **chastening, God dealeth with you as with sons; for what son is he whom the father chasteneth not? But if ye be without chastisement, whereof all are partakers, then are ye bastards, and not sons. (Hebrews 12:5–8)**

These are Jesus' words from the Book of Revelation. He would like to make you rich, but you are limiting what he can do for you. You cannot receive anything from God while you are breaking his rules.

> **Because thou sayest, I am rich, and increased with goods, and have need of nothing; and knowest not that thou art wretched, and miserable, and poor, and blind, and naked: I counsel thee to buy of me gold tried in the fire, that thou mayest be rich; and white raiment, that thou mayest be clothed, and that the shame of thy nakedness do not appear; and anoint thine eyes with eye salve, that thou mayest see. As many as I love, I rebuke and chasten: be zealous therefore, and repent. (Revelation 3:17–19)**

## THE DESIRE OF YOUR HEART

Did you know that God will give you the things you desire? That is what Jesus said in Mark 11:24 "What things soever ye desire, when ye pray, believe that ye receive them, and ye shall have them." What do you have to do to receive these things? Have faith in the Lord, that he keeps his word. Have the confidence that comes from obedience to God. What are the desires of your heart? God will reveal them to you. They certainly would include love, peace, joy, and fellowship with God. The heart that is right toward God gets what it desires.

When your heart is pure, and you are in fellowship with God, you will not ask for things you cannot have that are outside the will of God. "Selah" is a direction to pause and fully realize what you have heard.

> **Thou hast given him his heart's desire, and hast not withholden the request of his lips. Selah. (Psalm 21:2)**

As long as you are doing right, you can expect good things from God.

> The desire of the righteous is only good: but the expectation of the wicked is wrath. (Proverbs 12:23)

Delight in the Lord, and you'll know the specific desires of your heart. Commit yourself to him and trust him. Then he will cause those things to happen. Your relationship with God will be apparent to everyone.

> Delight thyself also in the Lord; and he shall give thee the desires of thine heart. Commit thy way unto the Lord; trust also in him; and he shall bring it to pass. And he shall bring forth thy righteousness as the light, and thy judgment as the noonday. (Psalm 37:4–6)

You show your reverence for the Lord by doing what He says in his word. You have to follow his instructions before he will fulfill the desires of your heart.

> The Lord is righteous in all his ways, and holy in all his works. The Lord is nigh unto all them that call upon him, to all that call upon him in truth. He will fulfill the desire of them that fear him: he also will hear their cry, and will save them. The Lord preserveth all them that love him: but all the wicked will he destroy. My mouth shall speak the praise of the Lord: and let all flesh bless his holy name for ever and ever. (Psalm 145:17–21)

This verse explains that fear is the opposite of faith. It causes evil things to happen, just as faith in God causes good things to happen.

> The fear of the wicked, it shall come upon him: but the desire of the righteous shall be granted. (Proverbs 10:24)

## ETERNAL LIFE

Eternal life is the kind of life God has. It is far superior to ordinary human life. It is spiritual life that goes on forever. The Bible tells that this new kind of life is only available through Jesus Christ. Though your mortal body will die, your soul and spirit will continue to live with him.

In this passage, Jesus explained this concept of spiritual birth to a religious leader named Nicodemus. These well-known verses make one thing clear. Believing in Jesus gives you life.

> **And as Moses lifted up the serpent in the wilderness, even so must the Son of man be lifted up: that whosoever believeth in him should not perish, but have eternal life. For God so loved the world, that he gave his only begotten Son, that whosoever believeth in him should not perish, but have everlasting life. (John 3:14–16)**

The Bible is the written word of God. And it is all about Jesus, the Living Word of God. The Holy Spirit speaks of him throughout the Bible.

> **Search the scriptures: for in them ye think ye have eternal life: and they are they which testify of me. (John 5:39)**

Eternal life is a gift from God. You do not have to earn it.

> **For the wages of sin is death; but the gift of God is eternal life through Jesus Christ our Lord. (Romans 6:23)**

This verse reveals the truth that Eternal Life is a Person. And that Person is Jesus.

> **And we know that the Son of God is come, and hath given us an understanding, that we may know him that is true,**

**and we are in him that is true, even in his Son Jesus Christ. This is the true God, and eternal life. (1 John 5:20)**

## THE FAITH

"The Faith" is the doctrine of Jesus Christ as it is revealed in the Bible. It includes his teachings, the things he has commanded you to do, and valuable information concerning fellowship with him. It is God's own truth about his Son, and it enables you to know him by knowing his ways. The purpose of the Bible is to introduce you to Jesus and to teach you the things you need to know about him. Many truths throughout the Bible fit together to reveal what he is like, what he thinks, and what he has done for you. Your only access to God is through faith in Jesus. Jesus has made a way for you to benefit from his sinless life and to participate in his perfect sacrifice. If you believe God's testimony concerning his Son and apply his ideas to your life, then you are in "the faith."

You can easily tell for yourself whether or not you are in the faith. Either you have the Holy Spirit living in you, or you do not. A "reprobate" is someone who does not meet this requirement for being in the faith.

**Examine yourselves, whether ye be in the faith; prove your own selves. Know ye not your own selves that Jesus Christ is in you, except ye be reprobates? (2 Corinthians 13:5)**

When you are in the faith, Jesus will come to live in you and empower you to live by faith.

**I am crucified with Christ: nevertheless I live; yet not I, but Christ liveth in me: and the life which I now live in the flesh I live by the faith of the Son of God, who loved me, and gave himself for me. (Galatians 2:20)**

To "depart from the faith" is to abandon the doctrine of Christ and accept some idea that exalts itself against the knowledge of God.

> Now the Spirit speaketh expressly, that in the latter times some shall depart from the faith, giving heed to seducing spirits, and doctrines of devils; (1 Timothy 4:1)

Your behavior will reveal whether you are in the faith, or not. If your family is in need and you ignore them, it's likely that the Spirit of God is not alive in you. God is love and he will cause you to have mercy and compassion for those in need.

> But if any provide not for his own, and specially for those of his own house, he hath denied the faith, and is worse than an infidel. (1 Timothy 5:8)

Your most valuable resource is the Bible. Everything you need to know can be found within its pages. It will teach you how to live in the faith. It will cause you to continue in a right relationship and favor with God and man. It will cause you to prosper and be in health.

> But continue thou in the things which thou hast learned and hast been assured of, knowing of whom thou hast learned them; and that from a child thou hast known the holy scriptures, which are able to make thee wise unto salvation through faith which is in Christ Jesus. All scripture is given by inspiration of God, and is profitable for doctrine, for reproof, for correction, for instruction in righteousness: that the man of God may be perfect, thoroughly furnished unto all good works. (2 Timothy 3:14–17)

When you are in the faith, you are different from the people of the world. It is easy to love people who are like you racially or socially. However, when you are in the faith, you are impartial in your love for others.

> My brethren, have not the faith of our Lord Jesus Christ, the Lord of glory, with respect of persons. For if there

> come unto your assembly a man with a gold ring, in goodly apparel, and there come in also a poor man in vile raiment; And ye have respect to him that weareth the gay clothing, and say unto him, Sit thou here in a good place; and say to the poor, Stand thou there, or sit here under my footstool: Are ye not then partial in yourselves, and are become judges of evil thoughts? (James 2:1–4)

The truth is something that never changes. Jesus Christ is the same yesterday, today, and forever. The Bible is not really difficult to understand. It had to be written by men, but God told them what to say. It does not need to be re-interpreted by modern man.

> Knowing this first, that no prophecy of the scripture is of any private interpretation. For the prophecy came not in old time by the will of man: but holy men of God spake as they were moved by the Holy Ghost. (2 Peter 1:20–21)

## FORGIVENESS OF ALL SINS

Under the Old Covenant, you had to keep the Law of Moses or die. Technically it would be impossible for you to keep from breaking some small part of it. God's point is that you are a sinner and you need a Savior who will do for you what you cannot possibly do for yourself. Jesus paid your death penalty so you won't have to pay it. All your sins are forgiven—past, present, and future. Because you have received him as your Savior, you will live forever. God has raised you from the dead to a new and different kind of life.

This passage celebrates the mercy of God. He has done away with the punishment for your sins.

> The Lord is merciful and gracious, slow to anger, and plenteous in mercy. He will not always chide: neither will he keep his anger for ever. He hath not dealt with us after our sins; nor rewarded us according to our iniquities. For as

> the heaven is high above the earth, so great is his mercy toward them that fear him. As far as the east is from the west, so far hath he removed our transgressions from us. (Psalm 103:8–12)

God says in Isaiah that he not only forgives your sins, but he also forgets them.

> I, even I, am he that blotteth out thy transgressions for mine own sake, and will not remember thy sins. (Isaiah 43:25)

These words were written centuries before Jesus was born in the flesh. Micah spoke of God's great mercy in disposing of all your sins.

> Who is a God like unto thee, that pardoneth iniquity, and passeth by the transgression of the remnant of his heritage? He retaineth not his anger for ever, because he delighteth in mercy. He will turn again, he will have compassion upon us; he will subdue our iniquities; and thou wilt cast all their sins into the depths of the sea. (Micah 7:18–19)

Paul preached this sermon at Antioch. He explained that there is no forgiveness of sins apart from Jesus.

> Be it known unto you therefore, men and brethren, that through this man is preached unto you the forgiveness of sins: And by him all that believe are justified from all things, from which ye could not be justified by the law of Moses. (Acts 13:38–39)

Sin is an attitude of the heart. To confess your sins is to agree with God that you have sinned. God can create a clean heart and renew a right spirit within you.

> If we confess our sins, he is faithful and just to forgive us our sins, and to cleanse us from all unrighteousness. (1 John 1:9)

## GOD'S HELP

Being in fellowship with God is similar to being on the internet with him. When you talk to him, he will answer. You have to stay on-line with him because you need him all the time. God knows you and loves you. When you ask for help, he will respond. Do not wait until you have a major problem, and then come running to God. Do not avoid him because of sin. As soon as you realize that you have committed a sin, ask him to forgive you and he will. Receive his forgiveness and cleansing from it. Your relationship with God is the most valuable thing you have. Do not trade it in for anything on Earth.

Asa was a King of Judah. The Bible says that he did that which was right in the eyes of the Lord. His people were facing certain destruction and he led them in this prayer. God answered the prayer and destroyed their enemies.

> And Asa cried unto the Lord his God, and said, Lord, it is nothing with thee to help, whether with many, or with them that have no power: help us, O Lord our God; for we rest on thee, and in thy name we go against this multitude. O Lord, thou art our God; let not man prevail against thee. (2 Chronicles 14:11)

When your heart is right before God, he actively seeks ways to help you.

> For the eyes of the Lord run to and fro throughout the whole earth, to show himself strong in the behalf of them whose heart is perfect toward him. (2 Chronicles 16:9)

God's protection doesn't apply to everyone. It only applies to those who fear the Lord.

> The angel of the Lord encampeth round about them that fear him, and delivereth them. (Psalm 34:7)

In order to receive God's help, you have to be good. The Bible teaches you how to go about doing that.

> The steps of a good man are ordered by the Lord: and he delighted in his way. Though he fall, he shall not be utterly cast down: for the Lord upholdeth him with his hand. (Psalm 37:23–24)

This passage is your assurance that God will help you. Every time you face a challenge, remember these words.

> God is our refuge and strength, a very present help in trouble. Therefore will not we fear, though the earth be removed, and though the mountains be carried into the midst of the sea; Though the waters thereof roar and be troubled, though the mountains shake with the swelling thereof. Selah. (Psalm 46:1–3)

The prerequisite to receiving God's help is to love him. Loving the Lord is the same thing as fearing the Lord. They both mean keeping his commandments.

> Because he hath set his love upon me, therefore will I deliver him. (Psalm 91:14)

Having faith in God is acting like you believe what he said. Anything less than that is not faith, it is fear. This is where God has promised to help you.

> Fear thou not; for I am with thee: be not dismayed; for I am thy God: I will strengthen thee; yea, I will help thee; yea, I will uphold thee with the right hand of my righteousness.... For I the Lord will hold thy right hand, saying unto thee, fear not; I will help thee. (Isaiah 41:10, 13)

## GOD'S REST

Work is important, but God never intended that you work all the time. He set the example of working first, and then resting. He created the heavens and the earth, then he rested. After Jesus completed his work on the cross, he sat down at the right hand of the Father. God gave his people the Law. Jesus fulfilled the Law. The Jews continue to work, attempting to keep the Law of Moses, which can never save them. They continue to observe the letter of the law and their own tradition, but they have rejected their own Messiah. Salvation is not based on works, but on faith in Jesus. Your salvation is based on his righteousness, not yours. Faith is observing the spirit of the law from the heart. The power of the Holy Spirit enables you to do that. You are in Christ and he is God's rest.

This is where God established the principle of rest.

> Thus the heavens and the earth were finished, and all the host of them. And on the seventh day God ended his work which he had made; and he rested on the seventh day from all his work which he had made. And God blessed the seventh day, and sanctified it: because that in it he had rested from all his work which God created and made. (Genesis 2:1–3)

This saying is consistent with Jesus' words, "For my yoke is easy, and my burden is light." Transgressors could have gone the easy way, but they chose the hard way instead.

> The way of transgressors is hard. (Proverbs 13:15)

"Milk" is spiritual food for baby Christians. Spiritual babies can handle only a few basic truths. Many Christians never reach spiritual maturity. Thus, they do not know about God's rest, and they do not receive its benefits.

> Whom shall he teach knowledge? And whom shall he make to understand doctrine? them that are weaned from the milk, and drawn from the breasts. For precept must be upon precept, precept upon precept; line upon line, line upon line; here a little, and there a little: for with stammering lips and another tongue will he speak to this people. To whom he said, This is the rest wherewith ye may cause the weary to rest; and this is the refreshing: yet they would not hear. (Isaiah 28:9–12)

God's rest is not for everyone. Some love their old habits so much, they cannot give them up and enter into God's rest.

> Thus saith the Lord, Stand ye in the ways, and see, and ask for the old paths, where is the good way, and walk therein, and ye shall find rest for your souls. But they said, We will not walk therein. Also I set watchmen over you, saying, Hearken to the sound of the trumpet. But they said, We will not hearken. Therefore hear, ye nations, and know, O congregation, what is among them. Hear, O earth; behold, I will bring evil upon this people, even the fruit of their thoughts, because they have not hearkened unto my words, nor to my law, but rejected it. (Jeremiah 6:16–19)

These are Jesus' words. His commandments are much easier to keep than the Law of Moses.

> Come unto me, all ye that labor and are heavy laden, and I will give you rest. Take my yoke upon you, and learn of me,

> for I am meek and lowly in heart: and ye shall find rest unto your souls. For my yoke is easy, and my burden is light. (Matthew 11:28–30)

Clearly Jesus is the God of the Old Testament, and he spoke through David. David wrote a psalm that invited everyone to enter God's rest.

> Again he limiteth a certain day, saying in David, Today, after so long a time; as it is said, Today if ye will hear his voice, harden not your hearts. For if Jesus had given them rest, then would he not afterward have spoken of another day. There remaineth therefore a rest to the people of God. For he that is entered into his rest, he also hath ceased from his own works, as God did from his. Let us labor therefore to enter into that rest, lest any man fall after the same example of unbelief. (Hebrews 4:7–11)

## HEAVEN

Heaven is the place where God lives. It's where you'll go when you die. It could be on another planet. It could be in a parallel universe or another dimension. Theoretical physicists are among the smartest people in the world. They have faith in these things which can't be proven and cannot be seen. But they refuse to believe in God until they have tangible evidence of his existence. You know that heaven exists because you have placed your faith in God and you believe the Bible. You know that the only way to get to heaven is through Jesus Christ. It is a real place and it is filled with people you know and love. Someday you will be reunited with them, and you will live with God forever.

The Bible clearly states that there is a place where you will go after you die.

> For I know that thou wilt bring me to death, and to the house appointed for all living. (Job 30:23)

These are Jesus' words to you. He promised to take you home to live with him.

> **Let not your heart be troubled: ye believe in God, believe also in me. In my Father's house are many mansions: if it were not so, I would have told you. I go to prepare a place for you. And if I go and prepare a place for you, I will come again, and receive you unto myself; that where I am, there ye may be also. (John 14:1–3)**

Jesus prayed this prayer for you, just before he was crucified.

> **Neither pray I for these alone, but for them also which shall believe on me through their word;...Father, I will that they also, whom thou hast given me, be with me where I am. (John 17:20, 24)**

Two thieves were crucified on either side of Jesus. This is the record of what the three of them said to each other. "Paradise," or "Abraham's Bosom," was the place of the righteous dead at that time.

> **And one of the malefactors which were hanged railed on him, saying, If thou be Christ, save thyself and us. But the other answering rebuked him, saying, Dost not thou fear God, seeing thou art in the same condemnation? And we indeed justly; for we receive the due reward of our deeds: but this man hath done nothing amiss. And he said unto Jesus, Lord, remember me when thou comest into thy kingdom. And Jesus said unto him, Verily I say unto thee, Today shalt thou be with me in paradise. (Luke 23:39–43)**

This verse says that heaven will exceed all your expectations.

> **But as it is written, Eye hath not seen, nor ear heard, neither have entered into the heart of man, the things**

**which God hath prepared for them that love him. (1 Corinthians 2:9)**

Heaven is where God is. This verse describes what heaven is like.

**And God shall wipe away all tears from their eyes; and there shall be no more death, neither sorrow, nor crying, neither shall there be any more pain: for the former things are passed away. (Revelation 21:4)**

## THE HOLY SPIRIT

The Holy Spirit is God. He's equal to the Father and the Son. Jesus is God in human form. The Holy Spirit is Jesus in spirit form. He lives within every believer in Christ. He teaches you all things, and leads you in the ways of God. He reveals God's ideas to you. He gives you love, joy, peace, and self-control. He gives you the desire to please God by obeying him. If none of these things are going on in you, you do not have the Holy Spirit. If you have not changed at all since you became a Christian, you don't have the Holy Spirit. And if you don't have the Holy Spirit, then you are not saved. "Now if any man have not the Spirit of Christ, he is none of his."The following two verses tell us that the Holy Spirit is a gift. God gives it to his children. This is Jesus' explanation of how things work in his kingdom.

**If ye then, being evil, know how to give good gifts unto your children: how much more shall your heavenly Father give the Holy Spirit to them that ask him? (Luke 11:13)**

On the Day of Pentecost, the Holy Spirit descended from heaven upon Jesus' disciples. They spilled out into the street and spoke the word of God with boldness. Peter preached about Jesus to the people who had killed him. The word of God affected them strongly. They asked Peter what they should do. This was his answer to them.

> Then Peter said unto them, Repent, and be baptized every one of you in the name of Jesus Christ for the remission of sins, and ye shall receive the gift of the Holy Ghost. (Acts 2:38)

In this passage Peter speaks for himself and the other Apostles. They were eyewitnesses to the things Jesus said and did. The Holy Ghost is also a witness that these things are true.

> And we are his witnesses of these things; and so is also the Holy Ghost, whom God hath given to them that obey him. (Acts 5:32)

In the story of Abraham and Isaac, Abraham said that God would provide himself a sacrifice, and God provided a ram to be that sacrifice. God requires that you love others, but he furnishes you the love that you need through his Spirit.

> The love of God is shed abroad in our hearts by the Holy Ghost which is given unto us. (Romans 5:5)

The Holy Spirit changes your attitude. You start to notice other people's needs. You overlook their shortcomings. You do not waste your life thinking about how hurt and angry you are. You experience love, joy, and peace instead.

> But ye are not in the flesh, but in the Spirit, if so be that the Spirit of God dwell in you. Now if any man have not the Spirit of Christ, he is none of his....But if the Spirit of him that raised up Jesus from the dead dwell in you, he that raised up Christ from the dead shall also quicken your mortal bodies by his Spirit that dwelleth in you. (Romans 8:9, 11)

This verse makes it plain that Jesus is the Holy Spirit.

> **Now the Lord is that Spirit: and where the Spirit of the Lord is, there is liberty. (2 Corinthians 3:17)**

Jesus is the last Adam and He is that Spirit that lives within you.

> **And so it is written, The first man Adam was made a living soul; the last Adam was made a quickening spirit. (2 Corinthians 15:45)**

When Jesus is alive in you, you'll know it.

> **And hereby we know that he abideth in us, by the Spirit which he hath given us. (1 John 3:24)**

## INHERITANCE

When Jesus died, he left you an inheritance. Part of that inheritance is reserved for you in heaven, but there's another part of it here on the Earth. The Bible is God's last will and testament. It explains what he expects you to do and also defines the reward you will receive for obedience. There is a relationship between the two. If you will do this, then you will receive that. The Bible is filled with God's great and precious promises. They give you access to all the good things in life. To receive your inheritance, exert your faith. Make loving your neighbor a way of life.

As a child of God, you are a joint—heir with Jesus.

> **The Spirit itself beareth witness with our spirit, that we are the children of God: and if children, then heirs; heirs of God, and joint-heirs with Christ. (Romans 8:16–17)**

This passage groups unrighteous people together. The past tense in the phrase, "And such were some of you," implies that those things are no longer part of your life.

> Know ye not that the unrighteous shall not inherit the kingdom of God? Be not deceived: neither fornicators, nor idolaters, nor adulterers, nor effeminate, nor abusers of themselves with mankind, nor thieves, nor covetous, nor drunkards, nor revilers, nor extortioners, shall inherit the kingdom of God. And such were some of you: but ye are washed, but ye are sanctified, but ye are justified in the name of the Lord Jesus, and by the Spirit of our God. (1 Corinthians 6:9–11)

The Lord always rewards you for serving him. He also chastens you when you rebel against him. You cannot sin without paying for it.

> Servants, obey in all things your masters according to the flesh; not with eye service, as men pleasers; but in singleness of heart, fearing God; and whatsoever ye do, do it heartily, as to the Lord, and not unto men; knowing that of the Lord ye shall receive the reward of the inheritance: for ye serve the Lord Christ. But he that doeth wrong shall receive for the wrong which he hath done: and there is no respect of persons. (Colossians 3:22–25)

The Bible clearly states that there is an inheritance for you in heaven.

> Blessed be the God and Father of our Lord Jesus Christ, which according to his abundant mercy hath begotten us again unto a lively hope by the resurrection of Jesus Christ from the dead, to an inheritance incorruptible, and undefiled, and that fadeth not away, reserved in heaven for

> you, who are kept by the power of God through faith unto salvation ready to be revealed in the last time.
> (1 Peter 1:3–5)

It takes both faith and patience to receive what God has promised in his word.

> For God is not unrighteous to forget your work and labor of love, which ye have shown toward his name, in that ye have ministered to the saints, and do minister. And we desire that every one of you do show the same diligence to the full assurance of hope unto the end: that ye be not slothful, but followers of them who through faith and patience inherit the promises. (Hebrews 6:10–12)

## JUDGMENT

For most people, life is like being in a shopping mall filled with everything you want. It appears that everything is free. So you start grabbing everything you see. Then, you find out that nothing is free. You have to pay for everything. After you have paid out everything you have, you find that you are still in debt.

Sins don't have visible price tags, but they do have built-in penalties. Sin is anything that hurts you and the people you love. For example, adultery destroys marriages and families. There is a judgment from God for every sin, but the good news is that God is in the business of forgiving sin. He sent Jesus to deliver you from the power of sin. When you turn away from a particular sin, he will cleanse you from it. The Holy Ghost has the power to deliver you from every sin.

Remember what Deuteronomy 6:25 says. "And it shall be our righteousness, if we observe to do all these commandments before the Lord our God, as he hath commanded us." God judges you by the thoughts and intentions of your heart. He knows whether you are trying to obey him or not. Your words and deeds determine the circumstances of your life.

> Then hear thou from heaven, and do, and judge thy servants, by requiting the wicked, by recompensing his way upon his own head; and by justifying the righteous, by giving him according to his righteousness. (2 Chronicles 6:23)

It is more important to please God than anyone else. The Lord is the most powerful and influential Being in the universe.

> Many seek the ruler's favor; but every man's judgment cometh from the Lord. (Proverbs 29:26)

When you sin, you lose. If you persist in sinning, God will chasten you.

> Fear God, and keep his commandments: for this is the whole duty of man. For God shall bring every work into judgment, with every secret thing, whether it be good, or whether it be evil. (Ecclesiastes 12:13–14)

God is just. He does not punish anyone undeservedly. Men complain about the circumstances of their lives that they have brought upon themselves, but, in truth, you bring those circumstances on yourself when you sin.

> Wherefore doth a living man complain, a man for the punishment of his sins? (Lamentations 3:39)

Judging other people is more than just disapproving of their actions. It is pointing out their shortcomings and correcting them. It is trying to do God's job. God will judge you for punishing other people.

> Judge not, that ye be not judged. (Matthew 7:1)

It's not your job to execute judgment on others. You are not allowed to punish other people for their sins. If you do, you are usurping God's authority. You are playing God. God says that He will repay your enemies for mistreating you.

> For we know him that hath said, Vengeance belongeth unto me, I will recompense, saith the Lord. And again, the Lord shall judge his people. It is a fearful thing to fall into the hands of the living God. (Hebrews 10:30–31)

Instead of judging other people, judge yourself. If you are guilty of a particular sin, then stop doing it. When you turn away from a sin, that ends the chastening for it.

> For if we would judge ourselves, we should not be judged. But when we are judged, we are chastened of the Lord, that we should not be condemned with the world. (1 Corinthians 11:31–32)

The fact that Jesus has forgiven your sins doesn't mean that you have a license to sin.

> But we are sure that the judgment of God is according to truth against them which commit such things. And thinkest thou this, O man, that judgest them which do such things, and doest the same, that thou shalt escape the judgment of God? (Romans 2:2–3)

You will eventually have to stand before the Lord and be judged for everything you have done.

> For we must all appear before the judgment seat of Christ; that every one may receive the things done in his body, according to that he hath done, whether it be good or bad. (2 Corinthians 5:10)

When you are in Christ, you are no longer under the Law of Moses. You are judged according to God's Law of Liberty. You know in your heart the difference between right and wrong.

> **So speak ye, and so do, as they that shall be judged by the law of liberty. (James 2:12)**

## JUSTIFICATION

Jesus took your sins and gave you the benefits of his sinless life. Because he has justified you before God, you get to live forever. Because of God's great mercy, you get treated just like Jesus, just as though you had never sinned. Nothing you do in life will improve upon what Jesus has done for you. He has also set you free from guilt and condemnation.

Faith is actively obeying the word of God. Being a doer of the word shows God that you really do believe him.

> **For not the hearers of the law are just before God, but the doers of the law shall be justified. For when the Gentiles, which have not the law, do by nature the things contained in the law, these, having not the law, are a law unto themselves: which show the work of the law written in their hearts, their conscience also bearing witness, and their thoughts the meanwhile accusing or else excusing one another. (Romans 2:13–15)**

Your justification is based on faith. You are declared righteous before God because you believe his word.

> **Therefore by the deeds of the law there shall no flesh be justified in his sight: for by the law is the knowledge of sin. But now the righteousness of God without the law is manifested, being witnessed by the law and the prophets; even the righteousness of God which is by faith of Jesus Christ unto all and upon all them that believe: for there is**

> **no difference: For all have sinned, and come short of the glory of God; Being justified freely by his grace through the redemption that is in Christ Jesus. (Romans 3:20–24)**

Martin Luther was a Bible Believer. The realization that a person could be justified by faith aside from works is what motivated him to nail his 95 Theses to the door of the church in Wittenberg, which began the Protestant Reformation.

> **Knowing that a man is not justified by the works of the law, but by the faith of Jesus Christ, even we have believed in Jesus Christ, that we might be justified by the faith of Christ, and not by the works of the law: for by the works of the law shall no flesh be justified. (Galatians 2:16)**

Long before Martin Luther, Abraham exhibited his faith through his willingness to give God everything he had, even the son he loved. This was not a work of the law. Abraham knew that God would not do anything to hurt him. This was a work of faith. It showed that he loved God.

> **Was not Abraham our father justified by works, when he had offered Isaac his son upon the altar? Seest thou how faith wrought with his works, and by works was faith made perfect? And the Scripture was fulfilled which saith, Abraham believed God, and it was imputed unto him for righteousness: and he was called the Friend of God. Ye see then how that by works a man is justified, and not by faith only. (James 2:21–24)**

## THE KINGDOM OF GOD

Jesus preached and taught about the kingdom of God. Matthew, Mark, Luke, and John proclaim the good news that this kingdom is available to everyone. The kingdom of God is not a physical kingdom. It is a spiritual place. To enter God's kingdom, you have to be born of God's Spirit. Jesus lived in that place of fellowship with God. The Holy Spirit was his constant companion. The Bible teaches you how to live like Jesus did. He gave you the benefit of his sinless life, so you can be in fellowship with God. Then, he gave you his Holy Spirit to be your constant companion. You are a citizen of heaven, and you are a part of the kingdom of God.

Seeking first the kingdom of God means putting Jesus' interests ahead of your own. Instead of building a little kingdom of your own, you're building up his kingdom. Your highest priority should be to promote the kingdom of God. Then, you will not ever have to worry about your own needs. Jesus promised that he would provide these material things for you.

> **Therefore take no thought, saying, What shall we eat? or, What shall we drink? or, Wherewithal shall we be clothed? (For after all these things do the Gentiles seek) for your heavenly Father knoweth that ye have need of all these things. But seek ye first the kingdom of God, and his righteousness; and all these things shall be added unto you. (Matthew 6:31–33)**

The people of the world cannot comprehend the kingdom of God. They are spiritually dead. They do not have the Holy Spirit to open their eyes and ears to God's word.

> **And he said unto them, Unto you it is given to know the mystery of the kingdom of God: but to them which are without, all these things are done in parables: That seeing they may see, and not perceive; and hearing they may hear, and not understand. (Mark 4:11–12)**

It's God's will to give you the kingdom of God and everything that comes with it.

> Fear not, little flock; for it is your Father's good pleasure to give you the kingdom. (Luke 12:32)

"John" is John the Baptist. He was the last of the Old Testament prophets. He was the forerunner of Jesus who proclaimed that the kingdom of God is at hand.

> The law and the prophets were until John: since that time the kingdom of God is preached, and every man presseth into it. (Luke 16:16)

In order to enter God's kingdom you must be born into it. Jesus was born of the Holy Spirit, and so are you. You were born spiritually when you first believed in Jesus.

> Jesus answered and said unto him, Verily, verily, I say unto thee, Except a man be born again, he cannot see the kingdom of God. (John 3:3)

Paul preached about the kingdom to the very end of his life. In Rome, he was under house arrest and couldn't go out to preach. People came to him so they could hear the word of God. He told them how the scriptures were fulfilled in Jesus. He preached what Jesus preached, the kingdom of God. Some of the people believed and some did not.

> But we desire to hear of thee what thou thinkest: for as concerning this sect, we know that everywhere it is spoken against. And when they had appointed him a day, there came many to him into his lodging; to whom he expounded and testified the kingdom of God, persuading them concerning Jesus, both out of the law of Moses, and out of the prophets, from morning till evening. And some believed the things which were spoken, and some believed not. (Acts 28:22–24)

## THE LAMB OF GOD

The last of the plagues in Egypt was the death of the firstborn. God provided a way for his people to survive it. Two elements were required, faith and blood. It took faith to follow God's instructions, and it took trust that those instructions would work. God's people took the blood of a lamb and applied it to the doors of their houses. Upon seeing the blood, the Death Angel "passed over" that house. Jewish people still celebrate the Passover. It was a symbol of Jesus' substitutionary sacrifice for you. Jesus is the Lamb of God. Egypt represents the world in which you live. When you believed in Jesus, you applied the blood of Jesus to your heart. He saved you from spiritual death. He has also set you free from slavery to sin.

Jesus came to John the Baptist to be baptized. This was what John said about Jesus.

> **The next day John seeth Jesus coming unto him, and saith, Behold the Lamb of God, which taketh away the sin of the world. (John 1:29)**

All lambs sacrificed to God had to be physically perfect, without spot or blemish. Jesus was without sin, spiritually perfect.

> **And if you call on the Father, who without respect of persons judgeth according to every man's work, pass the time of your sojourning here in fear: Forasmuch as ye know that ye were not redeemed with corruptible things, as silver and gold, from your vain conversation received by tradition from your fathers; But with the precious blood of Christ, as of a lamb without blemish and without spot: (1 Peter 1:17–19)**

The Apostle John had a vision of heaven. This is part of what he saw there.

> **And I beheld, and I heard the voice of many angels round about the throne and the beasts and the elders: and the number of them was ten thousand times ten thousand, and thousands of thousands; saying with a loud voice, Worthy is the Lamb that was slain to receive power, and riches, and wisdom and strength, and honor, and glory, and blessing. (Revelation 5:11–12)**

## LAW

"The Law" is the written word of God. It's not just the Ten Commandments. Everyone who breaks the law is under a sentence of death. That included everyone except for Jesus. God gave the law to show how perfect a man must be to be acceptable to him. Jesus fulfilled the law by loving God and loving his neighbor. Now that you are in Christ, you are under a different law, God's Law of Liberty. You have a tremendous amount of liberty, but you are still accountable to God. You do not have to follow a rigid set of rules. You get to use your creativity instead. Sin consists of knowing what to do and not doing it. Sin always costs you dearly because it affects your fellowship with God. That's what gives you all the good things in life. Your love, peace and joy come from fellowship with God. Getting your prayers answered does, too. You do not want anything to limit what God can do for you, so listen to the voice of the Holy Spirit guiding you. Whatever is not of faith is sin.

This psalm describes the man who is blessed by God. He does two things that cause him to succeed. He delights in the word of God and he meditates on it constantly. Meditating is communing with God in your heart.

> **But his delight is in the law of the Lord; and in his law doth he meditate day and night. And he shall be like a tree planted by the rivers of water, that bringeth forth his fruit in his season; his leaf also shall not wither; and whatsoever he doeth shall prosper. (Psalm 1:2–3)**

The purpose of the law is to show you that you need Jesus to save you from death.

> **Wherefore the law was our schoolmaster to bring us unto Christ, that we might be justified by faith. But after that faith is come, we are no longer under a schoolmaster: for ye are all the children of God by faith in Christ Jesus. (Galatians 3:24–26)**

When you're keeping the Lord's commandment from the heart, you are fulfilling the law.

> **For, brethren, ye have been called unto liberty; only use not liberty for an occasion to the flesh, but by love serve one another. For all the law is fulfilled in one word, even in this; thou shalt love thy neighbor as thyself. (Galatians 5:13–14)**

Because you are in Christ, the Law does not apply to you anymore. You are under grace.

> **Knowing this, that the law is not made for a righteous man, but for the lawless and disobedient, for the ungodly and for sinners, for unholy and profane, for murderers of fathers and murderers of mothers, for manslayers, for whoremongers, for them that defile themselves with mankind, for men stealers, for liars, for perjured persons, and if there be any other thing that is contrary to sound doctrine; according to the glorious gospel of the blessed God, which was committed to my trust. (1 Timothy 1:9–11)**

## THE LIVING WORD OF GOD

If a man is good, his word is good, but God goes far beyond that. His word is full of power. It causes what he says to happen. That's how God created the heavens and the Earth. He spoke them into existence. Jesus is the Living Word of God. The Bible is the written word of God. The Bible is the written word about the Living Word. Jesus was God in human flesh. The Holy Spirit was always with him. The Holy Spirit is everywhere at the same time. He lives continuously within your heart. The Bible says that he will never leave you nor forsake you.

This passage tells us plainly that Jesus is the Word of God, and that He is the Creator.

> In the beginning was the Word, and the Word was with God, and the Word was God. The same was in the beginning with God. All things were made by him; and without him was not any thing made that was made. (John 1:1–3)

Jesus is the Word of God made flesh. John refers to the time he saw Jesus in his glory. His face was like the sun and his clothing was white as light.

> And the Word was made flesh, and dwelt among us, (and we beheld his glory, the glory as of the only begotten of the Father,) full of grace and truth. (John 1:14)

You know some things about Jesus through the Bible, but he knows everything about you.

> For the word of God is quick and powerful, and sharper than any two-edged sword, piercing even to the dividing asunder of soul and spirit, and of the joints and marrow, and is a discerner of the thoughts and intents of the heart. Neither is there any creature that is not manifest in his sight: but all things are naked and opened unto the eyes of him with whom we have to do. (Hebrews 4:12–13)

This John's vision of Jesus at the end of the age as recorded in the Book of Revelation. It reveals the fact that Jesus is the Word of God.

> **And I saw heaven opened, and behold a white horse; and he that sat upon him was called Faithful and True, and in righteousness he doth judge and make war. His eyes were as a flame of fire, and on his head were many crowns; and he had a name written, that no man knew, but he himself. And he was clothed with a vesture dipped in blood: and his name is called The Word of God. (Revelation 19:11–13)**

## MARRIAGE

My wife and I know that God put us together. Just before we met, each of us had asked God to send somebody. I had just moved to Memphis, and didn't know anybody there. In loneliness and desperation, I cried out to God, "Will you please send me a girl who will be my friend?" At the same time, Marie had asked God, "Will you please send me a guy who will love me for me?" I showed up at her church, of all places. It was love at first sight. She was the answer to my prayer, and I was the answer to hers. He gave us much more than we expected. Instead of sending a girl to be my friend, he gave me the woman who would be my wife. After more than forty years of marriage, she is still my best friend and I still love her for her.

I did not think that we would actually experience all those things that are mentioned in the wedding vows, but we have gone through most of them. We've experienced more "poorer" than "richer." We've cared for each other in sickness and in health. Like all married couples, we've had some difficult times. We've made it through them because we know the Lord. He has never let us down. Without him, our marriage wouldn't have survived.

Early on in our marriage, I heard a sermon that changed my life. Our pastor, Brother Paul, explained how marriage is a picture of the Lord's relationship with the believer. It's the husband's job to love the wife as Christ loved the church, and to give up his life for her. He explained that love is more than just a feeling. It's doing the things that have to be done. If you tell your wife that you love her, and you don't work and pay the bills, then you're a liar. If you say that you love the

Lord, and you never do anything he says, you're a liar. He caused me to realize how selfish and self-centered I was. I thought that the whole world revolved around me. The things that I wanted took priority over everything and everybody else. I didn't understand what love was until it was explained to me in this way. I realized how greatly I had failed as both a husband and a Christian.

I changed my mind and changed my life. I started loving my wife the way Jesus loved me, which is unconditionally. It doesn't matter what she does or what she says, I just love her anyway. She doesn't have to do anything to earn my love and affection. I practiced loving my children the same way. Then, I extended this love to other members of my family, and my church family. I was doing what the Lord requires of me and enjoying it. My wife Marie had always loved me in that way. She loved me, and she loved her neighbor as herself. She made me want to be like her. She taught me how to love.

This is what the Bible says about the first marriage, that of Adam and Eve. The archaic word "meet" means appropriate or suitable. God puts couples together that suit each other.

> **And the Lord God said, It is not good that the man should be alone; I will make him an help meet for him. (Genesis 2:18)**

"Leaving father and mother," means putting your marriage ahead of your relationship with your parents. If a conflict arises between the two, the marriage has to come first.

> **Therefore shall a man leave his father and his mother, and shall cleave unto his wife: and they shall be one flesh. (Genesis 2:24)**

The Lord expects you to be satisfied with your own wife.

> **Let thy fountain be blessed: and rejoice with the wife of thy youth. Let her be as the loving hind and pleasant roe; let**

> **her breasts satisfy thee at all times; and be thou ravished always with her love. And why wilt thou, my son, be ravished with a strange woman, and embrace the bosom of a stranger? For the ways of man are before the eyes of the Lord, and he pondereth all his goings. (Proverbs 5:18–21)**

This three-fold cord is the secret of success in marriage. The first strand of the cord is my relationship with the Lord. The second is Marie's relationship with him. The third strand is our relationship with each other. One strand might weaken, but all three aren't going to fail at the same time. When both partners are married to the Lord, that marriage will last.

> **Two are better than one; because they have a good reward for their labor. For if they fall, the one will lift up his fellow: but woe to him that is alone when he falleth; for he hath not another to help him up. Again, if two lie together, then they have heat: but how can one be warm alone? And if one prevail against him, two shall withstand him; and a threefold cord is not quickly broken. (Ecclesiastes 4:9–12)**

In my own life, I have experienced the truth of this verse. God blessed me by giving me Marie to be my wife. She's the most loving person I've ever known. It's because of her godly influence that I'm a believer in Jesus today.

> **Whoso findeth a wife findeth a good thing, and obtaineth favor of the Lord. (Proverbs 18:22)**

This is the advice of King Solomon, the wisest man who ever lived, except for Jesus. When you enjoy living with your wife and enjoy your work, life is good.

> **Live joyfully with the wife whom thou lovest all the days of the life of thy vanity, which he hath given thee under**

> **the sun, all the days of thy vanity: for that is thy portion in this life, and in thy labor which thou takest under the sun. (Ecclesiastes 9:9)**

Marie and I sincerely believe that God put us together. We used to say that it takes both of us to make one person.

> **But from the beginning of the creation God made them male and female. For this cause shall a man leave his father and mother, and cleave to his wife; and they twain shall be one flesh: so then they are no more twain, but one flesh. What therefore God hath joined together, let not man put asunder. (Mark 10:6–9)**

God looks at a man and his wife as a single entity.

> **Nevertheless neither is the man without the woman, neither the woman without the man, in the Lord. (1 Corinthians 11:11)**

Never marry anyone who is not a believer in Jesus. It takes hard work and obedience to God to create a happy marriage. A non-believer isn't going to do the necessary work, and he is certainly not going to obey God.

> **Be ye not unequally yoked together with unbelievers: for what fellowship hath righteousness with unrighteousness? And what communion hath light with darkness? (2 Corinthians 6:14)**

It's the husband's job to love his wife the way Jesus loves the Church. That includes providing for her and caring for her. As a husband, you have no right to judge your wife, or to punish her, or to humiliate her. You have to love like Jesus loves. When you truly love your wife, she will respond to that love. She will bloom like the delicate flower that she is.

> **Husbands, love your wives, even as Christ also loved the church, and gave himself for it. (Ephesians 5:25)**

The Golden Rule always works. You get back what you give out. We love Jesus because he first loved us. When you love your wife, she will love you back.

> **Nevertheless let every one of you in particular so love his wife even as himself; and the wife see that she reverence her husband. (Ephesians 5:33)**

## THE NEW BIRTH

When you believe in your heart that Jesus is Lord, you are born by the Spirit of God. The Holy Spirit comes to live in you. In order to understand the things of God, you must have experienced this new birth. In order to receive anything from God, you must be born again. Galatians 4:19 says, "My little children, of whom I travail in birth again until Christ be formed in you." This is one of the mysteries of God. You are born in him, and he is born in you. The new birth makes the difference between life and death, heaven and hell.

Nicodemus was a religious leader who came to learn from Jesus in secret. Jesus explained the new birth.

> **Jesus answered and said unto him, Verily, verily, I say unto thee, Except a man be born again, he cannot see the kingdom of God. Nicodemus saith unto him, How can a man be born when he is old? Can he enter the second time into his mother's womb, and be born? Jesus answered, Verily, verily, I say unto thee, Except a man be born of water and of the Spirit, he cannot enter into the kingdom of God. That which is born of the flesh is flesh; and that which is born of the Spirit is spirit. Marvel not that I said unto thee, Ye must be born again. (John 3:3–7)**

When you experience the new birth, you become a new creation.

> Therefore if any man be in Christ, he is a new creature: old things are passed away; behold, all things are become new. (2 Corinthians 5:17)

Your physical body is perishable. The new birth lasts forever.

> Being born again, not of corruptible seed, but of incorruptible, by the word of God, which liveth and abideth for ever. (1 Peter 1:23)

When you are born again, you will have a desire to do what's right.

> If ye know that he is righteous, ye know that every one that doeth righteousness is born of him. (1 John 2:29)

Jesus was born by the Holy Spirit. When you believe in Jesus, you are born spiritually by that same Spirit.

> Whosoever believeth that Jesus is the Christ is born of God: and every one that loveth him that begat loveth him also that is begotten of him....For whatsoever is born of God overcometh the world: and this is the victory that overcometh the world, even our faith. Who is he that overcometh the world, but he that believeth that Jesus is the Son of God? This is he that came by water and blood, even Jesus Christ; not by water only, but by water and blood. And it is the Spirit that beareth witness, because the Spirit is truth. For there are three that bear record in heaven, the Father, the Word, and the Holy Ghost: and these three are one. And there are three that bear witness in earth, the spirit, and the water, and the blood: and these

**three agree in one. If we receive the witness of men, the witness of God is greater: for this is the witness of God which he hath testified of his Son. (1 John 5:1,4–9)**

## THE NEW COVENANT

The Old Covenant was a contract between God and His people. It was based on the Law he gave them through Moses on Mount Sinai. Jesus fulfilled the Law and the Old Covenant, and established the New Covenant. You are a participant in this covenant. It's a contract between Jesus and God. It is based on the blood Jesus shed for you, and it has better promises. In order to receive the things God promises, you must be willing to do all that Jesus commanded you. All these things are summarized by one Commandment, to love your neighbor as yourself. The Holy Spirit in you will empower you to do this. God is full of mercy. He has provided everything you need to keep the Lord's commandment. You just have to supply the willingness to do so.

When you are keeping the Lord's commandment, the Holy Spirit will teach you everything you need to know.

**All the paths of the Lord are mercy and truth unto such as keep his covenant and his testimonies. For thy name's sake, O Lord, pardon mine iniquity; for it is great. What man is he that feareth the Lord? Him shall he teach in the way that he shall choose. His soul shall dwell at ease; and his seed shall inherit the earth. The secret of the Lord is with them that fear him; and he will show them his covenant. (Psalm 25:10–14)**

In the Old Testament, God spoke through his prophet Jeremiah and specifically stated that he would establish a New Covenant with his people.

**Behold, the days come, saith the Lord, that I will make a new covenant with the house of Israel, and with the house**

> of Judah: not according to the covenant that I made with their fathers in the day that I took them by the hand to bring them out of the land of Egypt; which my covenant they brake, although I was an husband unto them, saith the Lord: but this shall be the covenant that I will make with the house of Israel; After those days, saith the Lord, I will put my law in their inward parts, and write it in their hearts; and will be their God, and they shall be my people.
> (Jeremiah 31:31–33)

The Holy Spirit teaches you how to do right. You are free to keep the spirit of the law from the heart. You do not have to superficially observe the letter of the law.

> Forasmuch as ye are manifestly declared to be the epistle of Christ ministered by us, written not with ink, but with the Spirit of the living God; not in tables of stone, but in fleshy tables of the heart...Who also hath made us able ministers of the new testament; not of the letter, but of the spirit: for the letter killeth, but the spirit giveth life.
> (2 Corinthians 3:3, 6)

Under the New Covenant, God can show you more mercy. He can forgive your sins and forget them.

> For I will be merciful to their unrighteousness, and their sins and their iniquities will I remember no more. In that he saith, A new covenant, he hath made the first old. Now that which decayeth and waxeth old is ready to vanish away.
> (Hebrews 8:12–13)

## RECOMPENSE

Righteousness consists of doing what the Bible says. Righteous behavior always produces good things. Recompense is payback for what you've done. Going against God's word always causes you trouble. Abusing other people always causes you pain. Everyone wants to be loved and respected. Treat them with respect, and they will usually respect you in return. People who show disrespect to others get angry when they are disrespected. Treat everyone the way you want to be treated. The Golden Rule is the secret of success in every area of life.

Always do what is right. Then the Lord will be constantly rewarding you for the good things you have done.

> The Lord rewarded me according to my righteousness; according to the cleanness of my hands hath he recompensed me. For I have kept the ways of the Lord, and have not wickedly departed from my God. (2 Samuel 22:21–22)

The circumstances of your life are determined by your behavior.

> For the work of a man shall he render unto him, and cause every man to find according to his ways. Yea, surely God will not do wickedly, neither will the Almighty pervert judgment. (Job 34:11–12)

Always do what is right, and you will receive good things in abundance. Evildoers are repaid with evil. That is the currency they deal in, and they are repaid in kind.

> Behold, the righteous shall be recompensed in the earth: much more the wicked and the sinner. (Proverbs 11:31)

The condition of your heart determines what happens to you in life. God knows your intentions as well as what you are thinking.

> The heart is deceitful above all things, and desperately wicked: who can know it? I the Lord search the heart, I try

> **the reins, even to give every man according to his ways, and according to the fruit of his doings. (Jeremiah 17:9–10)**

You do not have the right to mistreat people, or to punish them. You have to love them. You are not allowed to execute your judgment on them. That is God's department.

> **But he that doeth wrong shall receive for the wrong which he hath done: and there is no respect of persons. (Colossians 3:25)**

## REDEMPTION

To redeem something is to recover it after it has been lost. When Adam sinned, every human being was lost to the enemy. Jesus, the second Adam, has made it possible for everyone to be redeemed. But this redemption only applies to those who will accept it. It is a free gift to everyone who believes in Jesus. But there is a world full of people who do not believe in him. He came to seek and to save that which was lost. He redeemed you from Satan by his obedience unto death.

You are the redeemed of the Lord. He bought you back from the enemy with his own blood.

> **Let the redeemed of the Lord say so, whom he hath redeemed from the hand of the enemy. (Psalm 107:2)**

Jesus has bought you, and you belong to him. He'll be with you wherever you go.

> **But now thus saith the Lord that created thee, O Jacob, and he that formed thee, O Israel, Fear not: for I have redeemed thee, I have called thee by thy name; thou art mine. When thou passeth through the waters, I will be with thee; and through the rivers, they shall not overflow**

> thee: when thou walkest through the fire, thou shalt not be burned; neither shall the flame kindle upon thee. (Isaiah 43:1–2)

Because of Adam's sin, you were sentenced to death. But now you get to live forever because of Jesus' righteousness.

> Christ hath redeemed us from the curse of the law, being made a curse for us: for it is written, Cursed is every one that hangeth on a tree: that the blessing of Abraham might come on the Gentiles through Jesus Christ; that we might receive the promise of the Spirit through faith. (Galatians 3:13–14)

Your "vain conversation" is your old lifestyle. The blood of Jesus has redeemed you from that, and has given you a new purpose, new hope, and new desires.

> And if ye call on the Father, who without respect of persons judgeth according to every man's work, pass the time of your sojourning here in fear: forasmuch as ye know that ye were not redeemed with corruptible things, as silver and gold, from your vain conversation received by tradition from your fathers; but with the precious blood of Christ, as of a lamb without blemish and without spot.
> (1 Peter 1:17–19)

## THE RIGHTEOUSNESS OF CHRIST

It was World War Two, and going to war was an exciting adventure for an eighteen-year-old farm boy from Tennessee. He volunteered to became a paratrooper and was assigned to the 101st Airborne Division know as the Screaming Eagles. He saw action in Normandy, Belgium, and Holland. He volunteered for several missions in which they parachuted behind enemy lines. On the way to his last combat jump, he was really scared. In desperation, he cried out to God, "Jesus, please help me stay alive." He was part of a five man crew firing a 75mm howitzer. It blew up, and he was the only survivor. But he was badly wounded. Far behind enemy lines, he was as good as dead. As he lay there broken and bleeding, a British Army officer appeared and noticed that he was still alive. Moved by compassion, he took off his own coat and covered the wounded man with it. A British ambulance crew showed up. When they spotted that coat, they assumed that one of their officers had been hit. The wounded American was given the best of care, the same that a British Officer would have received. He woke in the hospital back in England where they were calling him "Sir."

That American soldier was my dad. His story illustrates perfectly what Jesus has done for you. Just as he saved my dad from physical death, he has saved you from spiritual death. He has covered you with the coat of his righteousness. You get the benefit of his sinless life. And God treats you just the same as if you were his Son.

One of many names for Jesus in the Bible is The Lord Our Righteousness. This name reveals the only way a man can be in right-standing with God

> **And this is his name whereby he shall be called, The Lord Our Righteousness. (Jeremiah 23:6)**

Even though God's promises defied logic, Abraham believed them anyway. He honored God and his word. In return, God substituted what Abraham had (faith) for something he could never earn or deserve (righteousness.)

> **For what saith the scripture? Abraham believed God, and it was counted unto him for righteousness. (Romans 4:3)**

The righteousness of Christ is available to everyone who believes in Jesus. You are a child of Abraham when you follow his example and take God at his word.

> For the promise, that he should be the heir of the world, was not to Abraham, or to his seed, through the law, but through the righteousness of faith....Therefore it is of faith, that it might be by grace; to the end the promise might be sure to all the seed; not to that only which is of the law, but to that also which is of the faith of Abraham; who is the father of us all. (Romans 4:13, 16)

Jesus' obedience reversed the effects of Adam's disobedience. That's why he is called the Second Adam. The righteousness of Christ has replaced Adam's legacy of sin and death.

> For if by one man's offense death reigned by one; much more they which receive abundance of grace and of the gift of righteousness shall reign in life by one, Jesus Christ. Therefore as by the offense of one, judgment came upon all men to condemnation; even so by the righteousness of one the free gift came upon all men unto justification of life. For as by one man's disobedience many were made sinners, so by the obedience of one shall many be made righteous. (Romans 5:17–19)

Your salvation does not depend on how good you are. It is based on how good Jesus is. When you believe God's testimony concerning his son Jesus, you receive the righteousness of Christ. When you believe in your heart that Jesus is the Son of God, you will affirm that belief with your words. You will say with your mouth what you believe in your heart.

> That if thou shalt confess with thy mouth the Lord Jesus, and shalt believe in thine heart that God hath raised him from the dead, thou shalt be saved. For with the heart man believeth unto righteousness; and with the mouth confession is made unto salvation. (Romans 10:9–10)

When you believe that Jesus is the Lord, and that the Bible is God's word, you will base your life on these truths. That is how you demonstrate your faith in God.

> **Even as Abraham believed God, and it was accounted to him for righteousness. Know ye therefore that they which are of faith, the same are the children of Abraham. (Galatians 3:6–7)**

Salvation is a free gift from God, and so is the faith you use to receive it.

> **For by grace are ye saved through faith; and that not of yourselves: it is the gift of God: not of works, lest any man should boast. (Ephesians 2:8–9)**

Your salvation is based entirely on the righteousness of Christ.

> **And be found in him, not having mine own righteousness, which is of the law, but that which is through the faith of Christ, the righteousness which is of God by faith: (Philippians 3:9)**

You are saved by what Jesus has done, not by anything you could ever do. This is because of God's great mercy.

> **Not by works of righteousness which we have done, but according to his mercy he saved us, by the washing of regeneration, and renewing of the Holy Ghost; which he shed on us abundantly through Jesus Christ our Savior. (Titus 3:5–6)**

## SONSHIP

Jesus said that those who do his Father's will are members of his family. The Bible says that Jesus is the firstborn of many brethren. The world measures you by how much money you have. In God's family, you are known by how much you give of yourself. Jesus set a very high standard. He gave his own flesh and blood as a sacrifice for your sins. When you give something of yourself in doing God's will, you are acting like God's son. You resemble Jesus.

When you were born again, you became part of God's family. God accepts you just as you are and treats you like his son.

> Yet the number of the children of Israel shall be as the sand of the sea, which cannot be measured nor numbered; and it shall come to pass, that in the place where it was said unto them, Ye are not my people, there it shall be said unto them, Ye are the sons of the living God. (Hosea 1:10)

Jesus, the Son of God, has given you the power to be like him.

> He was in the world, and the world was made by him, and the world knew him not. He came unto his own, and his own received him not. But as many as received him, to them gave he power to become the sons of God, even to them that believe on his name: which were born, not of blood, nor or the will of the flesh, nor of the will of man, but of God. (John 1:10–13)

When you are led by the Holy Spirit, you are acting like a son of God. The name "Abba" is the same as our word "Daddy."

> For as many as are led by the Spirit of God, they are the sons of God. For ye have not received the spirit of bondage again to fear; but ye have received the Spirit of

adoption, whereby we cry, Abba, Father. The Spirit itself beareth witness with our spirit, that we are the children of God. (Romans 8:14–16)

It's faith in Jesus that makes you a child of God.

For ye are all the children of God by faith in Christ Jesus. (Galatians 3:26)

The Lord really hates it when you complain. Remember what the Bible said about God's people in the desert, "And when the people complained, it displeased the Lord: and the Lord heard it; and his anger was kindled;"( Numbers 11:1). God's will for you is that you act like a son of God.

Do all things without murmurings and disputings: That ye may be blameless and harmless, the sons of God, without rebuke, in the midst of a crooked and perverse nation, among whom ye shine as lights in the world. (Philippians 2:14–15)

When you're born again, you'll have the desire to do what's right.

If ye know that he is righteous, ye know that every one that doeth righteousness is born of him. (1 John 2:29)

God loves you and accepts you as a son. The world hates you just as they hated Jesus. One day you will be like Jesus.

Behold, what manner of love the Father hath bestowed upon us, that we should be called the sons of God: therefore the world knoweth us not, because it knew him not. Beloved, now are we the sons of God, and it doth not yet appear what we shall be: but we know that, when he

> shall appear, we shall be like him; for we shall see him as he is. And every man that hath this hope in him purifieth himself, even as he is pure. (1 John 3:1–3)

## THE SPIRIT OF TRUTH

The Spirit of Truth is one of many names for the Holy Spirit. He's the third Person of the Holy Trinity. He's the equal of the Father and the Son. You're created in God's image. You have a soul that consists of your mind, your heart, and your will. You live in a body. Your spirit is the part of you that comes from God. The Spirit of Truth communicates with you through your heart, your mind and your spirit.

Jesus' definition of loving him is to keep his commandments. He promised to send the Spirit of Truth to live in you.

> If ye love me keep my commandments, and I will pray the Father, and he shall give you another Comforter, that he may abide with you forever; even the Spirit of truth; whom the world cannot receive, because it seeth him not, neither knoweth him: but ye know him; for he dwelleth with you, and shall be in you.(John 14:15–17)

"Comforter" means advisor or counselor. The Spirit of Truth is the author of the Bible. He will prompt you to remember what he wrote and teach you what it means. He will teach you how to apply God's word to your life.

> But the Comforter, which is the Holy Ghost, whom the Father will send in my name, he shall teach you all things, and bring all things to your remembrance, whatsoever I have said unto you. (John 14:26)

The Holy Spirit does not talk about himself. He directs all glory, honor, and praise to Jesus.

> Howbeit when he, the Spirit of truth, is come, he will guide you into all truth: for he shall not speak of himself; but whatsoever he shall hear, that shall he speak: and he will show you things to come. He shall glorify me: for he shall receive of mine, and shall show it unto you. All things that the Father hath are mine: therefore said I, that he shall take of mine, and shall show it unto you. (John 16:13–15)

If you don't have the Holy Spirit living in you, then you have not been born again. You are spiritually dead.

> So then they that are in the flesh cannot please God. But ye are not in the flesh, but in the Spirit, if so be that the Spirit of God dwell in you. Now if any man have not the Spirit of Christ, he is none of his. (Romans 8:8–9)

"The world" consists of everything and everyone who opposes God. The Holy Spirit is more powerful than anything in the world. He tells you what's true and what's false.

> Ye are of God, little children, and have overcome them: because greater is he that is in you, than he that is in the world. They are of the world: therefore speak they of the world, and the world heareth them. We are of God: he that knoweth God heareth us; he that is not of God heareth not us. Hereby know we the spirit of truth, and the spirit of error. (1 John 4:4–6)

## SPIRITUAL BREAD

Jesus said, you do not live by bread alone but by every word that proceedeth out of the mouth of God. Just as your body needs food to survive, your mind and your emotions need God's word. In his model prayer, Jesus said, ask the Father to give you your daily bread. Like the manna God provided in the wilderness, his word is fresh and new each day. All you have to do is gather it.

God watched to see who would follow his instructions in gathering manna. He's watching you to see if you're basing your life on his word or not.

> Then said the Lord unto Moses, Behold I will rain bread from heaven for you; and the people shall go out and gather a certain rate every day, that I may prove them, whether they will walk in my law, or no. (Exodus 16:4)

God's people left Egypt and lived in the wilderness. He fed them with manna, which was bread from heaven. Jesus is the Bread of Life. You feed on him figuratively when you do what the Bible tells you.

> And he humbled thee, and suffered thee to hunger, and fed thee with manna, which thou knewest not, neither did thy fathers know; that he might make thee know that man doth not live by bread only, but by every word that proceedeth out of the mouth of the Lord doth man live. (Deuteronomy 8:3)

When Satan tempted Jesus, he did not follow Satan's line of thought. He said what God's written word said on the subject of bread. You have to be thoroughly familiar with God's word, to know how to respond when you are tempted.

> And when the tempter came to him, he said, If thou be the Son of God, command that these stones be made bread. But he answered and said, It is written, Man shall not live by bread alone, but by every word that proceedeth out of the mouth of God. (Matthew 4:3–4)

Jesus explained to his disciples that manna was a symbol for him. He is the bread that came down from heaven and the Word of God.

God's Word accomplished the thing that he intended it to do. You can live your life by every word that came from God. You can feed on a fresh supply of God's Word every day.

> Then Jesus said unto them, Verily, verily I say unto you, Moses gave you not that bread from heaven; but my Father giveth you the true bread from heaven. For the bread of God is he which cometh down from heaven, and giveth life unto the world. Then said they unto him, Lord, evermore give us this bread. And Jesus said unto them, I am the bread of life: he that cometh to me shall never hunger; and he that believeth on me shall never thirst. (John 6:32–35)

"Eating his flesh" and "drinking his blood" are metaphors. When you live according to God's word, you are "eating his flesh." When your sins are covered by the blood of his sacrifice, you are "drinking his blood." Because of these two elements, you are alive in Christ, and he is alive in you.

> I am the living bread which came down from heaven: if any man eat of this bread, he shall live for ever: and the bread that I will give is my flesh, which I will give for the life of the world....He that eateth my flesh, and drinketh my blood, dwelleth in me, and I in him. (John 6:51, 56)

At the Last Supper, Jesus explained that the Passover meal was a picture of the New Covenant. He established the Lord's Supper as an ordinance of the Church. The bread and wine represent his body and his blood. Discerning the Lord's body is applying God's word to your life. Drinking the cup is applying Jesus' blood to the doorposts of your heart.

> For I have received of the Lord that which also I delivered unto you, that the Lord Jesus, the same night in which he was betrayed took bread: and when he had given thanks,

> **he brake it, and said, Take, eat: this is my body, which is broken for you: this do in remembrance of me. After the same manner also he took the cup, when he had supped, saying, This cup is the new testament in my blood: this do ye, as oft as ye drink it, in remembrance of me.. . . But let a man examine himself, and so let him eat of that bread, and drink of that cup. For he that eateth and drinketh unworthily, eateth and drinketh damnation to himself; not discerning the Lord's body. For this cause many are weak and sickly among you, and many sleep. For if we would judge ourselves, we should not be judged. (1 Corinthians 11:23–25; 28–31)**

## SPIRITUAL DRINK

God delivered the Children out of Egypt, a place of slavery to sin. They spent forty years wandering in the desert. They lived on manna. They drank water from a supernatural Rock that traveled with them. This Rock was a symbol for the Christ, like the Ark in the story of Noah. God did not intend for them to wander around the desert until they died. But they did it anyway. It was God's will for them to enter the Promised Land. Yet they refused to go. The desert is a place of spiritual immaturity. The Children of Israel were not willing to do what God told them to do. As long as you refuse to obey God, your circumstances will stay the same. Your life will be filled with frustration and disappointment. Your fear and unbelief limit what God can do for you. Your hopes and dreams will die with you in the desert.

This is God's lament to his people through the prophet Isaiah.

> **O that thou hadst hearkened to my commandments! Then had thy peace been as a river, and thy righteousness as the waves of the sea. (Isaiah 48:18)**

God's word is as essential to your life as water. In Jeremiah, the Lord says he is the fountain of living waters. Water represents God's word. A "broken cistern" is a false religion that does not contain the truth of the word of God.

> For my people have committed two evils; they have forsaken me, the fountain of living waters, and hewed them out cisterns, broken cisterns, that can hold no water. (Jeremiah 2:13)

In the time of Jesus, Jews treated Samaritans as an inferior race. A Samaritan woman was surprised that Jesus would even speak to her. He met her at a well where he asked her for a drink of water.

> Jesus answered and said unto her, If thou knewest the gift of God, and who it is that saith to thee, Give me to drink; thou wouldest have asked of him, and he would have given thee living water....But whosoever drinketh of the water that I shall give him shall never thirst; but the water that I shall give him shall be in him a well of water springing up into everlasting life. (John 4:10, 14)

Jesus prophesied about you. You have God's living water flowing out of you because you believe in him. To the people around you, you are like that spiritual Rock in the desert.

> In the last day, that great day of the feast, Jesus stood and cried, saying, If any man thirst, let him come unto me, and drink. He that believeth on me, as the scripture hath said, out of his belly shall flow rivers of living water. (But this spake he of the Spirit, which they that believe on him should receive: for the Holy Ghost was not yet given; because that Jesus was not yet glorified. (John 7:37–39)

A supernatural Rock went along with the children of Israel. It provided them water in the desert. When the Holy Spirit revealed to Peter that Jesus is the Messiah, Jesus said, "Upon this rock I will build my church." The rock he was talking about was not Peter. It was the rock of revelation of knowledge that Peter had received from the Holy Spirit. The Holy Spirit revealed the same truth to you. That is what made you a believer in Jesus.

> **Moreover, brethren, I would not that ye should be ignorant, how that all our fathers were under the cloud, and all passed through the sea; and were all baptized unto Moses in the cloud and in the sea; and did all eat the same spiritual meat; and did all drink the same spiritual drink: for they drank of that spiritual Rock that followed them: and that Rock was Christ. (1 Corinthians 10:1–4)**

This verse says that you experience things figuratively that the Children of Israel experienced literally. "Ensamples" means examples.

> **Now all these things happened unto them for ensamples: and they are written for our admonition, upon whom the ends of the world are come. (1 Corinthians 10:11)**

## SPIRITUAL MEAT

Spiritual meat is truth from the Word of God that you need to know. Incorporating God's word into your life is like eating meat. It nourishes you spiritually and it causes you to grow. When you were a baby Christian, you needed the sincere milk of the word. As you add more of God's concepts to your life, you'll prosper. You will be doing more of God's will as it is revealed to you. The more of it you do, the more you will want to do. You will be searching the scriptures to find more things to apply to your life. That is how you reach maturity as a believer in Christ

Spiritual meat is God's own truth. You'll recognize it when you hear it.

> **For the ear trieth words, as the mouth tasteth meat. (Job 34:3)**

Jesus explained to his disciples that eating meat symbolized doing God's will.

> In the meanwhile his disciples prayed him, saying, Master, eat. But he said unto them, I have meat to eat that ye know not of. Therefore said the disciples one to another, Hath any man brought of him aught to eat? Jesus said unto them, My meat is to do the will of him that sent me and to finish his work. (John 4:31–34)

Make it your goal to do everything Jesus commanded. That's how you show your love for him.

> Labor not for the meat that perisheth but for that meat which endureth unto everlasting life, which the Son of man shall give unto you: for him hath God the Father sealed. Then said they unto him, What shall we do, that we might work the works of God? Jesus answered and said unto them, This is the work of God, that ye believe on him whom he hath sent. (John 6:27–29)

Jesus speaks to those who have spiritual ears, and he reveals the meaning of his word to everyone who asks him. "Eating my flesh" and "Drinking my blood" are figurative. Doing God's word is "eating his flesh." "Drinking his blood" is applying Jesus' blood sacrifice to your life.

> For my flesh is meat indeed, and my blood is drink indeed. He that eateth my flesh, and drinketh my blood, dwelleth in me, and I in him. As the living Father hath sent me, and I live by the Father: so he that eateth me, even he shall live by me. (John 6:55–57)

Spiritual infants can't handle spiritual meat. As long as you are a baby Christian, you will continue to live in the desert where your diet will consist of the simple manna.

> **Anyone who lives on milk, being still an infant, is not acquainted with the teaching about righteousness. But solid food is for the mature, who by constant use have trained themselves to distinguish good from evil. (Hebrews 5:13–14 NIV)**

## THE VOICE OF GOD

The voice of God is not an audible voice. It is the voice of your conscience. You can always tell God's voice by what is being said. God's voice will always be consistent with what the Bible says. God is not going to tell you anything that conflicts with his word. You know that the Bible says not to commit murder. If a voice told you to kill someone, you would know immediately that it was not the voice of God. If a voice causes you to be confused, it is not the voice of God because the Bible says that God is not the author of confusion. If a voice makes you afraid, you know it is not the voice of God. The Bible says that God has not given us the spirit of fear. If a voice takes away your peace, it is not the voice of God. Psalm 85, verse 8, says that God will speak peace unto his people.

A message from God will be something of substance, something that is useful, and something that makes sense. It will be something that you need to know. The Holy Spirit will remind you of some incident or verse from the Bible. Then, he will explain how it applies to you. Most of the time he will be responding to something you have asked him. When God speaks to you, his words will stand out. They will be out of context with what you were thinking. Most of the time, you will hear the voice of God when you are quiet and alone with him.

God gave Elijah a great victory over the prophets of Baal. But when Jezebel threatened to kill him, he ran away and hid in a cave. God spoke directly to him there. God's still small voice isn't loud or spectacular like the wind or an earthquake. It is normal and natural like the voice of a friend.

> **And he said, Go forth, and stand upon the mount before the Lord. And, behold, the Lord passed by, and a great and**

> strong wind rent the mountains, and brake in pieces the rocks before the Lord; but the Lord was not in the wind: and after the wind an earthquake; but the Lord was not in the earthquake: and after the earthquake a fire; but the Lord was not in the fire: and after the fire a still small voice. And it was so, when Elijah heard it, that he wrapped his face in his mantle and went out, and stood in the entering of the cave. And, behold, there came a voice unto him, and said, What doest thou here, Elijah? (1 Kings 19:11–13)

God speaks to you while you are asleep, and teaches you things you need to know. The Holy Spirit will counsel you in every area of life.

> For God speaketh once, yea twice, yet man perceiveth it not. In a dream, in a vision of the night, when deep sleep falleth upon men, in slumberings upon the bed; Then he openeth the ears of men, and sealeth their instruction, that he may withdraw man from his purpose, and hide pride from man. He keepeth back his soul from the pit, and his life from perishing by the sword. (Job 33:14–18)

Your conscience usually speaks to you just before you go to sleep at night.

> I will bless the Lord, who hath given me counsel: my reins also instruct me in the night seasons. (Psalms 16:7)

You always have to watch what you say. You cannot say everything you think. Limit the things you say to agree with what the Bible says.

> Thou hast proved mine heart; thou hast visited me in the night; thou has tried me, and shalt find nothing; I am purposed that my mouth shall not transgress. Concerning the works of men, by the word of thy lips I have kept me from the paths of the destroyer. (Psalm 17:3–4)

This verse explains how God guides you in your daily life. You hear the voice of God with your spiritual ears.

> **And thine ears shall hear a word behind thee, saying. This is the way, walk ye in it, when ye turn to the right hand, and when ye turn to the left. (Isaiah 30:21)**

When the Lord speaks to you, you will know it. He will talk to you about things that you have asked him about. He will never say anything that contradicts the Bible. Knowing the Bible thoroughly will keep you from listening to the wrong voice.

> **To him the porter openeth; and the sheep hear his voice: and he calleth his own sheep by name, and leadeth them out. And when he putteth forth his own sheep, he goeth before them, and the sheep follow him, for they know his voice. And a stranger will they not follow, but will flee from him: for they know not the voice of strangers. (John 10:3–5)**

## THE WILL OF GOD

God's will and his word are the same. If you want to know God's will concerning anything, read what the Bible says about it. In First Timothy 2:3-4, we are told that it's God's will that every person be saved. But people still reject the salvation God provided them. You have a free will so you can make this choice. Why would God tell you to choose life if you did not have the ability to choose something else? God does not violate your will and impose his will on you.

The disciples asked Jesus to teach them to pray. He gave them this model prayer. Jesus revealed that God's will is not always done on Earth. He would not have told you to ask God for something that is already in effect. He said to ask for God's will to be done in your situation.

> After this manner therefore pray ye: Our Father which art in heaven, Hallowed be thy name. Thy kingdom come. Thy will be done in earth, as it is in heaven. (Matthew 6:9–10 )

It's God's will for everyone to be saved, but not everyone will go along with God's will.

> Even so it is not the will of your Father which is in heaven that one of these little ones should perish. (Matthew 18:14)

God's free gift of salvation doesn't automatically apply to everyone. It rightfully belongs to everyone who believes in Jesus.

> And this is the will of him that sent me, that every one which seeth the Son, and believeth on him, may have everlasting life: and I will raise him up at the last day. (John 6:40 )

God's will for you is that you rejoice and pray and give thanks to him in every situation.

> Rejoice evermore. Pray without ceasing. In every thing give thanks: for this is the will of God in Christ Jesus concerning you. (1 Thessalonians 5:16–18)

It is not God's will for some to be lost and others saved. The same opportunity is available to all, to choose either life or death.

> For this is good and acceptable in the sight of God our Savior; Who will have all men to be saved, and to come unto the knowledge of the truth. (1 Timothy 2:3–4)

> For so is the will of God, that with well doing ye may put to silence the ignorance of foolish men: as free, and not

> **using your liberty for a cloak of maliciousness, but as the servants of God. (1 Peter 2:15–16)**

It seems like Jesus is taking a long time before returning. Because of God's great mercy, he is giving people more time to be saved. "Repentance" means changing your mind and changing your direction.

> **The Lord is not slack concerning his promise, as some men count slackness; but is long suffering to us-ward, not willing that any should perish, but that all should come to repentance. (2 Peter 3:9)**

## THE WRITTEN WORD OF GOD

Jesus is the Living Word of God. The Bible is the written word of God. So the Bible is the written word about the Living Word. That's why they agree so perfectly. The more you read about Jesus, the better you know him. Eventually he becomes so real, it's as if he has stepped out of the pages of the Bible. He is not a historical figure or a fictional hero. He is real and he is alive today. He makes your life as a believer enjoyable and exciting. It is not a life of drudgery and hardship. It's the adventure of your life. It's having the Creator of the universe as your best friend. It's discovering the extent of the love he has for you. It's receiving the good things he has in store for you.

God spoke through Isaiah concerning His word. He said that his word always accomplishes what he intends it to do. Jesus is that word sent by God. He is that bread from heaven, which nourishes you. God's word is powerful and effective.

> **For as the rain cometh down, and the snow from heaven, and returneth not thither, but watereth the earth, and maketh it bring forth and bud, that it may give seed to the sower, and bread to the eater: so shall my word be that goeth forth out of my mouth: it shall not return unto me**

> void, but it shall accomplish that which I please, and it shall prosper in the thing whereto I sent it. (Isaiah 55:9–10)

Jesus explained an important truth to the religious leaders of his day. All the Hebrew Scriptures, the Law and the Prophets were written about him.

> And the Father himself, which hath sent me, hath borne witness of me. Ye have neither heard his voice at any time, nor seen his shape. And ye have not his word abiding in you: for whom he hath sent, him ye believe not. Search the Scriptures; for in them ye think ye have eternal life: and they are they which testify of me. And ye will not come to me, that ye might have life. (John 5:37–40)

The Bible presents the doctrine of Christ. It is much different from the doctrines of men. When there is a conflict between the two, always go with what the Bible says.

> All scripture is given by inspiration of God, and is profitable for doctrine, for reproof, for correction, for instruction in righteousness: That the man of God may be perfect, thoroughly furnished unto all good works. (2 Timothy 3:16–17)

This is Paul's advice to the young preacher, Timothy. He told him to preach the word of God. That is excellent advice for every preacher.

> Preach the word; be instant in season, out of season; reprove, rebuke, exhort with all long-suffering and doctrine. (2 Timothy 4:2)

It is true that men wrote the Bible. But God told them what to say. He inspired all of their words.

> Knowing this first, that no prophecy of the scripture is of any private interpretation. For the prophecy came not in old time by the will of man: but holy men of God spake as they were moved by the Holy Ghost. (2 Peter 1:20–21)

## YOUR HIGH PRIEST

Jesus is your High Priest. Because he lived as a man, he knows how you feel. He knows what temptations you face. He knows that you are weak and fail him often. When you are in trouble, come to Jesus. He has already made the perfect sacrifice for you. Now, he is interceding for you before the throne of God. He is representing you before God like a defense attorney.

The Bible says, come boldly to the throne of grace to obtain mercy. It does not say come and be rejected. Grace is favor from God that you do not deserve.

> Seeing then that we have a great high priest, that is passed into the heavens, Jesus the Son of God, let us hold fast our profession. For we have not an high priest which cannot be touched with the feeling of our infirmities; but was in all points tempted like as we are, yet without sin. Let us therefore come boldly unto the throne of grace, that we may obtain mercy, and find grace to help in time of need. (Hebrews 4:14–16)

Jesus lives forever. Presently, he's with God in heaven, where he is interceding for you.

> And they truly were many priests, because they were not suffered to continue by reason of death: But this man, because he continueth ever, hath an unchangeable priesthood. Wherefore he is able also to save them to the uttermost that come unto God by him, seeing he ever liveth to make intercession for them. (Hebrews 7:23–25)

The New Covenant is better than the Old because Jesus is the mediator of it. In him you have forgiveness of sin and justification by grace.

> **But now hath he obtained a more excellent ministry, by how much also he is the mediator of a better covenant, which was established upon better promises. For if that first covenant had been faultless, then should no place have been sought for the second. (Hebrews 8:6–7)**

Jesus, your High Priest, made one perfect offering to God. He sacrificed himself. You are no longer separated from God because of sin. His act of love covers a multitude of sins.

> **Then said he, Lo, I come to do thy will, O God. He taketh away the first, that he may establish the second. By the which will we are sanctified through the offering of the body of Jesus Christ once for all. And every priest standeth daily ministering and offering oftentimes the same sacrifices, which can never take away sins: But this man, after he had offered one sacrifice for sins for ever, sat down on the right hand of God; From henceforth expecting till his enemies be made his footstool. For by one offering he hath perfected for ever them that are sanctified. (Hebrews 10:9–14)**

## YOUR SAVIOR

Jesus is different from all other prophets and spiritual teachers. He is unique because he is God. Even though he lived as a man, he is also God. He is alive. He knows you and loves you. He is the only person who's qualified to be your Savior. He died so that you can live.

The Book of Isaiah was written more than seven hundred years before Jesus was born. This passage shows that the God of the Old Testament and Jesus are the same person. The Trinity is not difficult to understand when you think of it like this: I am a father, but I am also a son. I am still one person. The relationship is the only thing that is different.

> I, even I, am the Lord; and beside me there is no savior. I have declared, and have saved, and I have showed, when there was no strange god among you: therefore ye are my witnesses, saith the Lord, that I am God. Yea, before the day was I am he; and there is none that can deliver out of my hand: I will work, and who shall let it? (Isaiah 43:11–13)

In order to have access to the Living God, you must come through Jesus because he is God's son. There are no other ways to God or to heaven other than through Jesus.

> Jesus saith unto him, I am the way, the truth, and the life: no man cometh unto the Father, but by me. (John 14:6)

Jesus is the only begotten Son of God, and the only Savior of the world.

> Neither is there salvation in any other: for there is none other name under heaven given among men, whereby we must be saved. (Acts 4:12)

Because of Adam's sin, you were born a sinner. Because of Jesus, God considers you to be righteous.

> Therefore as by the offense of one judgment came upon all men to condemnation; even so by the righteousness of one the free gift came upon all men unto justification of life. For as by one man's disobedience many were made sinners, so by the obedience of one shall many be made righteous. (Romans 5:18–19)

The Bible clearly states that Jesus is God.

> We trust in the living God, who is the Savior of all men, specially of those that believe. (1 Timothy 4:10)

Even though Jesus was God, he was still obedient to God. This was part of his fulfilling of the Law.

> Who in the days of his flesh, when he had offered up prayers and supplications with strong crying and tears unto him that was able to save him from death, and was heard in that he feared; though he were a Son, yet learned he obedience by the things which he suffered; and being made perfect, he became the author of eternal salvation unto all them that obey him. (Hebrews 5:7–9)

PART TWO

# Things God Expects You To Do

In order to receive the things of God that are listed in Part One, you must obey the Word of God. There's a big difference between believing in Jesus and just saying that you do. If you truly believe that Jesus is God, you will value the things that he says. If the Spirit of God lives in you, you will want to do what he tells you. This is what Jesus says to everyone who believes in him.

> And why call ye me, Lord, Lord, and do not the things which I say? Whosoever cometh to me, and heareth my sayings, and doeth them, I will show you to whom he is like: He is like a man which built an house, and digged deep, and laid the foundation on a rock: and when the flood arose, the stream beat vehemently upon that house, and could not shake it: for it was founded upon a rock. But he that heareth, and doeth not, is like a man that without a foundation built an house upon the earth; against which the stream did beat vehemently, and immediately it fell; and the ruin of that house was great. (Luke 6:46–49)

## TO ABIDE IN CHRIST

"To abide in Christ" means that you live there. You're there all the time. You're don't just stop by to visit once in a while. When you abide in Jesus, he will live his life through you. Ada was my wife's mother. She based her everyday life on the Bible and it was obvious to everyone who knew her that Jesus lived through her. She told us, "you might be the only Bible some people will ever read." People were drawn to her because they knew that she loved them, and they loved her back. She was an excellent Bible.

You cannot bear any fruit unless you are connected to the Lord. Life flows from him to you.

> Abide in me, and I in you. As the branch cannot bear fruit of itself, except it abide in the vine; no more can ye, except ye abide in me. I am the vine, ye are the branches: He that abideth in me, and I in him, the same bringeth forth much fruit: for without me ye can do nothing. (John 15:4–5)

When you abide in Christ, you are glorifying God. When your will and God's will are the same, he will grant your requests.

> If ye abide in me, and my words abide in you, ye shall ask what ye will, and it shall be done unto you. Herein is my Father glorified, that ye bear much fruit; so shall ye be my disciples. (John 15:7–8)

This is the Lord's definition of abiding in Christ. It is living a life of love.

> If ye keep my commandments, ye shall abide in my love; even as I have kept my Father's commandments, and abide in his love. (John 15:10)

The reward of your obedience is having Jesus come to life in you.

> I am crucified with Christ: nevertheless I live; yet not I, but Christ liveth in me: and the life which I now live in the flesh I live by the faith of the Son of God, who loved me, and gave himself for me. (Galatians 2:20)

This is how you can tell if the Lord is alive in you, or not.

> And hereby we do know that we know him, if we keep his commandments. He that saith, I know him, and keepeth not his commandments is a liar, and the truth is not in him. But whoso keepeth his word, in him verily is the love of God perfected: hereby know we that we are in him. (1 John 2:3–5)

The Holy Spirit is the author of the Bible and he is alive in you. He will teach you everything you need to know.

> But the annointing which ye have received of him abideth in you and ye need not that any man teach you: but as the same annointing teacheth you of all things, and is truth, and is no lie, and even as it hath taught you, ye shall abide in him. (1 John 2:27)

When you are keeping the Love Commandment, the Spirit of God will manifest himself to you.

> And this is his commandment, that we should believe on the name of his Son Jesus Christ, and love one another, as he gave us commandment. And he that keepeth his commandments dwelleth in him, and he in him. And hereby we know that he abideth in us, by the Spirit which he hath given us. (1 John 3:23–24)

When you have the desire to love your neighbor, you can be assured that Jesus is alive in you. People just do not do that on their own apart from God.

> If we love one another, God dwelleth in us, and his love is perfected in us. Hereby know we that we dwell in him, and he in us, because he hath given us of his Spirit. (1 John 4:12–13)

Jesus is love personified. He wants you to be like him and he empowers you to do so.

> God is love; and he that dwelleth in love dwelleth in God, and God in him. (1 John 4:16)

## TO ASK FOR WHAT YOU WANT

When your will and God's will are the same, you will not ask for things you cannot have. When you are doing what the Bible says, you are a righteous person doing righteousness. The things that you desire will be consistent with God's will. You will be confident that God will grant your requests.

Wicked people do not expect God to give them anything. They think that God is angry with them and they are right.

> The desire of the righteous is only good: but the expectation of the wicked is wrath. (Proverbs 11:23)

Do not repeat the same prayer over and over. God knows what you need. When he answers your prayer, be sure to thank him. That is part of the respect that he deserves.

> But when ye pray, use not vain repetitions, as the heathen do: for they think that they shall be heard for their much speaking. Be not ye therefore like unto them: for your

> Father knoweth what things ye have need of, before ye ask him. (Matthew 6:7–8)

This is what your life will be like when your will is the same as God's.

> Ask, and it shall be given you; seek, and ye shall find; knock, and it shall be opened unto you: For every one that asketh receiveth; and he that seeketh findeth; and to him that knocketh it shall be opened. (Matthew 7:7–8)

Jesus said that you can ask God for the things you want, and he will give them to you.

> Whatsoever ye shall ask the Father in my name, he will give it you. Hitherto have ye asked nothing in my name: ask, and ye shall receive, that your joy may be full. (John 16:23–24)

God is extremely generous. He provides everything you need.

> He that spared not his own son, but delivered him up for us all, how shall he not with him also freely give us all things? (Romans 8:32)

Make your requests to God. You can ask him for anything you want.

> Be careful for nothing; but in every thing by prayer and supplication with thanksgiving let your requests be made known unto God. (Philippians 4:6)

God is better than any human father. He is not poor and weak. He is not mean and stingy. He doesn't have you depending on him, and then let you down. This verse says to come to God and obtain mercy. It does not say come to God and be rejected by him.

> **Let us therefore come boldly unto the throne of grace, that we might obtain mercy, and find grace to help in time of need. (Hebrews 4:16)**

If you do not receive what you have requested, there is a reason. Usually it is because of some kind of sin. God hates sin. He cannot reward it. He cannot be involved in it. Unless your heart is right before God, you will not receive anything from him.

> **From whence come wars and fightings among you? come they not hence, even of your lusts that war in your members? Ye lust, and have not: ye kill, and desire to have, and cannot obtain: ye fight and war, yet ye have not, because ye ask not. Ye ask, and receive not, because ye ask amiss, that ye may consume it upon your lusts. (James 4:1–3)**

You can only receive the things you need in life through Jesus.

> **According as his divine power hath given unto us all things that pertain unto life and godliness, through the knowledge of him that hath called us to glory and virtue: (2 Peter 1:3)**

When your heart is right before God, you will have the right motives. You will please God by keeping his commandments. Then he will give you the things you desire.

> **Beloved, if our heart condemn us not, then have we confidence toward God. And whatsoever we ask, we receive of him, because we keep his commandments, and do those things that are pleasing in his sight. (1 John 3:21–22)**

## TO BE CONVERTED

I thought I was saved when I was a kid, but I was mistaken. I had asked Jesus to save me from Hell. I had walked an aisle, shaken a preacher's hand, and joined a church. I considered myself a Christian. I believed in the existence of Jesus, but I did not have a personal relationship with him. I was still the same self-centered person I had always been. I was glad to take everything God would give me, but I was not willing to give him anything in return. I had one foot in God's kingdom and the other in the world. Going to college, being in the Army, and socializing with non-believers had nearly destroyed what little faith I had. But I was fascinated by the Bible, and God took an interest in me. He took me under his wing, and taught me everything I needed to know.

God sent a new pastor to our church. Brother Paul was different from any preacher I had ever heard. He preached the Bible. I heard the pure unadulterated word of God for the first time in my life. It changed my life forever. Brother Paul told that it was essential to make a commitment to God. He said, if you believe in Jesus, act like it. If you don't believe in him, don't bother pretending that you do. You are not fooling anybody. You are especially not fooling God. To be converted is to make up your mind, once and for all, that you're going to stick with Jesus, no matter what. It was like being married to him. I was twenty-seven, when I was converted. I decided that I would follow Jesus for the rest of my life and do whatever he commanded me to do. That was the beginning of my walk with the Lord which I have continued unto the present day.

This is a Psalm of David that talks about God's word. It's sweeter than honey and more precious than gold. It saves you from death and it tells you how to receive God's rewards.

> **The law of the Lord is perfect, converting the soul: the testimony of the Lord is sure, making wise the simple. The statutes of the Lord are right, rejoicing the heart:**

> the commandment of the Lord is pure, enlightening the eyes. The fear of the Lord is clean, enduring for ever: the judgments of the Lord are true and righteous altogether. More to be desired are they than gold, yea, than much fine gold: sweeter also than honey and the honeycomb. Moreover by them is thy servant warned: and in keeping of them there is great reward. (Psalm 19:7–11)

Being converted is a necessary part of being a son of God. You have to be teachable like a child in order to be trained by the Holy Spirit.

> At the same time came the disciples unto Jesus, saying, Who is the greatest in the kingdom of heaven? And Jesus called a little child unto him, and set him in the midst of them, and said, Verily I say unto you, except ye be converted, and become as little children, ye shall not enter into the kingdom of heaven. Whosoever therefore shall humble himself as this little child, the same is greatest in the kingdom of heaven. (Matthew 18:1–4)

Repentance is changing your mind and changing your direction. It is changing your way of thinking concerning sin. It is realizing that sins are not desirable and glamorous. They are inconvenient, sleazy and they cost you a lot. Conversion is changing your way of life to be consistent with God's word. It is like you were walking one way, then you turned and started going the other direction. Then you are headed toward God instead of away from him.

> Repent ye therefore, and be converted, that your sins may be blotted out, when the times of refreshing shall come from the presence of the Lord; and he shall send Jesus Christ, which before was preached unto you. (Acts 3:19–20)

## TO BE FAITHFUL

To be faithful is to be reliable and to always keep your word. Jesus is always faithful to you. This is one of the Lord's character traits that you must develop. He promised to reward you for being faithful to him. That means keeping his Word as well as your own. Faithfulness is one aspect of the fruit of the Holy Spirit. He empowers you to be faithful to God.

God preserves every one who is faithful to him.

> O love the Lord, all ye his saints: for the Lord preserveth the faithful, and plentifully rewardeth the proud doer. (Psalm 31:23)

People think of themselves as faithful, but they're not.

> Most men will proclaim every one his own goodness: but a faithful man who can find? (Proverbs 20:6 )

If you want to be blessed by God, then be faithful to his word.

> A faithful man shall abound with blessings: but he that maketh haste to be rich shall not be innocent. (Proverbs 28:20)

If God gives you something to say, tell it exactly the way you heard it. That is a part of being faithful to God.

> The prophet that hath a dream, let him tell a dream; and he that hath my word, let him speak my word faithfully. What is the chaff to the wheat? saith the Lord. (Jeremiah 23:28)

This is the one of Jesus' teachings called the Parable of the Talents. A talent was a specific amount of money. In this parable Jesus used differing amounts of money to represent God's gifts. You are a faithful servant of the Lord when you use your gifts effectively.

> After a long time the lord of those servants cometh, and reckoneth with them. And so he that had received five talents came and brought another five talents saying, Lord, thou deliveredst unto me five talents: behold, I have gained beside them five talents more. His lord said unto him, Well done, thou good and faithful servant: thou hast been faithful over a few things, I will make thee ruler over many things: enter thou into the joy of thy lord. (Matthew 25:19–21)

Jesus said that if a man is dishonest in minor things, he will be dishonest in major things too. "Mammon" is money. The things God provides are more valuable than money. They are the true riches in life.

> He that is faithful in that which is least is faithful also in much: and he that is unjust in the least is unjust also in much. If therefore ye have not been faithful in the unrighteous mammon, who will commit to your trust the true riches? And if ye have not been faithful in that which is another man's, who shall give you that which is your own? (Luke 16:10–12)

A steward is a person in charge of something valuable. You are a steward of the things of God. He requires that you be faithful to him.

> Let a man so account of us, as of the ministers of Christ, and stewards of the mysteries of God. Moreover it is required in stewards, that a man be found faithful. (1 Corinthians 4:1–2)

## TO BE GODLY

Jesus is God in human form. God's will for you is for you to be like him, to be motivated by love instead of selfishness. That is your destiny. The Holy Spirit will empower you to be like Jesus. You have to cooperate with him, and it takes time. You will have to stop giving in to the desires of your flesh. But it's definitely worth your trouble because "godliness is profitable unto all things."

First Corinthians, Chapter Thirteen, is called the "love chapter." It gives you the specifics of God's definition of love. "Charity" is the archaic word for this kind of love.

> **For we know in part, and we prophesy in part. But when that which is perfect is come, then that which is in part shall be done away. When I was a child, I spake as a child, I understood as a child, I thought as a child: but when I became a man, I put away childish things. For now we see through a glass, darkly; but then face to face: now I know in part; but then shall I know even as also I am known. And now abideth faith, hope, charity, these three; but the greatest of these is charity. (1 Corinthians 13:9–13)**

As you continue to express God's love, you will get better at it, and you will become more like Jesus. It is like looking at the Lord's reflection in a mirror and having your face change to look like his.

> **But we all, with open face beholding as in a glass the glory of the Lord, are changed into the same image from glory to glory, even as by the Spirit of the Lord. (2 Corinthians 3:18)**

Being like Jesus will get you everything. It's the only way you can have access to God.

> **But refuse profane and old wives' fables, and exercise thyself rather unto godliness. For bodily exercise profiteth**

> little: but godliness is profitable unto all things, having promise of the life that now is, and of that which is to come. (1 Timothy 4:7–8)

God's will is for you to be like Jesus. You become like him by loving your neighbor. This is the prerequisite to receiving what God has promised.

> According as his divine power hath given unto us all things that pertain unto life and godliness, through the knowledge of him that hath called us to glory and virtue: Whereby are given unto us exceeding great and precious promises: that by these ye might be partakers of the divine nature, having escaped the corruption that is in the world through lust. (2 Peter 1:3–4)

The following is a list of desirable traits. You have to work at making them part of your life.

> And beside this, giving all diligence, add to your faith virtue; and to virtue knowledge; and to knowledge temperance; and to temperance patience; and to patience godliness; and to godliness brotherly kindness; and to brotherly kindness charity. For if these things be in you and abound, they make you that ye shall neither be barren nor unfruitful in the knowledge of our Lord Jesus Christ. (Peter 1:5–8)

## TO BELIEVE ON HIM

Believing on Jesus is more than just believing that he exists. It means accepting his teachings and following his example. It's adopting his ideas as your own and basing your life on them. Supporters of abortion don't just believe that abortion exists. They think abortions are good things, and they encourage women to have them. Marxists believe in the teachings of

Karl Marx. Darwinists believe in the teachings of Charles Darwin. They choose to accept these men's ideas, and they reject the teachings of Jesus. The name of Jesus is above every name that is given among men. There are millions of people who are Christians in name only. They're part of a Christian culture. They believe that Jesus is real, but they have no relationship with him. They have not received him as their Savior and Lord.

This passage is about Jesus. Without him, you're dead. Believing on him gives you life.

> **For he whom God hath sent speaketh the words of God: for God giveth not the Spirit by measure unto him. The Father loveth the Son, and hath given all things into his hand. He that believeth on the Son hath everlasting life: and he that believeth not the Son shall not see life; but the wrath of God abideth on him. (John 3:34–36)**

In Philippi, Paul and Silas were in prison. At midnight, they were singing praises to God when an earthquake opened the doors of their prison. Their behavior caused the jailer to become a believer. This was what he asked them.

> **Sirs, what must I do to be saved? And they said, Believe on the Lord Jesus Christ, and thou shalt be saved, and thy house. And they spake unto him the word of the Lord, and to all that were in his house. (Acts 16:30–32)**

This passage explains how you can be saved. When you accept Jesus as your Savior and Lord, he will accept you and make you part of his family.

> **But what saith it? The word is nigh thee, even in thy mouth, and in thy heart: that is, the word of faith, which we preach: That if thou shalt confess with thy mouth the Lord Jesus, and shalt believe in thine heart that God hath raised him from the dead, thou shalt be saved. For with the heart**

> man believeth unto righteousness; and with the mouth confession is made unto salvation. (Romans 10:8–10)

People do not just start keeping God's commandments on their own. The Holy Spirit gives them the desire to do so.

> Whosoever believeth that Jesus is the Christ is born of God: and every one that loveth him that begat loveth him also that is begotten of him. By this we know that we love the children of God, when we love God, and keep his commandments. (1 John 5:1–2)

Non-believers cannot imagine believing the things that you believe: that Jesus came to Earth and lived among men, that God raised him from the dead, and that you will live with him forever. You have the Holy Spirit as an inward witness. He confirms that these things are true, and so do the Scriptures. They contain the testimony of God and the testimony of those who witnessed these things.

> For there are three that bear record in heaven, the Father, the Word, and the Holy Ghost: and these three are one. And there are three that bear witness in earth, the spirit, and the water, and the blood: and these three agree in one. If we receive the witness of men, the witness of God is greater: for this is the witness of God which he hath testified of his Son. He that believeth on the Son of God hath the witness in himself: he that believeth not God hath made him a liar; because he believeth not the record that God gave of his Son. (1 John 5:7–10)

## TO CONTROL YOUR SPEECH

The words you speak reveal what is in your heart. Your destiny and your survival are based on what you say. Carefully control your words, because they can't be taken back. Don't tell everything that you know.

Don't give voice to everything you think. Don't give people "a piece of your mind." If you're always in agreement with what God says, you won't get yourself into trouble. Express your thoughts only when they are consistent with the Bible.

The following is one of David's conversations with God. He reaffirms the decision to watch what he says. He says that he has prevented his own destruction by restricting what he says.

> **Thou hast proved mine heart; thou hast visited me in the night; thou has tried me, and shalt find nothing; I am purposed that my mouth shall not transgress. Concerning the works of men, by the word of thy lips I have kept me from the paths of the destroyer. (Psalm 17:2–4)**

Choose things to say to others that encourage people and build them up. Always be positive. Speak words of life. Do not give voice to negative thoughts.

> **A wholesome tongue is a tree of life: but perverseness therein is a breach in the spirit. (Proverbs 15:4)**

The words that you speak determine what you receive in life. They also determine whether you live or die.

> **A man's belly shall be satisfied with the fruit of his mouth; and with the increase of his lips shall he be filled. Death and life are in the power of the tongue; and they that love it shall eat the fruit thereof. (Proverbs 18:20–21)**

There is a connection between your words and your lifespan. "Guile" means deceit.

> **What man is he that desireth life, and loveth many days, that he may see good? Keep thy tongue from evil, and thy lips from speaking guile. (Proverbs 34:12–13)**

This is a part of Jesus' teaching called the Parable of the Talents. It describes several men in similar situations with different outcomes. What made the difference? The good man based his actions on the truth and received a reward. The wicked man acted on what he thought was true. That which he received was consistent with what he said.

> Then he which had received the one talent came and said, Lord, I knew thee that thou art an hard man, reaping where thou hast not sown, and gathering where thou hast not strawed: and I was afraid, and went and hid thy talent in the earth: lo there thou hast that is thine. His lord answered and said unto him, Thou wicked and slothful servant, thou knewest that I reap where I sowed not, and gather where I have not strawed. Thou oughtest therefore to have put my money to the exchangers, and then at my coming I should have received mine own with usury. (Matthew 25:24–27)

When you believe that God's word is true, your words will reflect that belief. Your words are a demonstration of your faith.

> We having the same spirit of faith, according as it is written, I believed, and therefore have I spoken; we also believe, and therefore speak. (Ephesians 4:13)

Always tell the truth. Remember the Golden Rule. You don't want people lying to you, so don't lie to them.

> Wherefore putting away lying, speak every man truth with his neighbor: for we are members one of another. (Ephesians 4:25)

"Corrupt communication" means words that are hurtful or offensive "Edifying" is building up. Build people up, instead of tearing them down.

> Let no corrupt communication proceed out of your mouth, but that which is good to the use of edifying, that it may minister grace unto the hearers. (Ephesians 4:29)

This is a list of things to eliminate from your life. Don't give voice to them.

> But now ye also put off all these: anger, wrath, malice, blasphemy, filthy communication out of your mouth. (Colossians 3:8)

Be especially careful what you say to non-believers. You cannot win them to Christ by offending them.

> Walk in wisdom toward them that are without, redeeming the time. Let your speech be always with grace, seasoned with salt, that ye may know how ye ought to answer every man. (Colossians 4:5–6)

This is from Paul's letter to Titus, the leader of the believers in Crete. Paul advised him to speak evil of no one and to focus his attention on doing what is right.

> Put them in mind to be subject to principalities and powers, to obey magistrates, to be ready to every good work, to speak evil of no man, to be no brawlers, but gentle, showing all meekness unto all men. (Titus 3:1–2)

There are people who seem to be godly until they open their mouths. Their words reveal that their hearts are not right before God.

> If any man among you seem to be religious, and bridleth not his tongue, but deceiveth his own heart, this man's religion is vain. (James 1:26)

The word "perfect" means fully developed or mature.

> For in many things we offend all. If any man offend not in word, the same is a perfect man, and able also to bridle the whole body. Behold we put bits in the horses' mouths, that they obey us; and we turn about their whole body. (James 3:2–3)

I used to be very critical and judgmental of others. I was not keeping the Golden Rule, and it cost me dearly. You don't want others to say bad things about you, so don't do that to them.

> Speak not evil one of another, brethren. He that speaketh evil of his brother, speaketh evil of the law: but if thou judge the law, thou art not a doer of the law, but a judge. There is one lawgiver, who is able to save and to destroy: who art thou that judgest another? (James 4:11–12)

"The oracles of God" are the scriptures. Everything you say should be consistent with God's ideas as expressed in the Bible.

> If any man speak, let him speak as the oracles of God. (1 Peter 4:11)

## TO CONTROL YOUR THOUGHTS

The things you believe did not originate with you. You got them from somebody else. God originated all of the good ideas. He knows everything and he defines reality. Everything he says in the Bible is true. For example, you might think that something is impossible. But Jesus said in Mark 10:27, "With men it is impossible, but not with God: for with God all things are possible." So there's a conflict between two ideas. You are going to choose one of these thoughts. Which one are you going to accept, God's or somebody else's? You are not limited to thinking the way the world thinks. The Bible says that you have the mind of Christ.

You can think like Jesus thinks. You have to control what you think, or somebody else will. The world, the flesh, and the devil will never stop trying to impose their ideas on you. The Lord always gives you a choice. You get to choose whether you will think like him or not. Trading your thoughts for God's is wise. It is like trading some useless junk for silver and gold.

These are King David's words to his son, Solomon. David was a man after God's own heart. You can take his advice and apply it to your own life.

> **And thou, Solomon my son, know thou the God of thy father, and serve him with a perfect heart and with a willing mind: for the Lord searcheth all hearts, and understandeth all the imaginations of the thoughts: if thou seek him, he will be found of thee; but if thou forsake him, he will cast thee off for ever. (1 Chronicles 28:9)**

Most people choose to do things their own way instead of God's way. That puts them on the road to death and destruction.

> **There is a way which seemeth right unto a man, but the end thereof are the ways of death. (Proverbs 14:12)**

Your thoughts cannot compare to God's. He is brilliant. By adopting his thoughts as your own, you are applying his genius to your life.

> **Let the wicked forsake his way, and the unrighteous man his thoughts: and let him return unto the Lord, and he will have mercy upon him; and to our God, for he will abundantly pardon. For my thoughts are not your thoughts, neither are your ways my ways, saith the Lord. For as the heavens are higher than the earth, so are my ways higher than your ways, and my thoughts than your thoughts. (Isaiah 55:7–9)**

Most people are not willing to abandon their own ideas and follow God's leadership.

> **But this thing commanded I them, saying, Obey my voice, and I will be your God, and ye shall be my people: and walk ye in all the ways that I have commanded you, that it may be well unto you. But they hearkened not, nor inclined their ear, but walked in the counsels and in the imagination of their evil heart, and went backward, and not forward. (Jeremiah 7:23–24)**

The world totally rejects God's ideas. It's easy to go along with them. Renewing your mind is adopting God's ideas as your own. Worldly people think they know everything. This is one of the symptoms of pride. God gives grace to the humble, not the proud.

> **And be not conformed to this world: but be ye transformed by the renewing of your mind, that ye may prove what is that good, and acceptable, and perfect, will of God. For I say, through the grace given unto me, to every man that is among you, not to think of himself more highly than he ought to think; but to think soberly, according as God hath dealt to every man the measure of faith. (Romans 12:2–3)**

The greatest challenge you face is in taking charge of your own mind. This is the where the enemy engages you. He never stops trying to control what you think. You have to oppose him one thought at a time.

> **Casting down imaginations, and every high thing that exalteth itself against the knowledge of God, and bringing into captivity every thought to the obedience of Christ. (2 Corinthians 10:5)**

The best way to control your mind is to think about what the Bible says. You cannot think two thoughts at once. These positive thoughts will take the place of your old negative ones.

> **Finally, brethren, whatsoever things are true, whatsoever things are honest, whatsoever things are just, whatsoever things are pure, whatsoever things are lovely, whatsoever things are of good report; if there be any virtue, and if there be any praise, think on these things. (Philippians 4:8)**

## TO DELIGHT IN THE WORLD

Some of us are fascinated by the word of God and cannot get enough of it. Others have no interest in it. They know that they are going to heaven, and that is enough for them. They do not want anything else from God. Delighting in the Word of God is not for everyone. But if you consume massive quantities of the Word of God, and apply it to your life, God will reward you greatly.

"To delight in" something means to enjoy it immensely. "The law of the Lord" is the Bible. Delighting in God's word will always cause you to prosper. Those who are addicted to drinking think about drinking all the time. Those who are obsessed with sex think about sex all the time. If you thought about the Bible all the time, this is how your life would be.

> **Blessed is the man that walketh not in the counsel of the ungodly, nor standeth in the way of sinners, nor sitteth in the seat of the scornful. But his delight is in the law of the Lord; and in his law doth he meditate day and night. And he shall be like a tree planted by the rivers of water, that bringeth forth his fruit in his season; his leaf also shall not wither; and whatsoever he doeth shall prosper. (Psalm 1:1–3)**

This is one of the biggest surprises in the Bible. The Lord has promised that if you will delight yourself in him, he will give you the desires of your heart. What an amazingly generous God we serve!

> Trust in the Lord, and do good; so shalt thou dwell in the land, and verily thou shalt be fed. Delight thyself also in the Lord; and he shall give thee the desires of thine heart. (Psalm 37:3–4)

When you fear the Lord and delight in his commandments, this is what he gives you.

> Praise ye the Lord; blessed is the man that feareth the Lord, that delighteth greatly in his commandments. His seed shall be mighty upon earth: the generation of the upright shall be blessed. Wealth and riches shall be in his house: and his righteousness endureth for ever. Unto the upright there ariseth light in the darkness: he is gracious, and full of compassion and righteous. (Psalm 112:1–4)

You are not obligated to literally keep the Sabbath, because you are not under the Law of Moses. You are under God's law of liberty. The Sabbath symbolizes the things of God as opposed to worldly things. You are not limited to serving God one day a week. You can serve him everyday.

> If thou turn away thy foot from the Sabbath, from doing thy pleasure on my holy day; and call the Sabbath a delight, the holy of the Lord, honorable; and shalt honor him, not doing thine own ways, nor finding thine own pleasure, nor speaking thine own words: then shalt thou delight thyself in the Lord; and I will cause thee to ride upon the high places of the earth, and feed thee with the heritage of Jacob thy father: for the mouth of the Lord hath spoken it. (Isaiah 58:13–14)

## TO DEPART FROM EVIL

God says that to depart from evil is understanding. He knows that when you truly understand what the Bible says, you will do what it says. Most people love their sins so much that they just can't give them up. The smartest move you can make is to depart from evil. Make it a habit to do everything God's way. Your old bad habits will disappear. You will still have old temptations tugging at you to lead you astray. But God will empower you to overcome them. Are you willing to give up your favorite sins?

> And unto man he said, Behold, the fear of the Lord, that is wisdom, and to depart from evil is understanding. (Job 28:28)

Departing from evil actually is a matter of life and death.

> Depart from evil, and do good; and dwell for evermore.
> For the Lord loveth judgment, and forsaketh not his saints; they are preserved for ever; but the seed of the wicked shall be cut off. (Psalm 37:27–28)

Fools are those who rebel against God. Now that God has changed you on the inside, you can no longer rebel against him. You have an alliance with him. You love him and he is your friend.

> The fool hath said in his heart, there is no God. Corrupt are they, and have done abominable iniquity: there is none that doeth good. God looked down from heaven upon the children of men, to see if there were any that did understand, that did seek God. Every one of them is gone back: they are altogether become filthy; there is none that doeth good, no, not one. (Psalm 53:1–3)

Pay no attention to how things appear. Take God's word for it; things really are the way he says they are. This is one of God's secrets of good health. Do not even think about doing evil.

> Be not wise in thine own eyes: fear the Lord, and depart from evil. It shall be health to thy navel, and marrow to thy bones. (Proverbs 3:7–8)

An "abomination" is something that is intensely hated.

> The desire accomplished is sweet to the soul: but it is abomination to fools to depart from evil. (Proverbs 13:19)

The best way to eliminate evil is to replace it with good. Obeying God's word takes up the time that you used to spend doing evil things.

> By mercy and truth iniquity is purged: and by the fear of the Lord men depart from evil. (Proverbs 16:6)

## TO DO GOD'S WILL

God's word and his will are the same. When you're doing what the Bible says, you're doing God's will. You think and act differently from the people of the world. Those who heard Jesus in person were astonished at his doctrine. People are still astonished by the doctrine of Christ. It is very different from the religious traditions of men.

God spoke through the Prophet Isaiah. He explained that the fasting he desires is not literal but figurative. It is not going without food. It is spending your resources on behalf of others. It is providing food, clothing, and shelter to people in need. God's will is that you show love and compassion for others. When you become a blessing to others, God will bless you.

> Is not this the fast that I have chosen? To loose the bands of wickedness, to undo the heavy burdens, and to let the oppressed go free, and that ye break every yoke? Is it not to deal thy bread to the hungry, and that thou bring the poor that are cast out to thy house? When thou seest the

> naked, that thou cover him; and that thou hide not thyself from thine own flesh? Then shall thy light break forth as the morning, and thine health shall spring forth speedily: and thy righteousness shall go before thee; the glory of the Lord shall be thy reward. Then shalt thou call, and the Lord shall answer; thou shalt cry, and he shall say, Here I am. If thou take away from the midst of thee the yoke, the putting forth of the finger, and speaking vanity; and if thou draw out thy soul to the hungry, and satisfy the afflicted soul; then shall thy light rise in obscurity, and thy darkness be as the noonday: and the Lord shall guide thee continually, and satisfy thy soul in drought, and make fat thy bones: and thou shalt be like a watered garden, and like a spring of water, whose waters fail not. (Isaiah 58:6–11)

There are two prerequisites to being heard by God. You have to be one of his people and you have to be doing his will.

> Now we know that God heareth not sinners: but if any man be a worshipper of God, and doeth his will, him he heareth. (John 9:31)

If you are supposed to do something, then be sure that you do it. Do it for the Lord.

> Servants, be obedient to them that are your masters according to the flesh, with fear and trembling, in singleness of your heart, as unto Christ; not with eye service, as men pleasers; but as the servants of Christ, doing the will of God from the heart. Knowing that whatsoever good thing any man doeth, the same shall he receive of the Lord, whether he be bond or free. (Ephesians 6:5–8)

The term "the world" does not mean the environment. It refers to everything that opposes God and his word. It is the opposite of the kingdom of God.

> **Love not the world, neither the things that are in the world. If any man love the world, the love of the Father is not in him. For all that is in the world, the lust of the flesh, and the lust of the eyes, and the pride of life, is not of the Father, but is of the world. And the world passeth away, and the lust thereof: but he that doeth the will of God abideth for ever. (1 John 2:15–17)**

## TO DO GOOD WORKS

Your salvation is based on Jesus' works, not your own. But your works are evidence of the fact that you are saved. People who benefit from your good works will be thankful to God. Glory and shame are opposites. You are either bringing glory or shame to the cause of Christ.

The Bible plainly states that God will reward you for the good things you do.

> **Also unto thee, O Lord, belongeth mercy: for thou renderest to every man according to his work. (Psalm 62:12)**

The purpose of your life is to glorify God. Your good works will bring glory to God.

> **Let your light so shine before men, that they may see your good works, and glorify your Father which is in heaven. (Matthew 5:16)**

Jesus said that you can recognize false prophets by their fruits. They are not going to produce good works that bring glory to God. You are not going to see the fruit of the Spirit in their lives because they do not have the Spirit of God living in them.

> Beware of false prophets, which come to you in sheep's clothing, but inwardly they are ravening wolves. Ye shall know them by their fruits. Do men gather grapes of thorns, or figs of thistles? Even so every good tree bringeth forth good fruit; but a corrupt tree bringeth forth evil fruit. A good tree cannot bring forth evil fruit, neither can a corrupt tree bring forth good fruit. Every tree that bringeth not forth good fruit is hewn down, and cast into the fire. Wherefore by their fruits ye shall know them. (Matthew 7:15–20)

When you are a conduit to others, God will provide enough for you and for them. When people know that God is providing for them, they will be thankful to him.

> And God is able to make all grace abound toward you; that ye, always having all sufficiency in all things, may abound to every good work: (as it is written, he hath dispersed abroad; he hath given to the poor: his righteousness remaineth for ever. Now he that ministereth seed to the sower both minister bread for your food, and multiply your seed sown, and increase the fruits of your righteousness;) being enriched in every thing to all bountifulness, which causeth through us thanksgiving to God. For the administration of this service not only supplieth the want of the saints, but is abundant also by many thanksgivings unto God. (2 Corinthians 9:8–12)

This archaic term "to communicate" means to donate food, clothing, housing, or money directly to those in need.

> Charge them that are rich in this world, that they be not high-minded, nor trust in uncertain riches, but in the living God, who giveth us richly all things to enjoy; that they do good, that they be rich in good works, ready to distribute, willing to communicate. (1 Timothy 6:17–18)

This is how Christianity differs from all other religions. The others tell their followers they have to work their way to heaven. You don't have to do anything to earn your salvation. It is a free gift from God.

> Not by works of righteousness which we have done, but according to his mercy he saved us. (Titus 3:5 )

The Holy Spirit gives you the desire to do good works. All you have to do is to follow this desire. That is being led by the Spirit of God.

> This is a faithful saying, and these things I will that thou affirm constantly, that they which have believed in God might be careful to maintain good works. These things are good and profitable unto men. (Titus 3:8)

## TO DO WHAT IS RIGHT

Some say that we have no righteousness except that which Jesus has provided. They quote Isaiah 64:6, "Our righteousnesses are as filthy rags in God's sight." It is true that you cannot be saved by your own righteousness. Jesus paid for your salvation with his own blood. When you receive him by faith, you receive the benefit of his righteousness. That puts you in right-standing with God. But the term "righteousness" is used another way in the Bible. It means "doing what is right." Doing what is right makes you eligible to receive what God has promised. In addition to your positional righteousness, there is righteousness that you can either do or not do.

God defines your righteousness as "observing to do all" his commandments.

> **And it shall be our righteousness, if we observe to do all these commandments before the Lord our God, as he hath commanded us. (Deuteronomy 6:25)**

When you do what the Bible says, you are doing righteousness.

> **My tongue shall speak of thy word: for all thy commandments are righteousness. (Psalm 119:172)**

Jesus' finished work on the cross has reversed the effects of Adam's disobedience. He is the second Adam, and the rightful heir to the Earth. You are a joint-heir with him.

> **For if by one man's offense death reigned by one; much more they which receive abundance of grace and of the gift of righteousness shall reign in life by one, Jesus Christ. Therefore as by the offense of one judgment came upon all men to condemnation; even so by the righteousness of one the free gift came upon all men unto justification of life. For as by one man's disobedience many were made sinners, so by the obedience of one shall many be made righteous. (Romans 5:17–19)**

After you're born again, doing right comes naturally to you.

> **If you know that he is righteous, ye know that every one that doeth righteousness is born of him. (1 John 2:29)**

What people are like on the inside always shows on the outside. Believers in Jesus have an inner desire to do what is right. Non-believers have no interest in righteousness.

> Little children, let no man deceive you: he that doeth righteousness is righteous, even as he is righteous. He that committeth sin is of the devil; for the devil sinneth from the beginning. For this purpose the Son of God was manifested, that he might destroy the works of the devil. Whosoever is born of God doth not commit sin; for his seed remaineth in him: and he cannot sin, because he is born of God. In this the children of God are manifest, and the children of the devil: whosoever doeth not righteousness is not of God, neither he that loveth not his brother. (1 John 3:7–10)

## TO FORGIVE OTHERS

When you obey God, you benefit from his principle of reaping what you have sown. What you do for others will be done to you. For example, when you forgive others, you will be forgiven by God. Follow the example set by Jesus, and treat people better than they deserve to be treated.

When you are thinking about revenge, you cannot think about anything else. Never retaliate against anyone who hurts you. God says he will repay everyone who does you wrong.

> Say not, I will do so to him as he hath done to me: I will render to the man according to his work. (Proverbs 24:29)

God cannot reward you for being unforgiving. You cannot receive something that you withhold from others. Here is the good news. When you forgive other people and overlook their shortcomings, God will do the same for you.

> For if ye forgive men their trespasses, your heavenly Father will also forgive you: but if ye forgive not men their trespasses, neither will your Father forgive your trespasses. (Matthew 6:14–15)

Do not come to God and ask him for something when you have unforgiveness in your heart.

> And when ye stand praying, forgive, if ye have aught against any: that your Father also which is in heaven may forgive you your trespasses. (Mark 11:25)

Never hold a grudge. If someone hurts you, get over it and forgive him.

> Take heed to yourselves: If thy brother trespass against thee, rebuke him; and if he repent, forgive him. And if he trespass against thee seven times in a day, and seven times in a day turn again to thee, saying, I repent; thou shalt forgive him. (Luke 17:3–4)

Jesus prayed for the men who put him to death, and he forgave them. This is the high standard he has set for us to follow.

> And when they were come to the place, which is called Calvary, there they crucified him, and the malefactors, one on the right hand, and the other on the left. Then said Jesus, Father, forgive them; for they know not what they do. (Luke 23:33–34)

God reserves for himself the right to take revenge. If you attempt to do it yourself, you will be attempting to usurp his authority.

> Dearly beloved, avenge not yourselves, but rather give place unto wrath: for it is written, vengeance is mine; I will repay, saith the Lord. (Romans 12:19)

If you punish others for hurting you, you are also punishing yourself. Get rid of all negative feelings toward those who hurt you, forgive them and love them.

> Let all bitterness, and wrath, and anger, and clamor, and evil speaking, be put away from you, with all malice: and be ye kind one to another, tenderhearted, forgiving one another, even as God for Christ's sake hath forgiven you. (Ephesians 4:31–32)

## TO GIVE

God's concept of giving does not just apply to money. He expects you to give of your time and your talents. He expects that you will use the things he gives you to benefit others. Jesus gave everything he had. He submitted his body to torture and he shed his blood for you. He continually takes care of you because he loves you. He asks you to imitate him by giving something of yourself to people in need.

God promises that he will repay you the money you spend on the poor.

> He that hath pity on the poor lendeth unto the Lord; and that which he hath given will he pay him again. (Proverbs 19:17)

Giving to the poor will cause your own financial needs to be met. Pretending not to see their need will bring curses instead of blessings.

> He that giveth unto the poor shall not lack: but he that hideth his eyes shall have many a curse. (Proverbs 28:27)

Jesus said that his children do not have to pay tribute money to him.

> What thinkest thou, Simon? of whom do the kings of the earth take custom or tribute? of their own children, or of strangers? Peter saith unto him, Of strangers. Jesus saith unto him, Then are the children free. (Matthew 17:25–26)

When you give to others, God will give to you. Whatever you do for someone else determines what he will do for you. That is good news for everyone lives according to the Golden Rule; and bad news for those who mistreat other people.

> **Give, and it shall be given unto you; good measure, pressed down, and shaken together, and running over, shall men give into your bosom. For with the same measure that ye mete withal it shall be measured to you again. (Luke 6:38)**

Be motivated by love in everything you do, especially in your giving. Don't give because it's something you have to do. Give because you love God and you want to please him. Give to others because you love them.

> **Every man according as he purposeth in his heart, so let him give; not grudgingly, or of necessity: for God loveth a cheerful giver. (2 Corinthians 9:7)**

God's resources are limitless. He has promised to provide for all of your material needs.

> **But my God shall supply all your need according to his riches in glory by Christ Jesus. (Philippians 4:19)**

God requires that you take care of your family. That is what it means to be a man. A real man supports his wife and children. If your children are not receiving anything from their father, you won't be receiving anything from God, your Father.

> **But if any provide not for his own, and specially for those of his own house, he hath denied the faith, and is worse than an infidel. (1 Timothy 5:8)**

Talk is cheap. The Bible says to provide direct financial help to people in need.

> **What doth it profit, my brethren, though a man say he hath faith, and hath not works? Can faith save him? If a brother or sister be naked, and destitute of daily food, and one of you say unto them, depart in peace, be ye warmed and filled; notwithstanding ye give them not those things which are needful to the body; what doth it profit? (James 2:14–16)**

You glorify God when you are generous to people in need. They will thank God for helping them. Your job is to use the resources God has given you to meet the needs of his people. When you do your job, God's love will flow through you.

> **But whoso hath this world's good, and seeth his brother have need, and shutteth up his bowels of compassion from him, how dwelleth the love of God in him? (1 John 3:17)**

## TO GIVE THANKS

Your thankfulness to God is a demonstration of your faith in him. This is a continuous sacrifice; and it is the sacrifice that he desires. Make it a habit to be thankful to God, no matter what. If you complain, you are giving voice to unbelief instead of faith. It is like you are saying that you don't believe God, and you don't trust him. That attitude is the opposite of faith, and it has a negative effect.

There is a protocol for you to follow when approaching God. He desires for you to be thankful and joyful in his presence.

> **O come, let us sing unto the Lord: let us make a joyful noise to the rock of our salvation. Let us come before his presence with thanksgiving, and make a joyful noise unto him with psalms. (Psalm 95:1–2)**

Remember to thank God when you pray. This is a sacrifice that pleases him.

> When my soul fainted within me I remembered the Lord: and my prayer came in unto thee, into thine holy temple. They that observe lying vanities forsake their own mercy. But I will sacrifice unto thee with the voice of thanksgiving; I will pay that I have vowed. Salvation is of the Lord. (Jonah 2:7–9)

Paul and Silas went to prison for preaching about Jesus. Instead of complaining about their circumstances, they sang praises to God. They were thankful to be alive.

> And when they had laid many stripes upon them, they cast them into prison, charging the jailor to keep them safely: who, having received such a charge, thrust them into the inner prison, and made their feet fast in the stocks. And at midnight, Paul and Silas prayed, and sang praises unto God: and the prisoners heard them. And suddenly there was a great earthquake, so that the foundations of the prison were shaken: and immediately all the doors were opened, and every one's bands were loosed. (Acts 16:23–26)

Paul suffered hardships because he refused to stop preaching about Jesus. Thank God he never gave up. His preaching of the Gospel still echoes throughout the world.

> Of the Jews five times received I forty stripes save one. Thrice was I beaten with rods, once was I stoned, thrice I suffered shipwreck, a night and a day I have been in the deep; in journeyings often, in perils of waters, in perils of robbers, in perils by mine own countrymen, in perils by the heathen, in perils in the city, in perils in the wilderness, in perils in the sea, in perils among false brethren; in

> weariness and painfulness, in watchings often, in hunger and thirst, in fastings often, in cold and nakedness. Beside those things that are without, that which cometh upon me daily, the care of all the churches. (2 Corinthians 11:24–28)

Paul could have been bitter and angry after experiencing all these hardships. Here he summarizes what he learned from his experiences. Wherever you find yourself in life, make the best of it.

> Not that I speak in respect of want: for I have learned, in whatsoever state I am, therewith to be content. (Philippians 4:11)

"In every thing give thanks," means to continue to thank God in every circumstance.

> In every thing give thanks: for this is the will of God in Christ Jesus concerning you. (1 Thessalonians 5:18)

"Conversation" means lifestyle. "Covetousness" is greediness for money.

> Let your conversation be without covetousness; and be content with such things as ye have: for he hath said, I will never leave thee, nor forsake thee. (Hebrews 13:5)

Giving thanks to God is a sacrifice of praise. "To communicate" is to give directly to those in need. God is pleased with you when you do these things.

> By him therefore let us offer the sacrifice of praise to God continually, that is, the fruit of our lips giving thanks to his name. But to do good and to communicate forget not: for with such sacrifices God is well pleased. (Hebrews 13:15–16)

## TO KNOW THE LORD

Have you received Jesus as your Savior and Lord? If you have, then you know the Lord. Better than that, he knows you. Reading the Bible causes you to know the Lord. The deeper you go into God's word, the more he will reveal himself to you. It will be as though he stepped out of the pages of the Bible into your life. When you look for him, he will find you. The most rewarding experience you can have in life is to know the Lord.

To "glory in" a condition means to revel in it. Wisdom, riches, and might are nothing compared to having Jesus as your friend.

> Thus saith the Lord, Let not the wise man glory in his wisdom, neither let the mighty man glory in his might, let not the rich man glory in his riches: but let him that glorieth glory in this, that he understandeth and knoweth me, that I am the Lord which exercise loving-kindness, judgment and righteousness in the earth: for in these things I delight, saith the Lord. (Jeremiah 9:23–24)

You are a personal friend of Jesus, the Son of God. Why would you ever return to the weak and beggarly elements of this world?

> Howbeit then, when ye knew not God, ye did service unto them which by nature are no gods. But now, after that ye have known God, or rather are known of God, how turn ye again to the weak and beggarly elements, whereunto ye desire again to be in bondage? (Galatians 4:8–9)

Paul was the Apostle to the Gentiles. He certainly had a personal relationship with Jesus although he did not meet Jesus until after he was resurrected, just like you.

> For I know whom I have believed, and am persuaded that he is able to keep that which I have committed unto him against that day. (2 Timothy 1:12)

Some people sincerely believe that they are Christians when they are not Christians at all. Their works reveal that they don't have the Holy Spirit living in them. They have left out an important step in the process of becoming a Christian.

> Unto the pure all things all things are pure: but unto them that are defiled and unbelieving is nothing pure; but even their mind and conscience is defiled. They profess that they know God; but in works they deny him, being abominable, and disobedient, and unto every good work reprobate. (Titus 1:15–16)

When you know the Lord, you'll have the desire to keep his commandments.

> And hereby we do know that we know him, if we keep his commandments. He that saith, I know him, and keepeth not his commandments, is a liar, and the truth is not in him. (1 John 2:3–4 )

God empowers you to love others. But you have to exert yourself to get the job done. It can be difficult to love other people. But the more you practice it, the better you will be at it.

> Beloved, let us love one another: for love is of God; and every one that loveth is born of God, and knoweth God. He that loveth not knoweth not God; for God is love. (1 John 4:7–8)

## TO LOVE GOD

God's definition of loving him is keeping his commandments. He commanded you to love your neighbor as yourself. So, you love God when you love other people. By keeping one commandment, you fulfill them all. This is not as easy as it seems. You have to be nice to people who are mean and ugly to you. Whenever anyone hurts you, do not retaliate or hold a grudge against him. Just forgive him instead and let it go. Treat everyone the way you want to be treated. When you're not having an emotional reaction to everything that happens, you will be at peace on the inside. When you demonstrate that you love God, he can show you his love. Then you can experience the favor of God.

When you seek God and do what he says, he will demonstrate his love for you.

> I love them that love me; and those that seek me early shall find me. (Proverbs 8:17)

God is pleased with you when you observe these two commandments.

> There is one God; and there is none other but he: and to love him with all the heart, and with all the understanding, and with all the soul, and with all the strength, and to love his neighbor as himself, is more than all whole burnt offerings and sacrifices. (Mark 12:32–33)

Jesus' lesson about the Good Samaritan is an example of what it means to love your neighbor as yourself. Give your neighbor the kind of help that you would like to get.

> And, behold, a certain lawyer stood up, and tempted him, saying, Master, what shall I do to inherit eternal life? He said unto him, What is written in the law? How readest thou? And he answering said, Thou shalt love the Lord thy God with all thy heart, and with all thy soul, and with all thy strength, and with all thy mind; and thy neighbor as thyself. And he said unto him, Thou hast answered right: this do, and thou shalt live. But he, willing to justify himself, said unto Jesus, And who is my neighbor? And Jesus answering said, A certain man went down from Jerusalem

> to Jericho, and fell among thieves, which stripped him of his raiment, and wounded him, and departed, leaving him half dead. And by chance there came down a certain priest that way: and when he saw him, he passed by on the other side. And likewise a Levite, when he was at the place, came and looked on him, and passed by on the other side. But a certain Samaritan, as he journeyed, came where he was: and when he saw him, he had compassion on him, and went to him, and bound up his wounds, pouring in oil and wine, and set him on his own beast, and brought him to an inn, and took care of him. And on the morrow when he departed, he took out two pence, and gave them to the host, and said unto him, Take care of him; and whatsoever thou spendest more, when I come again, I will repay thee. Which now of these three, thinkest thou, was neighbor unto him that fell among the thieves? And he said, He that shewed mercy on him. Then said Jesus unto him, Go, and do thou likewise. (Luke 10:25–37)

This is the main thing that the Lord requires of you.

> If ye love me, keep my commandments. (John 14:15)

Your fellowship with God depends on the degree of love you have for him. He defines loving him as keeping his commandments.

> He that hath my commandments, and keepeth them, he it is that loveth me: and he that loveth me shall be loved of my Father, and I will love him, and will manifest myself to him. Judas saith unto him, not Iscariot, Lord, how is it that thou wilt manifest thyself unto us, and not unto the world? Jesus answered and said unto him, If a man love me, he will keep my words: and my Father will love him, and we will come unto him, and make our abode with him. (John 14:21–23)

This well-known verse does not apply to everyone. It only applies to those who love God. You show God that you love him when you base your life on his word.

**And we know that all things work together for good to them that love God, to them who are the called according to his purpose. (Romans 8:28)**

When you have experienced a miracle in your life, such as a gift of healing, you will know that God cares about you personally. And you will love him back. The best way to show God that you love him is to love his other children.

**We love him, because he first loved us....And this commandment have we from him, that he who loveth God love his brother also. (1 John 4:19, 21)**

Show God that you love him, by keeping his commandments.

**For this is the love of God, that we keep his commandments; and his commandments are not grievous. (1 John 5:3)**

## TO LOVE OTHERS

Your flesh tells you that if anyone hurts you, that gives you the right to hurt him in return. The world reinforces this attitude. God says that if anyone hurts you, forgive him. Forget about it and let it go. Show God that you love him by doing what he said. When you express your love for God, he will do the same for you. The Golden Rule is the secret of success, and it will work in every area of your life. Turning the other cheek is figurative, not literal. It is not a sign of weakness. It is a strategy for success. If you hurt someone, he will usually hold a grudge against you and wait for an opportunity to retaliate. If you treat everyone with kindness, most of them will return the favor. God is love, and when he fully indwells you, he will enable you to love other people.

These are the words of Jesus. The "law and the prophets" means the written word of God. His purpose is to fulfill the word of God. He continues to fulfill the word of God in you.

> Think not that I am come to destroy the law, or the prophets; I am not come to destroy, but to fulfill. (Matthew 5:17)

Jesus evaluates you by your love for others. In his word, he has listed some of the ways you can love others.

> Then shall the King say unto them on his right hand, come, ye blessed of my Father, inherit the kingdom prepared for you from the foundation of the world: for I was an hungered, and ye gave me meat: I was thirsty, and ye gave me drink: I was a stranger, and ye took me in: naked, and ye clothed me: I was sick, and ye visited me: I was in prison, and ye came unto me. Then shall the righteous answer him, saying, Lord, when saw we thee an hungered, and fed thee? or thirsty, and gave thee drink? When saw we thee a stranger, and took thee in? or naked, and clothed thee? Or when saw we thee sick, or in prison, and came unto thee? And the King shall answer and say unto you, Inasmuch as ye have done it unto one of the least of these my brethren, ye have done it unto me. (Matthew 25:34–40)

One of the Pharisees asked Jesus this question. The answer he received is very valuable information. Jesus explained that it is possible to fulfill the law of God by keeping two commandments.

> Master, which is the great commandment in the law? Jesus said unto him, Thou shalt love the Lord thy God with all thy heart, and with all thy soul, and with all thy mind. This is

**the first and great commandment. And the second is like unto it, Thou shalt love thy neighbor as thyself. On these two commandments hang all the law and the prophets. (Matthew 22:36–40)**

Jesus is your shepherd. He died so that you can live.

**I am the good shepherd: the good shepherd giveth his life for the sheep. (John 10:11)**

The very essence of Jesus' teaching is contained in the Love Commandment.

**A new commandment I give unto you, that ye love one another; as I have loved you, that ye also love one another. By this shall all men know that ye are my disciples, if ye have love one to another. (John 13:34–35)**

Jesus laid down his life for you literally. You lay down your life for others figuratively when you love them. Jesus said that when you obey him, you are his friend.

**This is my commandment, that ye love one another, as I have loved you. Greater love hath no man than this, that a man lay down his life for his friends. Ye are my friends, if ye do whatsoever I command you. (John 15:12–14)**

This is one of the most important truths in the Bible. By keeping the Lord's commandment, you are fulfilling the law.

**Owe no man any thing, but to love one another: for he that loveth another hath fulfilled the law. For this, thou shalt not commit adultery, thou shalt not kill, thou shalt not steal, thou shalt not bear false witness, thou shalt not covet; and if there be any other commandment, it is briefly**

> **comprehended in this saying, namely, thou shalt love thy neighbor as thyself. Love worketh no ill to his neighbor: therefore love is the fulfilling of the law. (Romans 13:9–10 )**

The Lord has commanded you to love others and this passage tells you how do it. It describes different aspects of God's love. This is the kind of love that God has toward you. And it's the kind of love that he expects you to demonstrate toward others. It goes beyond natural human love. If all of these characteristics apply to you, God will be pleased with you.

> **Love is patient, love is kind. It does not envy, it does not boast, it is not proud. It is not rude, it is not self-seeking, it is not easily angered, it keeps no record of wrongs. Love does not delight in evil but rejoices with the truth. It always protects, always trusts, always hopes, always perseveres. Love never fails. (1 Corinthians 13:4–8 NIV)**

When you keep the love commandment from the heart, you are fulfilling all the law.

> **For all the law is fulfilled in one word, even in this; thou shalt love thy neighbor as thyself. (Galatians 5:14)**

This is how to demonstrate that you are a believer in Christ.

> **If ye fulfill the royal law according to the scripture, thou shalt love thy neighbor as thyself, ye do well. (James 2:8)**

## TO OBSERVE TO DO ALL

God is pleased with you when you show him, "I will do everything you say, and I am not holding anything back." Abraham was willing to do everything that God told him, even when it defied logic. He demonstrated that he trusted God completely. He understood that there are no limits to what God can do. At the time that he offered his only son Isaac as a sacrifice, he told his servant that he and Isaac would return. In Hebrews 11:19, we find out that Abraham was "Accounting that God was able to raise him up, even from the dead." This is the kind of faith that God is looking for you to have. Most people think, "I can't do everything that God requires. It's impossible. I might as well give up." But attitude is everything. It is possible to meet God's expectations, and you know how to do it. Keeping the Love Commandment fulfills it all.

The Lord defines "our righteousness" as observing to do all his commandments.

> **And the Lord commanded us to do all these statutes, to fear the Lord our God, for our good always, that he might preserve us alive, as it is at this day. And it shall be our righteousness, if we observe to do all these commandments before the Lord our God, as he hath commanded us. (Deuteronomy 6:24–25)**

If you want to prosper, you will have to apply all of God's principles to your life.

> **And keep the charge of the Lord thy God, to walk in his ways, to keep his statutes, and his commandments, and his judgments, and his testimonies, as it is written in the law of Moses, that thou mayest prosper in all that thou doest, and withersoever thou turnest thyself: (1 Kings 2:3)**

You are responsible for creating your own prosperity. Success is a by-product of incorporating God's word into your life.

> **This book of the law shall not depart out of thy mouth; but thou shalt meditate therein day and night, that thou mayest observe to do all that is written therein: for then thou shalt make thy way prosperous, and then thou shalt have good success. (Joshua 1:8)**

In the following passage, Jesus told every believer to teach others to keep his commandments. It is called the Great Commission. Wherever you are, that is your mission field. The most effective way for you to teach others is by your own example.

> **And Jesus came and spake unto them, saying, All power is given unto me in heaven and in earth. Go ye therefore and teach all nations, baptizing them in the name of the Father, and of the Son, and of the Holy Ghost: teaching them to observe all things whatsoever I have commanded you: and, lo, I am with you always even unto the end of the world. Amen. (Matthew 28:18–20)**

## TO OVERCOME SATAN

Jesus defeated Satan at the cross when he shed his blood for you. That blood is the evidence that you belong to Jesus and are free from Satan's dominion. But Satan never stops trying to steal your faith. He wants to keep you afraid and worried, anxious and upset. You will have to overcome him daily. The devil hates you. He never gives, he takes. He doesn't come to bring you some fun, or deliver you from having to do things God's way. He wants to capture you and make you his slave. Every time he shows up, he's trying to steal something from you. He has a world full of temptations to lure you into sin. If he can't seduce you with lust, greed, or envy, then he will try to offend you and make you angry. But if you will refuse to take the bait, he is powerless against you. Do not open the door for Satan to come into your life. If you continue to hold onto even one pet sin, that is all you need. The devil cannot send you to hell when you belong to Jesus, but he can easily destroy your life on earth. Any involvement with sin will short-circuit your fellowship with God. You overcome Satan by staying in close fellowship with God. As long as you're obeying God, you are under his authority and protection. And you have nothing to fear. The word of God is your offensive weapon against the devil. It is also your most effective defensive weapon and your armor. To successfully overcome the devil, you must be very familiar with the Bible.

Jesus sent out seventy of his followers, in pairs, to go before him. He gave them power over Satan. They came back and told him that power had been very effective. Jesus has given you this same power.

> **And he said unto them, I beheld Satan as lightning fall from heaven. Behold, I give unto you power to tread on serpents and scorpions, and over all the power of the enemy: and nothing shall by any means hurt you. Notwithstanding in this rejoice not, that the spirits are subject unto you; but rather rejoice, because your names are written in heaven. (Luke 10:18–20)**

In this passage the Lord is speaking to Simon Peter. He explains that faith is the weapon that overcomes Satan. We know from Galatians 5:6 that "faith…worketh by love." You activate your faith by keeping the love commandment.

> **And the Lord said, Simon, Simon, behold, Satan hath desired to have you, that he may sift you as wheat: but I have prayed for thee, that thy faith fail not: and when thou art converted, strengthen thy brethren. (Luke 22:31–32)**

Jesus told us that all the devil ever does is steal, kill, and destroy.

> **The thief cometh not, but for to steal, and to kill, and to destroy: I am come that they might have life, and that they might have it more abundantly. ( John 10:10)**

Jesus called Satan the Prince of this world. He had nothing in Jesus because Jesus never sinned. You have successfully overcome Satan by making sure he has nothing in you.

> **Hereafter I will not talk much with you: for the prince of this world cometh, and hath nothing in me. (John 14:30)**

Never do anything evil, even when you are opposing evil.

> **Be not overcome of evil, but overcome evil with good. (Romans 12:21)**

When you keep the love commandment, the devil will retreat. When he sees you acting like Jesus, he knows that he is defeated.

> **Submit yourselves therefore to God. Resist the devil, and he will flee from you. (James 4:7)**

When you obey God, you are expressing your faith in him. If you are not a doer of the word, the devil will eat you alive.

> **Be sober, be vigilant; because your adversary the devil, as a roaring lion, walketh about, seeking whom he may devour: whom resist steadfast in the faith, knowing that the same afflictions are accomplished in your brethren that are in the world. (1 Peter 5:8)**

Jesus, the Word of God, empowers you to overcome the devil. He is that Holy Spirit who lives within you.

> **I have written unto you young men, because you are strong, and the word of God abideth in you, and ye have overcome the wicked one. (1 John 2:14)**

This is how to kick the devil out of your life. Forsake every sin that you are involved in and turn away from it.

> **We know that whosoever is born of God sinneth not; but he that is begotten of God keepeth himself, and that wicked one toucheth him not. (1 John 5:18)**

God has promised that one day Satan will be cast down. He will be overcome by the blood of Jesus and the testimony of those who believe in him.

> For the accuser of our brethren is cast down, which accused them before our God day and night. And they overcame him by the blood of the Lamb, and by the word of their testimony; and they loved not their lives unto the death. (Revelation 12:10–11)

## TO PLEASE GOD

Most people dedicate themselves to a life of self-indulgence. They love their sins and they do not want to give them up. You have the desire to please God, and you get to enjoy the benefits of pleasing him. They are quite substantial. You get to have fellowship with God, the creator of the universe. You have eternal life. You have the fruit of the Spirit, including love, joy, peace, faith, and self-control. You know that God hears your prayers, and that he will give you the desires of your heart.

This passage tells you how to please God. He knows that you love him when you demonstrate the willingness to do everything he requires.

> And now, Israel, what doth the Lord thy God require of thee, but to fear the Lord thy God, to walk in all his ways, and to love him, and to serve the Lord thy God with all thy heart and with all thy soul, to keep the commandments of the Lord, and his statutes, which I command thee this day for thy good? (Deuteronomy 10:12–13)

"Carnal" means fleshy. To have a carnal mind means to think like a non-believer. They are driven by their lusts. Your flesh will always advise you to indulge yourself. Follow the promptings of the Holy Spirit instead. It will be a different voice, the voice of your conscience.

> For to be carnally minded is death; but to be spiritually minded is life and peace. Because the carnal mind is enmity against God: for it is not subject to the law of God, neither indeed can be. So then they that are in the flesh cannot please God. But ye are not in the flesh, but in the Spirit, if so be that the Spirit of God dwell in you. Now if any man have not the Spirit of Christ, he is none of his. (Romans 8:6–9)

Believing in God is more than acknowledging his existence. It means believing that what he says is true. Faith is acting like you believe that it is true.

> But without faith it is impossible to please him: for he that cometh to God must believe that he is, and that he is a rewarder of them that diligently seek him. (Hebrews 11:6)

Pleasing God is the key to receiving the things you desire.

> And whatsoever we ask, we receive of him, because we keep his commandments, and do those things that are pleasing in his sight. (1 John 3:22)

## TO PRAISE THE LORD

God really hates it when you complain. When you complain, it's as if you are blaming God for what you have done. Complaining is the opposite of praising. It is focusing your attention on the problem instead of God, the problem solver. Change your thinking from negative to positive. Forget the past and focus on the present. Don't think about what is going wrong. Think about what is going right. Think about what God is doing for you right now and be thankful for that. Tell other people how good God is. These are ways of praising the Lord at all times. This is the difference between praise and worship. You praise God for the things he has done for you. You worship him because he is God.

The children of Israel complained against God when they were in the wilderness.

> **And when the people complained, it displeased the Lord: and the Lord heard it; and his anger was kindled; and the fire of the Lord burnt among them, and consumed them that were in the uttermost parts of the camp. (Numbers 11:1)**

According to the Bible, the Lord is present in the praises of his people. He is a Spirit.

> **But thou art holy, O Thou that inhabitest the praises of Israel. (Psalm 22:3)**

This is what God said concerning offerings. He does not need your money because he is richer than anyone else. He desires that you show that you appreciate the things that he has done for you.

> **Hear, O my people, and I will speak; O Israel, and I will testify against thee: I am God, even thy God. I will not reprove thee for thy sacrifices or thy burnt offerings, to have been continually before me. I will take no bullock out of thy house, nor he goats out of thy folds. For every beast of the forest is mine, and the cattle upon a thousand hills. I know all the fowls of the mountains: and the wild beasts of the field are mine. If I were hungry, I would not tell thee: for the world is mine and the fullness thereof. Will I eat the flesh of bulls, or drink the blood of goats? Offer unto God thanksgiving; and pay thy vows unto the most High: and call upon me in the day of trouble: I will deliver thee, and thou shalt glorify me. (Psalm 50:7–15)**

Praise is an offering that God accepts.

> Give unto the Lord, O ye kindreds of the people, give unto the Lord glory and strength. Give unto the Lord the glory due unto his name: bring an offering, and come into his courts. O worship the Lord in the beauty of holiness: fear before him, all the earth. (Psalm 96:7–9)

In these verses, God tells you how to conduct yourself in his presence. You are a "land."

> Make a joyful noise unto the Lord, all ye lands. Serve the Lord with gladness: come before his presence with singing. (Psalm 100:1–2)

What do you have that you didn't receive from God? What do you have of your own that you can give him? The answer is: praise and thanksgiving.

> What shall I render unto the Lord for all his benefits toward me? I will take the cup of salvation, and call upon the name of the Lord. I will pay my vows unto the Lord now in the presence of all his people....I will offer to thee the sacrifice of thanksgiving, and will call upon the name of the Lord. (Psalm 116:1–14, 17)

Another way of praising God is to tell everyone how excellent his word is.

> Accept, I beseech thee, the freewill offerings of my mouth, O Lord, and teach me thy judgments...My tongue shall speak of thy word: for all thy commandments are righteousness. (Psalm 119:108, 172)

Give God the praise that he deserves.

> **Render therefore to all their dues: tribute to whom tribute is due; custom to whom custom; fear to whom fear; honor to whom honor. (Romans 12:8)**

Another way to praise the Lord is to sing to him, even if you only do it silently. This will keep you from worrying and complaining. You cannot think negative thoughts while you are singing to God.

> **Speaking to yourselves in psalms and hymns and spiritual songs, singing and making melody in your heart to the Lord; giving thanks always for all things unto God and the Father in the name of our Lord Jesus Christ. (Ephesians 5:19–20)**

The "sacrifice of praise" means giving thanks to God for the things he has done for you.

> **By him therefore let us offer the sacrifice of praise to God continually, that is, the fruit of our lips giving thanks to his name. (Hebrews 13:15)**

Being a believer in Jesus puts you are in good company. Your good deeds glorify God. Your purpose in life is to glorify God.

> **But ye are a chosen generation, a royal priesthood, a holy nation, a peculiar people; that ye should show forth the praises of him who hath called you out of darkness into his marvelous light. (1 Peter 2:9)**

## TO PRAY

Most people are self-absorbed and spend all their time thinking about what they can get for themselves. They don't notice the needs of others. They don't realize that other people have hopes and dreams just as they do. When the Lord came into your life, he changed you on the inside.

You have a genuine interest in other people. You are not isolated from God, and you can communicate with him. It is not necessary to compose a formal structured prayer. Just talk to him like you would your earthly father. It is possible to maintain an ongoing conversation with God, similar to being on-line with him on the internet. Actually your whole life is your prayer to God. He knows your every thought and sees and hears everything you do. The way you spend your time shows the things you value the most, whether it is learning about God and doing what he says, or wasting your time doing nothing.

This is how to begin your prayer to God. Thank him and praise him, instead of presenting him your complaints.

> **Enter into his gates with thanksgiving, and into his courts with praise: be thankful unto him, and bless his name. (Psalm 100:4)**

God enjoys hearing from you.

> **The sacrifice of the wicked is an abomination to the Lord: but the prayer of the upright is his delight. (Proverbs 15:8)**

Any sin in your life sets up a barrier between you and God. The Holy Spirit will reveal them to you. In order to fellowship with God, you will have to turn away from them. Then you can receive God's forgiveness and his cleansing from all unrighteousness.

> **Your iniquities have separated between you and your God, and your sins have hid his face from you, that he will not hear. (Isaiah 59:2)**

God invites you to talk with him and ask him anything that you want to know.

> **Call unto me, and I will answer thee, and show thee great and mighty things, which thou knowest not. (Jeremiah 33:3)**

In this passage, Jesus explained some basic things about prayer. He said not to make a show out of praying but to do it privately. He said not to mindlessly repeat the same thing over and over. God knows what things you need, but he expects you to ask him for them.

> And when thou prayest, thou shalt not be as the hypocrites are: for they love to pray standing in the synagogues and in the corners of the streets, that they may be seen of men. Verily I say unto you, they have their reward. But thou, when thou prayest, enter into thy closet, and when thou hast shut thy door, pray to thy Father which is in secret; and thy Father which seeth in secret shall reward thee openly. But when ye pray, use not vain repetitions, as the heathen do: for they think that they shall be heard for their much speaking. Be not ye therefore like unto them: for your Father knoweth what things ye have need of, before ye ask him. (Matthew 6:5–8)

The following passage is called the Lord's Prayer. It's a model prayer for you to follow. You need food for your physical body daily, and you also need the Word of God. This spiritual daily bread is like the manna in the wilderness. It is all right to ask God for material things.

> After this manner therefore pray ye: Our Father which art in heaven, Hallowed be thy name. Thy kingdom come. Thy will be done in earth, as it is in heaven. Give us this day our daily bread. And forgive us our debts, as we forgive our debtors. And lead us not into temptation, but deliver us from evil: for thine is the kingdom, and the power, and the glory, for ever. Amen. (Matthew 6:9–13)

You can talk to God about anything; and, you can ask him for the things you want.

> Be careful for nothing; but in every thing by prayer and

> supplication with thanksgiving let your requests be made known unto God. (Philippians 4:6)

Praying for others is part of loving one another, as Jesus has commanded us. This passage explains how believers should pray for each other.

> Is any among you afflicted? let him pray. Is any merry? let him sing psalms. Is any sick among you? Let him call for the elders of the church; and let them pray over him, anointing him with oil in the name of the Lord: and the prayer of faith shall save the sick, and the Lord shall raise him up; and if he have committed sins, they shall be forgiven him. Confess your faults one to another, and pray one for another, that ye may be healed. The effectual fervent prayer of a righteous man availeth much. (James 5:13–16)

## TO PROFIT

Profiting is manifesting the fruit of the Spirit in every area of your life. It is bearing fruit in your personal life, your marriage, your family, and in your finances. It is growing in love and faith, righteousness and peace, and knowledge and wisdom. These blessings from God are more valuable than material things; but, they are the foundation on which material wealth is built.

This is what God says about his people. If they would keep his commandments, they would have righteousness and peace. This same promise of God applies to you.

> I, even I, have spoken; yea, I have called him: I have brought him, and he shall make his way prosperous. Come ye near unto me, hear ye this; I have not spoken in secret from the beginning; from the time that it was, there am I: and now the Lord God, and his spirit, hath sent me. Thus

> saith the Lord, thy Redeemer, the Holy One of Israel; I am the Lord thy God which teacheth thee to profit, which leadeth thee by the way that thou shouldest go. O that thou hadst hearkened to my commandments! Then had thy peace been as a river, and thy righteousness as the waves of the sea. (Isaiah 48:15–18 )

This is part of Jesus' teaching called The Sermon on the Mount. The things that you treasure in this life capture your heart. He urges you to treasure the things of God because they will last forever. Jesus said that he has reserved treasures in heaven for you.

> Lay not up for yourselves treasures upon earth, where moth and rust doth corrupt, and where thieves break through and steal: But lay up for yourselves treasures in heaven, where neither moth nor rust doth corrupt, and where thieves do not break through nor steal: for where your treasure is, there will your heart be also. (Matthew 6:19–21)

Being rich toward God makes more sense than piling up material possessions.

> And I will say to my soul, Soul, thou hast much goods laid up for many years; take thine ease, eat, drink, and be merry. But God said unto him, Thou fool, this night thy soul shall be required of thee: then whose shall those things be, which thou hast provided? So is he that layeth up treasure for himself, and is not rich toward God. (Luke 12:19–21)

Don't trade your mind, your emotions or your will for anything in the world.

> For what shall it profit a man, if he shall gain the whole world, and lose his own soul? (Mark 8:36)

Paul said to glorify God in everything you do. He revealed his strategy for winning people to the Lord.

> **Whether therefore ye eat, or drink, or whatsoever ye do, do all to the glory of God. Give none offense, neither to the Jews, nor to the Gentiles, nor to the church of God: even as I please all men in all things, not seeking mine own profit, but the profit of many, that they may be saved. (1 Corinthians 10:31–33)**

Paul's advice to the young preacher Timothy was to spend time in the word of God, reading it and discussing it. If you do the same, your profiting will appear to all.

> **Till I come, give attendance to reading, to exhortation, to doctrine. Neglect not the gift that is in thee, which was given thee by prophecy, with the laying on of the hands of the presbytery. Meditate upon these things; give thyself wholly to them; that thy profiting may appear to all. (1 Timothy 4:13–15)**

Faith is the catalyst that causes the word of God to work. Many people have heard the word of God who didn't act on it. They didn't use their faith and they did not receive anything from God.

> **For unto us was the gospel preached, as well as unto them: but the word preached did not profit them, not being mixed with faith in them that heard it. (Hebrews 4:2)**

## TO REPENT

Repentance is changing your mind about sin. It causes you to be repelled by sin instead of being attracted to it. It causes you to realize that sin is not glamorous or desirable at all. First, there is a general repentance in which you turn away from sin in general. Then, there is repentance from various personal sins. As you eliminate these from your life, you will discover sins that you didn't know you were committing. You could be filled with pride and not even know it. When the Holy Spirit reveals one of these sins to you, confess it to God. Confession is agreeing with God that it is sin. Repentance is turning away from it. God will forgive you of that sin and cleanse you from it. He will even take away the desire for it.

This is God's promise to all Christians. America can really use God's forgiveness and healing.

> If my people, who are called by my name, shall humble themselves and pray, and seek my face, and turn from their wicked ways; then will I hear from heaven, and will forgive their sin, and will heal their land. (2 Chronicles 7:14)

This is part of the sermon that Peter preached on the Day of Pentecost. The Holy Spirit had come to Earth from heaven and settled on the believers assembled in Jerusalem. The men who had killed Jesus were part of the crowd. Peter boldly told them to repent, to change their minds about Jesus, and accept him as the Messiah.

> Then Peter said unto them, Repent, and be baptized every one of you in the name of Jesus Christ for the remission of sins, and ye shall receive the gift of the Holy Ghost. For the promise is unto you, and to your children, and to all that are afar off, even as many as the Lord our God shall call. (Acts 2:38–39)

God is different from all other "gods." He is the One True God.

> Forasmuch then as we are the offspring of God, we ought not to think that the Godhead is like unto gold, or silver, or stone, graven by art and man's device. And the times of this ignorance God winked at; but now commandeth all men every where to repent: (Acts 17:29–30)

Sin always causes sorrow. Godly sorrow will cause you to turn away from sin. The Holy Spirit will show you the sins that you have committed.

> For godly sorrow worketh repentance to salvation not to be repented of, but the sorrow of the world worketh death. (2 Corinthians 7:10)

In the Old Testament, Esau sold his birthright to his brother Jacob for a single bowl of food. When he wanted to receive the blessing of the inheritance, he could not have it. He could not receive something that was not his. Do not be like Esau and trade the blessing of God for something of very little value.

> Lest there be any fornicator, or profane persons, as Esau, who for one morsel of meat sold his birthright. For ye know how that afterward, when he would have inherited the blessing, he was rejected: for he found no place of repentance, though he sought it carefully with tears. (Hebrews 12:16–17)

The Lord has promised that he will return for you and take you home with him. It seems to be taking a long time. That is because of God's great mercy. It is his will that none should perish. He is giving people more time to repent.

> The Lord is not slack concerning his promise, as some men count slackness; but is longsuffering to us-ward, not willing that any should perish, but that all should come to repentance. (2 Peter 3:9)

### TO RESEMBLE THE LORD

Renewing your mind with the word of God makes you think like Jesus. Being obedient to God's word makes you like Jesus. Loving other people makes you like Jesus. Being led by the Spirit of God makes you like Jesus. These things make you a disciple, a "disciplined one." The more you resemble Jesus, the better you will be at promoting his cause. You will be an asset to God instead of a liability.

This is what the Bible says about the origin of man. You did not evolve from lower forms of life. You were created by God in his image. You are a triune being. You are a spirit with a soul, and you live in a body.

> **And God said, Let us make man in our image, after our likeness: and let them have dominion over the fish of the sea, and over the fowl of the air, and over the cattle, and over all the earth, and over every creeping thing that creepeth upon the earth. So God created man in his own image, in the image of God created he him; male and female created he them. (Genesis 1:26–27)**

To be "holy" means to be different from the world, set apart for service to God.

> **For I am the Lord that bringeth you up out of the land of Egypt, to be your God: ye shall therefore be holy, for I am holy. (Leviticus 11:45)**

It is your destiny to be conformed to the image of Jesus. One day you will be like him.

> **For whom he did foreknow, he also did predestinate to be conformed to the image of his Son, that he might be the firstborn among many brethren. (Romans 8:29)**

You were condemned to death because of Adam's sin, but, because of Jesus' finished work on the cross, you get to live forever with him. Because of Jesus, you have been resurrected from the dead.

> But now is Christ risen from the dead, and become the firstfruits of them that slept. For since by man came death, by man came also the resurrection of the dead. For as in Adam all die, even so in Christ shall all be made alive. (1 Corinthians 15:20–22)

Adam was your earthly father, but now you are of Jesus. He has given spiritual life. Your citizenship is in heaven.

> The first man is of the earth, earthy: the second man is the Lord from heaven. As is the earthy, such are they also that are earthy: and as is the heavenly, such are they also that are heavenly. And as we have borne the image of the earthy, we shall also bear the image of the heavenly. (1 Corinthians 15:47–49 )

The more of God's word you apply to your life, the more you will resemble Jesus.

> But we all, with open face beholding as in a glass the glory of the Lord, are changed into the same image from glory to glory, even as by the Spirit of the Lord. (2 Corinthians 3:18)

As a believer in Christ, it is essential that you get along well with others.

> Follow peace with all men, and holiness, without which no man shall see the Lord: (Hebrews 12:14)

Pleasing God should be your highest priority. That is the mindset of Jesus.

> Forasmuch then as Christ hath suffered for us in the flesh, arm yourselves likewise with the same mind: for he that hath suffered in the flesh hath ceased from sin; That he

> **no longer should live the rest of his time in the flesh to the lusts of men, but to the will of God. (1 Peter 4:1–2)**

Jesus is Love in the flesh. When you excel at loving your neighbor, you will be like Jesus.

> **Whosoever shall confess that Jesus is the Son of God, God dwelleth in him, and he in God. And we have known and believed the love that God hath to us. God is love; and he that dwelleth in love dwelleth in God, and God in him. Herein is our love made perfect, that we may have boldness in the day of judgment: because as he is, so are we in this world. (1 John 4:15–17)**

## TO RETURN TO GOD

Some people become acquainted with Jesus when they are children, but they are lured away by the world, the flesh, and the devil. As long as you're alive, you can return to the Lord. He will always restore your fellowship with him. It does not matter what you might have done. God's love has no limits. Spiritual birth is like physical birth, in that once you are born, you can't be unborn. You do not stop being a child of God just because you fall into sin.

This passage is not only for the lost. It is for everyone who desires to be in fellowship with God.

> **Seek ye the Lord while he may be found, call ye upon him while he is near: Let the wicked forsake his way, and the unrighteous man his thoughts: and let him return unto the Lord, and he will have mercy upon him; and to our God, for he will abundantly pardon. (Isaiah 55:6–7)**

You might have committed a lot of sins, but God never gave up on you. Come back to Jesus. He will forgive you and restore you to fellowship with him.

> But if the wicked will turn from all his sins that he hath committed, and keep all my statutes, and do that which is lawful and right, he shall surely live, he shall not die. All his transgressions that he hath committed, they shall not be mentioned unto him: in his righteousness that he hath done he shall live. (Ezekiel 18:21, 22)

Your actions determine the circumstances of your life. Obeying God's word will change your circumstances. It will also change your destiny.

> Be ye not as your fathers, unto whom the former prophets have cried, saying, thus saith the Lord of hosts; Turn ye now from your evil ways, and from your evil doings: but they did not hear, nor hearken unto me, saith the Lord. Your fathers, where are they? and the prophets, do they live for ever? But my words and my statutes, which I commanded my servants the prophets, did they not take hold of your fathers? and they returned and said, Like as the Lord of hosts thought to do unto us, according to our ways, and according to our doings, so hath he dealt with us. (Zechariah 1:4–6)

The prodigal son collected his inheritance early and squandered it. When he came to the end of himself, he returned to his father. This earthly father was very happy to see his son. That is how God will react when you come back to him.

> And he arose, and came to his father. But when he was yet a great way off, his father saw him, and had compassion, and ran, and fell on his neck, and kissed him. And the son said unto him, Father, I have sinned against heaven, and in thy sight, and am no more worthy to be called thy son. But the father said to his servants, Bring forth the best robe, and put it on him; and put a ring on his hand, and shoes

> on his feet: and bring hither the fatted calf, and kill it; and let us eat, and be merry: for this my son was dead, and is alive again; he was lost, and is found. And they began to be merry. (Luke 15:20–24)

This is what God says about those who do not return to fellowship with God.

> For if after they have escaped the pollutions of the world through the knowledge of the Lord and savior Jesus Christ, they are again entangled therein, and overcome, the latter end is worse with them than the beginning. For it had been better for them not to have known the way of righteousness, than, after they have known it, to turn from the holy commandment delivered unto them. But it is happened unto them according to the true proverb, the dog is turned to his own vomit again; and the sow that was washed to her wallowing in the mire. (2 Peter 2:20–22)

## TO SEEK THE LORD

To seek the Lord is to come to him for answers to your questions. Seek the Lord when you have a problem. Seek the Lord when you don't know what to do. You can ask him anything, large or small. There is nothing that is too hard for him. He will tell you what to do in any situation. You have an advantage over the godly people who are mentioned in the Old Testament. All they had was the written word of God. You have the Holy Spirit alive in you to counsel you. Seeking the Lord is an ongoing process. As long as you continue in it, God will cause you to prosper. This verse refers to Uzziah. He became king of Judah when he was sixteen years old.

> We know that God is no respecter of persons. And he sought God in the days of Zechariah, who had understanding in

> the visions of God: and as long as he sought the Lord, God made him to prosper. (2 Chronicles 26:5)

Hezekiah was another godly king of Judah. We learn from his life experience that obedience to the word of God is an essential part of seeking the Lord.

> And thus did Hezekiah throughout all Judah, and wrought that which was good and right and truth before the Lord his God. And in every work that he began in the service of the house of God, and in the law, and in the commandments, to seek his God, he did it with all his heart, and prospered. (2 Chronicles 31:20–21 )

Fearing the Lord is obeying the general orders that are written in the Bible. Seeking the Lord is asking him for advice that applies specifically to you. Doing both of these at once will ensure that God will meet all your needs.

> O fear the Lord, ye his saints: for there is no want to them that fear him. The young lions do lack, and suffer hunger; but they that seek the Lord shall not want any good thing. (Psalm 34:9–10)

Most people do not understand how things work. They don't realize that cheaters get cheated, killers get killed, and thieves have their goods stolen. The evil things they do to others come back on them. They are repaid in kind.

> Evil men understand not judgment: but they that seek the Lord understand all things. (Proverbs 28:5)

God has a plan for your life. He will reveal it to you when you seek him and ask him about it.

> For I know the thoughts that I think toward you, saith the Lord, thoughts of peace, and not of evil, to give you an expected end. Then shall ye call upon me, and ye shall go and pray unto me, and I will hearken unto you. And ye shall seek me, and find me, when ye shall search for me with all your heart. (Jeremiah 29:11–13)

The Lord is always available to everyone who seeks him, especially his own children.

> That they should seek the Lord, if haply they might feel after him, and find him, though he be not far from every one of us: for in him we live, and move, and have our being; as certain of your own poets have said, for we are also his offspring. (Acts 17:27–28)

## TO SERVE THE LORD

Serving the Lord is allowing him to use you for the benefit of others. When you are a blessing to others, God will bless you. The name "Satan" means the opposer. It's a role that anyone can play. People who oppose you are only serving their own self-interests. The devil has deceived them into serving him. He takes advantage of their ignorance of the word of God. Don't let Satan use you as a weapon to hurt other people.

Three of Job's friends came to console him. One of them explained to Job that God rescues people from captivity.

> And if they be bound in fetters, and be holden in cords of affliction; then he showeth them their work, and their transgressions that they have exceeded. He openeth also their ear to discipline, and commandeth that they return from iniquity. If they obey and serve him, they shall spend their days in prosperity, and their years in pleasures. (Job 36:8–11)

God's will for you is that you serve the cause of Christ and prosper.

> Let them shout for joy, and be glad, that favor my righteous cause: yea, let them say continually, let the Lord be magnified, which hath pleasure in the prosperity of his servant. (Psalm 35:27)

When you are a servant of the Lord, he will protect you.

> No weapon that is formed against thee shall prosper, and every tongue that shall rise against thee in judgment thou shalt condemn. This is the heritage of the servants of the Lord, and their righteousness is of me, saith the Lord. (Isaiah 54:17)

The Apostles argued over which one of them was the greatest. This is what he told them.

> And there was also a strife among them, which of them should be accounted the greatest. And he said unto them, The kings of the Gentiles exercise lordship over them; and they that exercise authority upon them are called benefactors. But ye shall not be so: but he that is greatest among you, let him be as the younger; and he that is chief, as he that doth serve. For whether is greater, he that sitteth at meat, or he that serveth? Is not he that sitteth at meat? But I am among you as he that serveth. (Luke 22:24–27)

Men don't think like God thinks. It is impossible to please both God and men.

> For do I now persuade men, or God? Or do I seek to please men? For if I yet pleased men, I should not be the servant of Christ. (Galatians 1:10)

These are the Lord's instructions to those who want to be his servant. You must not argue and fight with others.

> And the servant of the Lord must not strive; but be gentle unto all men, apt to teach, patient; in meekness instructing those that oppose themselves; if God peradventure will give them repentance to the acknowledging of the truth; and that they may recover themselves out of the snare of the devil, who are taken captive by him at his will. (2 Timothy 2:24–26)

## TO TEACH GOD'S WORD

The most effective way to teach is to teach by example. Your children will do what they see you doing. When they see your personal relationship with the Lord, they will want one too. When they see you basing your life on the Lord's commandments, they will do the same. When the Holy Spirit lives strong in you, others will be drawn to you. You represent God. It is important that you bring him glory instead of shame. When others see that your life is better than theirs, they will want to be like you.

Nobody else is going to teach the Bible to your children. It is the most important subject matter in the world. You have to learn it yourself and teach it to your children.

> Hear, O Israel: the Lord our God is one Lord: and thou shalt love the Lord thy God with all thine heart, and with all thy soul, and with all thy might. And these words, which I command thee this day, shall be in thine heart: and thou shalt teach them diligently unto thy children, and shalt talk of them when thou sittest in thine house, and when thou walkest by the way, and when thou liest down, and when thou risest up. (Deuteronomy 6:4–7)

In the Old Testament, God told his people to "observe to do all" his commandments. Jesus used this same phrase when he gave us the Great Commission. Every seven years, the entire word of God was read aloud to the nation of Israel, so they would know what it says.

> When all Israel is come to appear before the Lord thy God in the place which he shall choose thou shalt read this law before all Israel in their hearing. Gather the people together, men, and women, and children, and thy stranger that is within thy gates, that they may hear, and that they may learn, and fear the Lord your God, and observe to do all the words of this law. (Deuteronomy 31:11–12)

Samuel was God's prophet and Saul became the first king of Israel. At that time, only prophets, kings and priests had direct access to the word of God.

> And as they were going down to the end of the city, Samuel said to Saul, Bid the servant pass on before us, (and he passed on,) but stand thou still a while, that I may show thee the word of God. (1 Samuel 9:27)

Ezra was a Bible teacher and a scribe. He was also a doer of the word.

> For Ezra had prepared his heart to seek the law of the Lord, and to do it, and to teach in Israel statutes and judgments. (Ezra 7:10)

Nehemiah and Ezra helped God's people to understand the word of God.

> So they read in the book in the law of God distinctly, and gave the sense, and caused them to understand the reading. (Nehemiah 8:8)

The people around you know if you are a doer of the word or not. Your children will follow your example whether it's good or bad. The Lord will judge your effectiveness as a Bible teacher.

> Whosoever therefore shall break one of these least commandments, and shall teach men so, he shall be called the least in the kingdom of heaven: but whosoever shall do and teach them, the same shall be called great in the kingdom of heaven. (Matthew 5:19)

## TO TRUST IN THE LORD

Instead of worrying about everything, trust Jesus for the outcome. He will look out for you. Worry is allowing yourself to be controlled by fear. Every time that fear arises, focus your attention on the word of God. Think like God thinks. Say what the Bible says. Jesus is your shepherd, and he is looking out for your best interest. There is nothing too hard for him. He will supply all your needs. He will cause all things to work together for your good. Make it your habit to depend on the Lord, and not on anything else.

Do not envy the people of the world. God will give you the things you desire. In this passage, God explains how you can receive the desires of your heart.

> Fret not thyself because of evildoers, neither be thou envious against the workers of iniquity. For they shall soon be cut down like the grass, and wither as the green herb. Trust in the Lord, and do good; so shalt thou dwell in the land, and verily thou shalt be fed. Delight thyself in the Lord; and he shall give thee the desires of thine heart. Commit thy way unto the Lord; trust also in him; and he shall bring it to pass. And he shall bring forth thy righteousness as the light, and thy judgment as the noonday. Rest in the Lord, and wait patiently for him: fret not thyself because of him who prospereth in his way,

> because of the man who bringeth wicked devices to pass. Cease from anger, and forsake wrath: fret not thyself in any wise to do evil. For evildoers shall be cut off: but those that wait upon the Lord, they shall inherit the earth. (Psalm 37:1–9)

Sometimes the best thing you can do is to do nothing. Ultimately God will triumph over everything that opposes him.

> Be still, and know that I am God: I will be exalted among the heathen, I will be exalted in the earth. (Psalm 46:10)

When you're afraid, trust God and praise him for the things he has done for you.

> What time I am afraid, I will trust in thee. In God I will praise his word, in God I have put my trust; I will not fear what flesh can do unto me. (Psalm 56:3–4)

Before you make a decision, ask God for his advice.

> Trust in the Lord with all thine heart; and lean not unto thine own understanding. In all thy ways acknowledge him, and he shall direct thy paths. (Proverbs 3:5–6)

Trusting the Lord will keep you away from the devil's snare.

> The fear of man bringeth a snare: but whoso putteth his trust in the Lord shall be safe. (Proverbs 29:25)

When you put your trust in God, he will know who you are.

> The Lord is good, a stronghold in the day of trouble; and he knoweth them that trust in him. (Nahum 1:7)

Each component of the armor of God is a portion of the word of God. It defeats the enemy every time it is used. To ensure victory, do everything that you are supposed to do. Then expect God to give you the victory.

> **Finally, my brethren, be strong in the Lord, and in the power of his might. Put on the whole armor of God, that ye may be able to stand against the wiles of the devil. For we wrestle not against flesh and blood, but against principalities, against powers, against the rulers of the darkness of this world, against spiritual wickedness in high places. Wherefore take unto you the whole armor of God, that ye may be able to withstand in the evil day, and having done all, to stand. (Ephesians 6:10–13)**

## TO WALK IN THE SPIRIT

Most people do what their human nature, their flesh, tells them to do. That is the way that seems right to a man, but is the way of death. You are making decisions everyday between life and death. Walking in the Spirit is doing everything God's way. God's Spirit tells you which way to go. He also empowers you to do what is right.

Your flesh never gives up. It never stops trying to dominate you. It never stops lusting for things you cannot have. You have to renew your mind with the word of God, and take control of your flesh. Following the promptings of the Holy Spirit will keep you from walking in the flesh.

> **I find then a law, that, when I would do good, evil is present with me. For I delight in the law of God after the inward man: but I see another law in my members, warring against the law of my mind, and bringing me into captivity to the law of sin which is in my members. (Romans 7:2–23)**

Your "walk" is your everyday behavior. You are living right when your walk is consistent with the Bible. You are walking in righteousness and obeying the Spirit of God.

> There is therefore now no condemnation to them which are in Christ Jesus, who walk not after the flesh, but after the Spirit. For the law of the Spirit of life in Christ Jesus hath made me free from the law of sin and death. For what the law could not do, in that it was weak through the flesh, God sending his own Son in the likeness of sinful flesh, and for sin, condemned sin in the flesh: that the righteousness of the law might be fulfilled in us, who walk not after the flesh, but after the Spirit. (Romans 8:1–4)

The most dangerous enemy you will ever face is your own flesh. It is like a spoiled child. It seizes every opportunity to take control of your life. Walking in the Spirit is the only way to keep your flesh from ruling your life.

> This I say then, Walk in the Spirit, and ye shall not fulfill the lust of the flesh. For the flesh lusteth against the Spirit, and the Spirit against the flesh: and these are contrary the one to the other; so that ye cannot do the things that ye would. But if ye be led of the Spirit, ye are not under the law. (Galatians 5:16–18)

You are crucifying your flesh, figuratively, when you ignore its demands. When you do that, you will manifest the following nine characteristics of the fruit of the Holy Spirit

> But the fruit of the Spirit is love, joy, peace, long-suffering, gentleness, goodness, faith, meekness, temperance: against such there is no law. And they that are Christ's have crucified the flesh with the affections and lusts. If we live in the Spirit, let us also walk in the Spirit. Let us not be desirous of vain glory, provoking one another, envying one another. (Galatians 5:22–26)

## TO WALK UPRIGHTLY

Fifty years ago, Americans knew God and the Bible very well. They knew that God will reward those who walk uprightly before him. They called this "living right." Whenever something good happened to a man, people would say to him," you must be living right." They knew that right living, not luck, caused good things to happen to people.

You can be filled with pride without realizing it. Because of your pride, you assume the right to be rude to others. That is an example of a presumptuous sin.

> Keep back their servant also from presumptuous sins; let them not have dominion over me: then shall I be upright, and I shall be innocent from the great transgression. (Psalm 19:13)

According to the word of God, walking uprightly will get you everything.

> Behold, O God our shield, and look upon the face of thine anointed. For a day in thy courts is better than a thousand. I had rather be a doorkeeper in the house of my God, than to dwell in the tents of wickedness. For the Lord God is a sun and shield: the Lord will give grace and glory: no good thing will he withhold from them that walk uprightly. O Lord of hosts, blessed is the man that trusteth in thee. (Psalm 84:9–12)

If you cause another person to fall, you will end up falling yourself.

> Whoso causeth the righteous to go astray in an evil way, he shall fall himself into his own pit: but the upright shall have good things in possession. (Proverbs 28:10)

Sinners don't like to be reminded that they are sinners. If they would only change their thinking and walk uprightly, God would bless them.

> Prophesy ye not, say they to them that prophesy: they shall not prophesy to them, that they shall not take shame. O thou that art named the house of Jacob, is the Spirit of the Lord straitened? Are these his doings? Do not my words do good to him that walketh uprightly? (Micah 2:6–7)

## TO WORK

The expression, "the world doesn't owe you a living," means that you must earn your own way in life. Every man has to work. Why would anyone think that he is too good to work? Why would anyone refuse to work and expect others to support him? God requires every man to work and to pay his own way. That is what it means to be a man, to support your wife and children. Since there's no escaping the fact that you have to work, the best thing you can do is find work you enjoy. Then your work will seem like play.

This was God's judgment on Adam for rebelling against him. God said that Adam would have to earn his living by the sweat of his brow. As one of his descendents, it applies to you. This passage makes it clear that God intends for every man to work.

> And unto Adam he said, Because thou hast hearkened unto the voice of thy wife, and hast eaten of the tree, of which I commanded thee, saying, Thou shalt not eat of it: cursed is the ground for thy sake; in sorrow shalt thou eat of it all the days of thy life; thorns also, and thistles shall it bring forth to thee; and thou shalt eat the herb of the field; in the sweat of thy face shalt thou eat bread, till thou return unto the ground; for out of it wast thou taken: for dust thou art, and unto dust shalt thou return. (Genesis 3:17–19)

Nehemiah and Ezra led God's people in rebuilding the walls of Jerusalem. This is what Nehemiah said about the people he led. This is the attitude that gets things done.

> **So built we the wall; and all the wall was joined together unto the half thereof: for the people had a mind to work. (Nehemiah 4:6)**

God is just, and he follows his own rules. He will not allow you to work without being paid for it.

> **Also unto thee, O Lord, belongeth mercy: for thou renderest to every man according to his work. (Psalm 62:12)**

Talk is cheap. It doesn't produce a paycheck. An undesirable job is better than no job at all. "Penury" is extreme poverty.

> **In all labor there is profit: but the talk of the lips tendeth only to penury. (Proverbs 14:23)**

Actual work always produces a harvest.

> **He that tilleth his land shall have plenty of bread: but he that followeth after vain persons shall have poverty enough. (Proverbs 28:19)**

"Planting" and "watering" refer to working in God's vineyard. He will reward you for the work you do for him.

> **Now he that planteth and he that watereth are one: and every man shall receive his own reward according to his own labor. (1 Corinthians 3:8)**

It is the Lord's idea for you to earn your own way. He requires that you provide for yourself and your family.

> And that ye study to be quiet, and to do your own business, and to work with your own hands, as we commanded you; that ye may walk honestly toward them that are without, and that ye may have lack of nothing. (1 Thessalonians 4:11–12)

God says in his word, "If any man will not work, neither shall he eat." It is morally wrong for an able-bodied man to be a burden to others. Anytime you are taking a free ride, it is on somebody else's back. Paul points out that, in Thessalonica, he provided his own food.

> Neither did we eat any man's bread for nought; but wrought with labor and travail night and day, that we might not be chargeable to any of you:...For even when we were with you, this we commanded you, that if any would not work, neither should he eat. For we hear that there are some which walk among you disorderly, working not at all, but are busybodies. Now them that are such we command and exhort by our Lord Jesus Christ, that with quietness they work, and eat their own bread. (2 Thessalonians 3:8,10–12)

Some of the Ephesians were thieves before they became believers, but Christians must not steal.

> Let him that stole steal no more: but rather let him labor, working with his hands the thing which is good, that he may have to give to him that needeth. (Ephesians 4:28)

PART THREE

# Good Things

**A good man out of the good treasure of the heart bringeth forth that which is good. (Luke 6:45)**

Jesus said that people are like trees. Good things come from good people, just as good fruit comes from good trees. When you receive God's word, you will receive everything that goes along with it. God's people are kind and patient. They are full of faith and joy, and they do things to benefit others. When you have a heart full of God's love, good things will happen to you. You will be like a tree growing by a river of water, bearing an abundance of fruit. Part Three is about the good things in life.

## CONFIDENCE

This is not self-confidence, but confidence in God. It is trusting that God will do what he says he will do. Walking in the light means staying close to God, and acknowledging him in everything you do. This kind of confidence comes from knowing that you are pleasing God. Get to know him. You can tell him everything about you. Confess your sins to him and repent of them. He will forgive you and cleanse you from all unrighteousness. They you can ask him for the things you desire and he will give them to you.

Confidence is the result of fearing God.

> In the fear of the Lord is strong confidence: and his children shall have a place of refuge. (Proverbs 14:26)

God says that your confidence in him will be richly rewarded.

> For ye had compassion of me in my bonds, and took joyfully the spoiling of your goods, knowing in yourselves that ye have in heaven a better and an enduring substance. Cast not away therefore your confidence, which hath great recompense of reward. (Hebrews 10:34–35)

Practicing love toward others is an essential part of receiving answers to your prayers.

> My little children, let us not love in word, neither in tongue; but in deed and in truth. And hereby we know that we are of the truth, and shall assure our hearts before him. For if our heart condemn us, God is greater than our heart, and knoweth all things. Beloved, if our heart condemn us not, then have we confidence toward God. And whatsoever we ask, we receive of him, because we keep his commandments, and do those things that are pleasing in his sight. (1 John 3:18–22)

When you please God by keeping Jesus' love commandment, his ears are open to your prayer. Since you are doing the will of God, you can ask him for the things you want.

> **And this is the confidence that we have in him, that, if we ask any thing according to his will, he heareth us: and if we know that he hear us, whatsoever we ask, we know that we have the petitions that we desired of him. (1 John 5:14–15)**

## COURAGE

Courage is standing up for God in the midst of a crooked and perverse generation. Courage is enduring ridicule for believing in Jesus and the Bible. Courage is continuing to believe that God's word will work when the situation seems hopeless. People of the world would like to intimidate you, make you afraid, and make you doubt yourself. Do not pay any attention to what they say. They have nothing. You have the power of God in you. The same Spirit that raised Jesus from the dead is alive in you. In order to succeed, you must have courage.

These are God's word of comfort to his people just before they entered the Promised Land. This same promise applies to you today, as you live your life for God.

> **Be strong and of a good courage, fear not, nor be afraid of them: for the Lord thy God, he it is that doth go with thee; he will not fail thee, nor forsake thee. (Deuteronomy 31:6)**

Joshua led God's people into the Promised Land. These were God's words to him. They contain the secret of success in every area of life. It is obedience to the word of God.

> **There shall not any man be able to stand before thee all the days of thy life: as I was with Moses, so I will be with thee: I will not fail thee, nor forsake thee. Be strong and of**

> a good courage: for unto this people shalt thou divide for an inheritance the land, which I sware unto their fathers to give them. Only be thou strong and very courageous, that thou mayest observe to do according to all the law, which Moses my servant commanded thee: turn not from it to the right hand or to the left, that thou mayest prosper whithersoever thou goest. (Joshua 1:5–7)

The Lord promised Joshua that he would always be with him. And he will always be with you.

> Have not I commanded thee? Be strong and of a good courage; be not afraid, neither be thou dismayed: for the Lord thy God is with thee whithersoever thou goest. (Joshua 1:9)

Those who do not know the Lord are always filled with fear. When you walk with God, you don't have to be afraid of anything.

> The wicked flee when no man pursueth: but the righteous are bold as a lion. (Proverbs 28:1)

## DILIGENCE

When my children were young, I posted a sign in the kitchen that explained the rules of the house. The sign read, "People are depending on you to do your job. If there's something you are supposed to do, do it. If there's something you are not supposed to do, don't do it." I think that this explains what diligence is. A diligent person knows what tasks need to be done and completes them in a timely fashion. It pleases God when you diligently apply his word to your life. Long life, health and riches go to the diligent.

Your heart is where you keep your secrets and the things that you love. Fill your heart so full of God's word that there is no room for anything else. Then you will enjoy good health.

> My son, attend to my words; incline thine ear unto my sayings. Let them not depart from thine eyes; keep them in the midst of thine heart. For they are life unto those that find them, and health to all their flesh. Keep thy heart with all diligence; for out of it are the issues of life. (Proverbs 4:20–23)

What is it that makes the difference between being rich and being poor? It is diligence.

> Treasure of wickedness profit nothing: but righteousness delivereth from death. The Lord will not suffer the soul of the righteous to famish: but he casteth away the substance of the wicked. He becometh poor that dealeth with a slack hand: but the hand of the diligent maketh rich. (Proverbs 10:2–4)

Your thoughts determine your financial condition. What you think about is what you will get. Be diligent in doing God's will, then expect to have plenty of everything.

> The thoughts of the diligent tend only to plenteousness; but of every one that is hasty only to want. (Proverbs 21:5)

Being diligent is always doing right. Success in life comes through diligence. "Mean men" means average, or ordinary men.

> Seest thou a man diligent in his business? He shall stand before kings; he shall not stand before mean men. (Proverbs 22:29)

In order to bear abundant fruit, you will have to develop the following character traits.

> According as his divine power hath given unto us all things that pertain unto life and godliness, through the knowledge

> of him that hath called us to glory and virtue: whereby are given unto us exceeding great and precious promises: that by these ye might be partakers of the divine nature, having escaped the corruption that is in the world through lust. And beside this, giving all diligence, add to your faith virtue; and to virtue knowledge; and to knowledge temperance; and to temperance patience; and to patience godliness; and to godliness brotherly kindness; and to brotherly kindness charity. For if these things be in you, and abound, they make you that ye shall neither be barren nor unfruitful in the knowledge of our Lord Jesus Christ. (2 Peter 1:3–8 )

## ENDURANCE

Endurance is doing what is right in spite of adversity. It's soldiering on through all kinds of hardships. You are going to face affliction and persecution just for being a believer in Christ. In the Bible this is called "the trying of your faith." What's good about these trials is that they prove that your faith is genuine. Gold is refined by having all of its impurities removed. The Lord will be with you when you go through this fire of purification; and, you will come forth as gold. The Lord will reward you and show you favor. Anybody can give up. It takes endurance to walk with God.

God has promised to reward you when you do things for him. "In due season," means in God's timing. "If we faint not," means, if we don't quit.

> Be not deceived; God is not mocked: for whatsoever a man soweth, that shall he also reap. For he that soweth to his flesh shall of the flesh reap corruption; but he that soweth to the Spirit shall of the Spirit reap life everlasting. And let us not be weary in well doing: for in due season we shall reap, if we faint not. As we have therefore opportunity, let us do good unto all men, especially unto them who are of the household of faith. (Galatians 6:7–10)

Paul compared endurance to running in a race.

> But this one thing I do, forgetting those things which are behind, and reaching forth unto those things which are before, I press toward the mark for the prize of the high calling of God in Christ Jesus. (Philippians 3:13–14)

Paul wrote to the young preacher Timothy and gave him this advice.

> But watch thou in all things, endure afflictions, do the work of an evangelist, make full proof of thy ministry. (2 Timothy 4:5)

"The spoiling of your goods," is losing some of your material assets. During the trying of your faith, you will experience some financial losses.

> But call to remembrance the former days, in which, after ye were illuminated, ye endured a great fight of afflictions; partly, whilst ye were made a gazingstock both by reproaches and afflictions; and partly, whilst ye became companions of them that were so used. For ye had compassion of me in my bonds, and took joyfully the spoiling of your goods, knowing in yourselves that ye have in heaven a better and an enduring substance. (Hebrews 10:32–34)

These are God's words of comfort to all believers who are being afflicted.

> Take, my brethren, the prophets, who have spoken in the name of the Lord, for an example of suffering affliction, and of patience. Behold, we count them happy which

> endure. Ye have heard of the patience of Job, and have seen the end of the Lord; that the Lord is very pitiful, and of tender mercy. (James 5:11)

## FAMILIES

When you receive Jesus as your Savior, you become a part of God's family. You become a part of Jesus' church along with all the other believers through the centuries. In order to love other Christians you have to be with them where they are. That means being a part of a local New Testament church. Do not try to get along without help from other Christians. That would make your life miserable. You need a church family. You need people to love and people who love you. If you do not already have a church home, go and find one.

> God setteth the solitary in families: he bringeth out those who are bound with chains: but the rebellious dwell in a dry land. (Psalm 68:6)

Jesus is that Holy Spirit who comes to life in you.

> My little children, of whom I travail in birth again until Christ be formed in you. (Galatians 4:19)

You are a member of God's own household, a citizen of heaven, and a part of the Kingdom of God. You are in good company. All of the godly people who are named in the Bible and everyone who believes in Jesus are now members of your family.

> For through him we both have access by one Spirit unto the Father. Now therefore ye are no more strangers and foreigners, but fellow citizens with the saints, and of the household of God; and are built upon the foundation of the apostles and prophets, Jesus Christ himself being

> the chief corner stone; in whom all the building fitly framed together groweth unto a holy temple in the Lord. (Ephesians 2:18–21)

One part of God's family is alive on the earth. The rest are with the Lord in heaven. One day you will be reunited with your loved ones there. You will see them again.

> For this cause I bow my knees unto the Father of our Lord Jesus Christ, of whom the whole family in heaven and earth is named, that he would grant you, according to the riches of his glory, to be strengthened with might by his Spirit in the inner man; that Christ may dwell in your hearts by faith; that ye, being rooted and grounded in love, may be able to comprehend with all saints what is the breadth, and length, and depth, and height; and to know the love of Christ, which passeth knowledge, that ye might be filled with all the fullness of God. (Ephesians 3:14–19)

## THE FEAR OF THE LORD

To fear the Lord doesn't mean actually being afraid of him. It means living a life that is based on the word of God. When you obey the Bible, you are obeying the Lord. He is the Word of God personified. God-fearing people demonstrate their faith by their behavior. The fact that they are taking God at his word is evident. Live as if you believe God and you will receive the things he promised. Live as if you don't believe the Bible and you will get nothing.

God's promise of protection does not extend to everyone. It applies to those who fear the Lord. God also promises that he will meet the material needs of those who fear him.

> The angel of the Lord encampeth round about them that fear him, and delivereth them. O taste and see that the Lord is good: blessed is the man that trusteth in him. O

> fear the Lord, ye his saints: for there is no want to them that fear him. The young lions do lack, and suffer hunger: but they that seek the Lord shall not want any good thing. (Psalm 34:7–10)

This verse explains how to go about fearing the Lord. Do not do things that you should not do. Do not say things that you should not say. Make it your goal to live in peace with everyone.

> Come, ye children, hearken unto me: I will teach you the fear of the Lord. What man is he that desireth life, and loveth many days, that he may see good? Keep thy tongue from evil, and thy lips from speaking guile. Depart from evil, and do good; seek peace, and pursue it. (Psalm 34:11–14)

This is how God defines the "fear of the Lord."

> The fear of the Lord is to hate evil: pride, and arrogancy, and the evil way, and the froward mouth, do I hate. (Proverbs 8:13)

Fearing the Lord will give you a long life.

> The fear of the Lord prolongeth days: but the years of the wicked shall be shortened. (Proverbs 10:27)

Fearing the Lord will keep you alive.

> The fear of the Lord is a fountain of life, to depart from the snares of death. (Proverbs 14:27)

Fearing the Lord will cause you to be content with your life, and it will keep evil away from you.

> The fear of the Lord tendeth to life: and he that hath it shall abide satisfied; he shall not be visited with evil. (Proverbs 19:23)

Fearing the Lord marks you as one of God's people.

> And they shall be my people, and I will be their God: And I will give them one heart, and one way, that they may fear me for ever, for the good of them, and of their children after them: And I will make an everlasting covenant with them, that I will not turn away from them to do them good; but I will put my fear in their hearts, that they shall not depart from me. (Jeremiah 32:38–40)

Search the scriptures to discover God's will for your life and you will understand the fear of the Lord.

> My son, if thou will receive my words, and hide my commandments with thee; so that thou incline thine ear unto wisdom, and apply thine heart to understanding; yea, if thou criest after knowledge, and liftest up thy voice for understanding; if thou seekest her as silver, and searchest for her as for hid treasures; then shalt thou understand the fear of the Lord, and find the knowledge of God. For the Lord giveth wisdom: out of his mouth cometh knowledge and understanding. (Proverbs 2:1–6)

## FELLOWSHIP

The Spirit of God lives within you. Your fellowship with God is in your heart and in your mind. But he still expects you to be part of a New Testament Church. You are obeying God when you have fellowship with other believers. You will be rewarded for your obedience. You will benefit the other believers and they will benefit you. God healed Job when he prayed for his friends. When you worship and pray with others, miracles happen.

When you obey God, he will reveal himself to you and have fellowship with you.

> He that hath my commandments, and keepeth them, he it is that loveth me: and he that loveth me shall be loved of my Father, and I will love him, and will manifest myself to him. Judas saith unto him, not Iscariot, Lord, how is it that thou wilt manifest thyself unto us, and not unto the world? Jesus answered and said unto him, If a man love me, he will keep my words: and my Father will love him, and we will come unto him, and make our abode with him. (John 14:21–23)

Any alliance you have with unbelievers is doomed from the start. They have different values and different motives. If they will not agree with God, they are not going to agree with you.

> Be ye not unequally yoked together with unbelievers: for what fellowship hath righteousness with unrighteousness? And what communion hath light with darkness? And what concord hath Christ with Belial? Or what part hath he that believeth with an infidel? And what agreement hath the temple of God with idols? for ye are the temple of the living God. (2 Corinthians 6:14–16)

You have to associate with other believers before you can love them.

> And let us consider one another to provoke unto love and to good works: not forsaking the assembling of ourselves together, as the manner of some is; but exhorting one another: and so much the more, as ye see the day approaching. (Hebrews 10:24–25)

This is what John the Apostle wrote about his fellowship with Jesus, the Word of God. This same Jesus makes himself available to fellowship with you.

> That which was from the beginning, which we have heard, which we have seen with our eyes, which we have looked upon, and our hands have handled, of the Word of life; (for the life was manifested, and we have seen it, and bear witness, and show unto you that eternal life, which was with the Father, and was manifested unto us;) that which we have seen and heard declare we unto you, that ye also may have fellowship with us: and truly our fellowship is with the Father, and with his Son Jesus Christ. (1 John 1:1–3)

When you are in fellowship with Jesus, you lose interest in sin. He gives you the desire to be with like-minded people.

> If we say that we have fellowship with him, and walk in darkness, we lie, and do not the truth: but if we walk in the light, as he is in the light, we have fellowship one with another, and the blood of Jesus Christ his Son cleanseth us from all sin. (1 John 1:6–7)

Jesus desires to come into your life and have fellowship with you.

> Behold, I stand at the door, and knock: if any man hear my voice, and open the door, I will come in to him, and will sup with him, and he with me. (Revelation 3:20)

## FRUIT OF RIGHTEOUSNESS

Jesus' sacrifice for you puts you in right-standing with God. The Holy Spirit gives you these nine things: love, joy, peace, patience, gentleness, goodness, faith, meekness, and self-control. These qualities will enable you to produce good works. You will find that you are doing what is right. You will gradually become more righteous, as God has called you to be. You will be producing righteousness like a tree bears fruit. You will be a tree of righteousness.

According to Jesus, false teachers cannot produce good fruit. You are not going to see fruits of the Spirit in false teachers, because the Holy Spirit is not in them.

> Beware of false prophets, which come to you in sheep's clothing, but inwardly they are ravening wolves. Ye shall know them by their fruits. Do men gather grapes of thorns, or figs of thistles? Even so every good tree bringeth forth good fruit; but a corrupt tree bringeth forth evil fruit. A good tree cannot bring forth evil fruit, neither can a corrupt tree bring forth good fruit. (Matthew 7:15–18)

Good people produce good things, and evil people produce evil things.

> For a good tree bringeth not forth corrupt fruit; neither doth a corrupt tree bring forth good fruit. For every tree is known by his own fruit. For of thorns men do not gather figs, nor of a bramble bush gather they grapes. A good man out of the good treasure of his heart bringeth forth that which is good; and an evil man out of the evil treasure of his heart bringeth forth that which is evil: for of the abundance of the heart his mouth speaketh. (Luke 6:43–45)

These are the words of Jesus. He has given you the job of loving people. As long as you are doing your job, you have his backing and support.

> Ye have not chosen me, but I have chosen you, and ordained you, that ye should go and bring forth fruit, and that your fruit should remain; that whatsoever ye shall ask

> of the Father in my name, he may give it you. These things I command you, that ye love one another. (John 15:16–17)

God sees you as "the righteousness of God" in Christ.

> For he hath made him to be sin for us, who knew no sin; that we might be made the righteousness of God in him. (2 Corinthians 5:21)

Practicing love toward others is doing righteousness. God will chasten you for not loving other people.

> Now no chastening for the present seemeth to be joyous, but grievous: nevertheless afterward it yieldeth the peaceable fruit of righteousness unto them which are exercised thereby. (Hebrews 12:11)

This passage describes what God's wisdom is like. Part of it is seeking peace with others.

> But the wisdom that is from above is first pure, then peaceable, gentle, and easy to be entreated, full of mercy and good fruits, without partiality, and without hypocrisy. And the fruit of righteousness is sown in peace of them that make peace. (James 3:17–18)

## A GOOD CONSCIENCE

Your conscience is that inner voice that tells you when you have done something wrong. A good conscience is one that works. When you were a child, your conscience worked very well. It would speak to you when you went to bed at night. Most adults have ignored their conscience for so long that they can barely hear it. Fellowship with God gets your conscience back into good working order. You will be able to hear it clearly and let it guide you.

This is part of Paul's defense before the Roman governor in Jerusalem. His testimony is that he believes the written word of God. He made it his goal to keep a clear conscience.

> But this I confess unto thee, that after the way which they call heresy, so worship I the God of my fathers, believing all things which are written in the law and in the prophets: and have hope toward God, which they themselves also allow, that there shall be a resurrection of the dead, both of the just and unjust. And herein do I exercise myself, to have always a conscience void of offense toward God, and toward men. (Acts 24:14–16)

"Having your conscience seared with a hot iron," means that to have overruled it so many times that it no longer works. When a person's conscience does not work, he cannot tell right from wrong, and he cannot tell the truth from a lie.

> Now the Spirit speaketh expressly, that in the latter times some shall depart from the faith, giving heed to seducing spirits, and doctrines of devils; speaking lies in hypocrisy; having their conscience seared with a hot iron; forbidding to marry, and commanding to abstain from meats, which God hath created to be received with thanksgiving of them which believe and know the truth. (1 Timothy 4:1–3)

Your conscience is a moral compass to guide you through this life.

> Pray for us: for we trust we have a good conscience, in all things willing to live honestly. (Hebrews 13:18)

Your conscience is a very reliable sin detector. You know the things you are supposed to do. Failing to do them is sin.

> **Therefore to him that knoweth to do good, and doeth it not, to him it is sin. (James 4:17)**

## GRACE

The term "grace" is used two ways in the Bible. It is the unmerited favor of God, as in, "by grace are you saved by faith" (Ephesians 2:8). Grace is when God does you a favor. For example, he saved you even though you did nothing to deserve it. If you were the friend of the President of the United States, he could show you great favor. But Jesus is greater than the President or any other man. There's no limit to his power or his resources. The other kind of grace means to have both the desire and the ability to do the will of God. "For it is God which worketh in you both to will and to do of his good pleasure" (Philippians 2:13). How do you receive this kind of grace? By honoring God by doing what the Bible says. When you humble yourself before God in this way, he will give you grace. He will supply you the willingness and the power to do God's will.

Jesus is the heir to this world, and you are a joint-heir with him. He has given you his righteousness as a free gift. All you have to do is receive it by faith.

> **For the promise, that he should be the heir of the world, was not to Abraham, or to his seed, through the law, but through the righteousness of faith. For if they which are of the law be heirs, faith is made void, and the promise made of none effect: because the law worketh wrath: for where no law is, there is no transgression. Therefore it is of faith, that it might be by grace; to the end the promise might be sure to all the seed; not to that only which is of the law, but to that also which is of the faith of Abraham; who is the father of us all. (Romans 4:13–16)**

Salvation is a gift of inestimable value, and God has given it to you because of his great mercy.

> For if through the offense of one many be dead, much more the grace of God, and the gift by grace, which is by one man, Jesus Christ, hath abounded unto many. (Romans 5:15)

Because of God's grace, sin has no power over you.

> Let not sin therefore reign in your mortal body, that ye should obey it in the lusts thereof. Neither yield ye your members as instruments of unrighteousness unto sin: but yield yourselves unto God, as those that are alive from the dead, and your members as instruments of righteousness unto God. For sin shall not have dominion over you: for ye are not under the law, but under grace. (Romans 6:12–14)

God will intervene in your life and provide everything you need.

> And God is able to make all grace abound toward you; that ye, always having all sufficiency in all things, may abound to every good work: (2 Corinthians 9:8)

Grace is God's part of the transaction. Faith is yours. It gives you access to God's favor.

> For by grace are ye saved through faith; and that not of yourselves: it is the gift of God: Not of works, lest any man should boast. (Ephesians 2:8–9)

God shows his favor toward those who please him by their humility. Humility is submitting yourself to God's authority.

> God resisteth the proud, but giveth grace unto the humble. (James 4:6)

## HARMONY

Everyone wants to be loved and respected. It is just as easy to be pleasant and agreeable as it is to be rude and mean. Try to get along with everyone. God will reward you for being a peacemaker. There are many built—in rewards for being nice to people. When you seek peace with everyone, you will be at peace within yourself. Your life will be more enjoyable.

This is a Psalm of David. God's annointing and his blessing are reserved for those who live in harmony with others.

> **Behold, how good and how pleasant it is for brethren to dwell together in unity! It is like the precious ointment upon the head, that ran down upon the beard, even Aaron's beard: that went down to the skirts of his garments; as the dew of Hermon, and as the dew that descended upon the mountains of Zion: for there the Lord commanded the blessing, even life for evermore. (Psalm 133)**

Jesus promised that if two believers agree on a thing and ask God for it, it will be done for them. The Bible says to let everything be established by two or three witnesses. The Bible is one witness. The Holy Spirit is another.

> **Again I say unto you, That if two of you shall agree on earth as touching any thing that they shall ask, it shall be done for them of my Father which is in heaven. For where two or three are gathered together in my name, there am I in the midst of them. (Matthew 18:19–20)**

Peter taught about Jesus in the temple, leading many in Jerusalem to become believers. The Chief Priest, rulers and elders arrested Peter and John. They threatened them and commanded them not to preach, or to even speak of Jesus. They were released and told the other disciples and all of them prayed together. This was their prayer on the day of Pentecost, in Jerusalem. The Holy Spirit sat upon each one of them as a flame of fire. They were all filled with the Holy Ghost. Your prayers are more effective when you are praying with other believers.

> And when they heard that, they lifted up their voice to God with one accord, and said, Lord, thou art God, which hast made heaven, and earth, and the sea, and all that in them is:...and now, Lord, behold their threatenings; and grant unto thy servants, that with all boldness they may speak thy word, . . and when they had prayed, the place was shaken where they were assembled together; and they were all filled with the Holy Ghost, and they spake the word of God with boldness. And the multitude of them that believed were of one heart and of one soul: . . .and with great power gave the apostles witness of the resurrection of the Lord Jesus: and great grace was upon them all. (Acts 4:24, 29, 31, 33)

Conflicting doctrines separate people and cause them to fight with each other. Avoid everyone whose doctrine is inconsistent with what the Bible teaches.

> Now I beseech you, brethren, mark them which cause divisions and offenses contrary to the doctrine which ye have learned; and avoid them. For they that are such serve not our Lord Jesus Christ, but their own belly; and by good words and fair speeches deceive the hearts of the simple. (Romans 16:17–18)

Make sure that your doctrine agrees with the doctrine of Jesus.

> Now I beseech you, brethren, by the name of our Lord Jesus Christ, that ye all speak the same thing, and that there be no divisions among you; but that ye be perfectly joined together in the same mind and in the same judgment. (1 Corinthians 1:10)

Your "conversation" is your lifestyle.

> **Only let your conversation be as it becometh the gospel of Christ: that whether I come and see you, or else be absent, I may hear of your affairs, that ye stand fast in one spirit, with one mind striving together for the faith of the gospel. (Philippians 1:27)**

Focus your attention on others instead of on yourself. Follow the example Jesus set and put the Love Commandment into action.

> **Fulfill ye my joy, that ye be likeminded, having the same love, being of one accord, of one mind. Let nothing be done through strife or vainglory; but in lowliness of mind let each esteem other better than themselves. Look not every man on his own things, but every man also on the things of others. Let this mind be in you, which was also in Christ Jesus: who, being in the form of God, thought it not robbery to be equal with God: but made himself of no reputation, and took upon him the form of a servant, and was made in the likeness of men: and being found in fashion as a man, he humbled himself, and became obedient unto death, even the death of the cross. (Philippians 2:2–8)**

## HEARING

God speaks to you through the voice of your conscience. He also speaks to you through his word, through circumstances, and through other people. He will communicate to you directly addressing your concerns. He is your personal counselor. It is your obedience to God that gives you access to him. If you ignore him, you won't be able to hear him. You must listen to God before he will listen to you.

Even though the word of God is easily available, there is a famine of hearing it. People run to and fro to satisfy their spiritual hunger and thirst. They don't know that it's God they are craving. They cannot hear him because they do not know him.

> Behold, the days come, saith the Lord God, that I will send a famine in the land, not a famine of bread, not a thirst for water, but of hearing the words of the Lord: and they shall wander from sea to sea, and from the north even to the east, they shall run to and fro to seek the word of the Lord, and shall not find it. In that day shall the fair virgins and young men faint for thirst. (Amos 8:11–13)

In the Parable of the Sower, Jesus explains how the devil reacts to the word of God. He always tries to steal it. It is a dangerous threat to him and his evil schemes.

> When any one heareth the word of the kingdom, and understandeth it not, then cometh the wicked one, and catcheth away that which was sown in his heart. This is he which received seed by the wayside. (Matthew 13:19)

"The dead" are people who are unsaved. They are physically alive but spiritually dead.

> Verily, verily, I say unto you, The hour is coming, and now is, when the dead shall hear the voice of the Son of God: and they that hear shall live. (John 5:25)

These verses explain that faith comes from hearing God's word. Hearing the preaching of truth from the Bible creates faith in God.

> How then shall they call on him in whom they have not believed? And how shall they believe in him of whom they have not heard? And how shall they hear without a preacher? And how shall they preach, except they be sent? As it is written, How beautiful are the feet of them

> **that preach the gospel of peace, and bring glad tidings of good things! But they have not all obeyed the gospel. For Esaias saith, Lord, who hath believed our report? So then faith cometh by hearing, and hearing by the word of God. (Romans 10:14–17)**

## HOPE

All people hope that good things will come their way, but this is just blind hope. It is not based on anything of substance. But your hope is based on God and the integrity of his word. You know that when you obey him, you will receive what he promised. Since God always keeps his word, the thing that you are hoping for is actually a certainty. You just have to wait for your hope to be fulfilled.

Disappointment makes you sick. Receiving what you desire insures your good health.

> **Hope deferred maketh the heart sick, but when the desire cometh, it is a tree of life. (Proverbs 13:12)**

Base your hope on Jesus. He will never let you down. Your eternal salvation is settled. The "salvation" in this passage refers to deliverance from a problem.

> **This I recall to my mind, therefore have I hope. It is of the Lord's mercies that we are not consumed, because his compassions fail not. They are new every morning: great is thy faithfulness. The Lord is my portion, saith my soul; therefore will I hope in him. The Lord is good unto them that wait for him, to the soul that seeketh him. It is good that a man should both hope and quietly wait for the salvation of the Lord. (Lamentations 3:21–26)**

This is the testimony of Paul the Apostle. He put everything he had into the cause of Christ.

> According to my earnest expectation and my hope, that in nothing I shall be ashamed, but that with all boldness, as always, so now also Christ shall be magnified in my body, whether it be by life, or by death. For to me to live is Christ, and to die is gain. (Philippians 1:20–21)

Our hope is in Jesus, who cannot lie and lives forever. When people ask you why you are full of hope, tell them some of the things that the Lord has done for you.

> But sanctify the Lord God in your hearts: and be ready always to give an answer to every man that asketh you a reason of the hope that is in you with meekness and fear: having a good conscience; that, whereas they speak evil of you, as of evildoers, they may be ashamed that falsely accuse your good conversation in Christ. (1 Peter 3:15–16)

## HUMILITY

I learned humility the hard way. When God first began to bless me, I immediately became filled with pride. My thinking was, why should I bother God with things I can do for myself? Instead of walking with the Lord, I was running ahead of him. I was entirely on my own. I forgot that the Bible says that without him I can do nothing. I was utterly defeated and financially ruined because of my own pride. I didn't know the meaning of the word humility. I had to submit myself to God's authority. I had to learn to have respect for everyone in authority over me. I had to learn that it is important to treat everyone with respect, and not to think that I am better than anyone else.

Saul was the first King of Israel. When he stopped being humble, God could not use him. This is what God told him through the Prophet Samuel. It is a good definition of humility. Think of yourself as small instead of great.

**And Samuel said, When thou wast little in thine own sight, wast thou not made the head of the tribes of Israel, and the Lord anointed thee king over Israel? (1 Samuel 15:17)**

When you humble yourself before the Lord, he will honor you.

**The fear of the Lord is the instruction of wisdom; and before honor is humility. (Proverbs 15:33)**

According to the Bible, there are two prerequisites to riches and honor.

**By humility and the fear of the Lord are riches, and honor, and life. (Proverbs 22:4)**

Humility and pride are opposites. Blowing your own horn is a symptom of pride.

**Let another man praise thee, and not thine own mouth; a stranger, and not thine own lips. (Proverbs 27:2)**

God requires three things of you—to do what is right, to be merciful, and to be humble.

**He hath showed thee, O man, what is good; and what doth the Lord require of thee, but to do justly, and to love mercy, and to walk humbly with thy God? (Micah 6:8)**

Jesus' disciples asked him which of them would be the greatest in his kingdom. This was his answer.

**Whosoever therefore shall humble himself as this little child, the same is greatest in the kingdom of heaven. (Matthew 18:4)**

"To be exalted" is to be lifted up. "To be abased" is to be brought down.

> For whosoever exalteth himself shall be abased; and he that humbleth himself shall be exalted. (Luke 14:11)

Do not think of yourself as better than anyone else, or smarter, or more deserving. This kind of thinking is evidence of pride.

> For I say, through the grace given unto me, to every man that is among you, not to think of himself more highly than he ought to think. (Romans 12:3)

After you have learned humility, God will exalt you.

> Humble yourself in the sight of the Lord, and he shall lift you up. (James 4:10)

Humility is the key to receiving God's grace. Grace is God's favor. God will do things for you that you could never do for yourself.

> Be clothed with humility: for God resisteth the proud, and giveth grace to the humble. Humble yourselves therefore under the mighty hand of God, that he may exalt you in due time. (1 Peter 5:5–6)

## INTEGRITY

Integrity is honesty. It is doing what's right. This is our family motto. "Always do right. This will gratify some people and astonish the rest." These words by Mark Twain are funny but they are true. Honesty really is the best policy in every area of life. You have to teach your children what is right and what is wrong. The world insists that everything is relative, that there is no such thing as absolute right, or absolute truth. But they are mistaken. God has the right to determine what is right and what is wrong. He has given us the Bible to teach us the difference between the two.

God "tries your hearts and reins" to see if you'll obey him.

> The Lord shall judge the people: judge me, O Lord, according to my righteousness, and according to mine integrity that is in me. Oh let the wickedness of the wicked come to an end; but establish the just: for the righteous God trieth the hearts and reins. My defense is of God, which saveth the upright in heart. (Psalm 7:8–10)

When you are operating in integrity, God will show you favor.

> By this I know that thou favorest me, because mine enemy doth not triumph over me. And as for me, thou upholdest me in mine integrity, and settest me before thy face for ever. (Psalm 41:11–12)

When it is your intention to do what's right, decision-making is easy. "Perverseness" is doing things that you know are wrong.

> The integrity of the upright shall guide them: but the perverseness of transgressors shall destroy them. (Proverbs 11:3)

When you do what's right, God will bless you. Your children will see that that the word of God is true. They will follow your example and God will bless them too.

> Counsel in the heart of man is like deep water; but a man of understanding will draw it out. Most men will proclaim every one his own goodness: but a faithful man who can find? The just man walketh in his integrity: his children are blessed after him. (Proverbs 20:5–7)

## JOY

Being happy is a choice that you make. You can make the decision to be happy every day. You can make a joyful noise unto the Lord even when you don't feel like it. That is literally a sacrifice of praise. It is an offering that pleases the Lord. When you are filled with God's Spirit, joy becomes a part of your life. It is part of the fruit that you bear. When you walk in the Spirit, you will also experience love, peace, patience, kindness, goodness, faithfulness, gentleness, and self-control.

First God's people rebuilt the walls of Jerusalem. Then, Nehemiah, Ezra, and the Levites taught them the word of the Lord. The people were sorry that they had disobeyed God. They understood how merciful he had been to them. God has given you many things. One of them is joy. The joy of the Lord is your strength too.

> And Nehemiah, which is the Tirshatha, and Ezra the priest the scribe, and the Levites that taught the people, said unto all the people. This day is holy unto the Lord your God; mourn not, nor weep. For all the people wept, when they heard the words of the law. Then he said unto them, Go your way, eat the fat, and drink the sweet, and send portions unto them for whom nothing is prepared: for this day is holy unto our Lord: neither be ye sorry; for the joy of the Lord is your strength. So the Levites stilled all the people, saying, Hold your peace, for the day is holy; neither be ye grieved. And all the people went their way to eat, and to drink, and to send portions, and to make great mirth, because they had understood the words that were declared unto them. (Nehemiah 8:9–12)

Make the decision every day that you are going to be joyful.

> This is the day which the Lord hath made; we will rejoice and be glad in it. (Psalm 118:24)

After you have experienced one of God's miracles, you will know what it is like to be filled with joy.

> When the Lord turned again the captivity of Zion, we were like them that dream. Then was our mouth filled with laughter, and our tongue with singing: then said they among the heathen, The Lord hath done great things for them. The Lord hath done great things for us; whereof we are glad. Turn again our captivity, O Lord, as the streams in the south. They that sow in tears shall reap in joy. He that goeth forth and weepeth, bearing precious seed, shall doubtless come again with rejoicing, bringing his sheaves with him. (Psalm 126)

Keep a joyful attitude even when things are going wrong.

> All the days of the afflicted are evil: but he that is of a merry heart hath a continual feast. (Proverbs 15:15)

Being joyful will keep you in good health.

> A merry heart doeth good like a medicine. (Proverbs 17:23)

Be joyful when you think about the things Jesus has done for you. He has made you righteous before God and has given you everlasting life.

> I will greatly rejoice in the Lord, my soul shall be joyful in my God; for he hath clothed me with the garments of salvation, he hath covered me with the robe of righteousness, as a bridegroom decketh himself with ornaments, and as a bride adorneth herself with her jewels. (Isaiah 61:10)

When God's Spirit is alive in you, he will furnish you with joy.

> If ye keep my commandments, ye shall abide in my love; even as I have kept my Father's commandments, and abide in his love. These things have I spoken unto you, that my joy might remain in you, and that your joy might be full. (John 15:10–11)

When you ask God for a specific thing and he gives it to you, that gives you something to be joyful about.

> Hitherto have ye asked nothing in my name: ask, and ye shall receive, that your joy may be full. (John 16:24)

Make it a habit to sing to the Lord. This is something that is pleasing to God. It is impossible to worry while you are singing to him.

> Let the word of Christ dwell in you richly in all wisdom; teaching and admonishing one another in psalms and hymns and spiritual songs, singing with grace in your hearts to the Lord. (Colossians 3:16)

When you are feeling joyful, show God the joy he has given you.

> Is any merry? Let him sing psalms. (James 5:13)

## KNOWLEDGE

Everything you need to know about life can be found in the Bible. The Holy Spirit is your guide. He will teach you anything you want to learn, anything that is worth knowing. He will tell you how to solve any problem you might have. He will teach you the way to longevity, prosperity and a happy life. His lessons are not mere theories. When you apply God's knowledge to your life, it will work. The way to obtain God's knowledge is to experience it in your own life.

Find out what God says to do, and then do exactly that. Knowing what the Bible says does not benefit you until you put it into practice.

> Bow down thine ear, and hear the words of the wise, and apply thine heart unto my knowledge. For it is a pleasant thing if thou keep them within thee; they shall withal be fitted in thy lips. That thy trust may be in the Lord, I have made known to thee this day, even to thee. Have not I written to thee excellent things in counsels and knowledge, that I might make thee know the certainty of the words of truth; that thou mightest answer the words of truth to them that send unto thee? (Proverbs 22:17–21)

The people of the world have rejected God's ideas. They prefer to believe their own theories.

> Hear the word of the Lord, ye children of Israel: for the Lord hath a controversy with the inhabitants of the land, because there is no truth, nor mercy, nor knowledge of God in the land. By swearing, and lying, and killing, and stealing, and committing adultery, they break out, and blood toucheth blood. Therefore shall the land mourn, and every one that dwelleth therein shall languish, with the beasts of the field, and with the fowls of heaven; yea, the fishes of the sea also shall be taken away. (Hosea 4:1–3)

What you don't know can kill you, even though you are one of God's people.

> My people are destroyed for lack of knowledge. (Hosea 4:6)

If you will do things God's way, you will succeed. You will be a living demonstration of the word of God in action.

> Now thanks be unto God, which always causeth us to triumph in Christ, and makest manifest the savor of his knowledge by us in every place. (2 Corinthians 2:14)

Wisdom is living a life that is consistent with the Bible.

> **Who is a wise man and endued with knowledge among you? Let him show out of a good conversation his works with meekness of wisdom. (James 3:13)**

## LIBERTY

Liberty is the freedom that Jesus gave you. He set you free from the law of sin and death and put you under God's law of liberty. That means that you do not have to observe the letter of the law superficially. You are free to observe the spirit of the law with your whole heart. You get to please God because you want to please him. You don't have to pretend to be something you are not, while living a secret life of selfishness. You have quit grasping for everything you can get for yourself. God judges you by the thoughts and intentions of your heart. You have been delivered from the power of sin. Don't let it boss you around. "Expedient" means appropriate.

> **All things are lawful unto me, but all things are not expedient: all things are lawful for me, but I will not be brought under the power of any. (1 Corinthians 6:12)**

The Holy Spirit gives you the desire to do what pleases God. All you have to do now is to follow that desire.

> **Now the Lord is that Spirit: and where the Spirit of the Lord is, there is liberty. (2 Corinthians 3:17)**

The Lord's commandment and the Golden Rule are two ways of expressing the same idea. When you make this concept a part of your life, you are fulfilling God's law.

> **For, brethren, ye have been called unto liberty; only use not liberty for an occasion to the flesh, but by love serve one**

> another. For all the law is fulfilled in one word, even in this; thou shalt love thy neighbor as thyself. (Galatians 5:13–14)

You know what God has commanded you to do. He will not bless you if you are not keeping his commandments.

> But be ye doers of the word, and not hearers only, deceiving your own selves. For if any be a hearer of the word, and not a doer, he is like unto a man beholding his natural face in a glass: for he beholdeth himself, and goeth his way, and straightway forgetteth what manner of man he was. But whoso looketh into the perfect law of liberty, and continueth therein, he being not a forgetful hearer, but a doer of the work, this man shall be blessed in his deed. (James 1:22–25)

Act like the free person you are. You will get back what you give. When you show mercy, you will get mercy.

> So speak ye, and so do, as they that shall be judged by the law of liberty. For he shall have judgment without mercy, that hath shewed no mercy. (James 2:12–13)

## LIFE

When God gave his people the Ten Commandments, he gave them the choice to either obey him or not. He gives you the same opportunity. You can choose life and the blessing of God or you can reject it. The Bible says that you were dead in your trespasses and sins. When you accepted God's free gift of salvation, he raised you from the dead. You chose life instead of death by accepting Jesus as your Savior and Lord. There is no life apart from God. You are alive because of your connection to him. Death is merely the absence of life. It is separation from God. Now that you have eternal life, you will never be separated from God again.

Some people don't want anything to do with God. He does not impose himself on them. They are free to reject him. Everyone has to make the same life or death decision. Accept Jesus and live, or reject him and die.

> I call heaven and earth to record this day against you, that I have set before you life and death, blessing and cursing: therefore choose life, that both thou and thy seed may live: that thou mayest love the Lord thy God, and that thou mayest obey his voice, and that thou mayest cleave unto him: for he is thy life, and the length of thy days. (Deuteronomy 30:19–20)

You are a part of Christ. You are part of his body in the Earth. You are dead to sin and alive to God. The wages of sin are death. That payment of death has been paid for you. You have been raised from the dead to experience a new kind of life. God's own Spirit empowers you to live that life.

> Now if we be dead with Christ, we believe that we shall also live with him: knowing that Christ being raised from the dead dieth no more; death hath no more dominion over him....Likewise reckon ye also yourselves to be dead indeed unto sin, but alive unto God through Jesus Christ our Lord. (Romans 6:8–9, 11)

Jesus reversed the damage caused by Adam's fall. Adam brought death into the world. Jesus brought resurrection from the dead.

> But now is Christ risen from the dead, and become the firstfruits of them that slept. For since by man came death, by man came also the resurrection of the dead. For as in Adam all die, even so in Christ shall all be made alive. (1 Corinthians 15:20–22)

Quickening is the experience that a woman has when she first feels her baby move within her. Spiritual quickening is when you become aware that Jesus is alive in you.

> **And so it is written, the first man Adam was made a living soul; the last Adam was made a quickening spirit. (1 Corinthians 15:45)**

## LOVE

Love is focusing your attention on others instead of on yourself. It is the "you" attitude that says, "I'm interested in you" instead of the "me" attitude that says, "What about me?" It is helping people in need instead of ignoring them. That is how Jesus lived his life. You needed a Savior and he supplied that need. That's how loving he is. He is the embodiment of love. His Spirit in you empowers you to be like him. That is what he meant when he commanded you to "Love one another as I have loved you."

The Holy Spirit provides you with the love for others that God requires you to have.

> **The love of God is shed abroad in our hearts by the Holy Ghost which is given unto us. (Romans 5:5)**

As a believer in Christ, it is your job to love your neighbor the way you love yourself. When you do that, you are acting like Jesus. You are following him.

> **For this, thou shalt not commit adultery, thou shalt not kill, thou shalt not steal, thou shalt not bear false witness, thou shalt not covet; and if there be any other commandment, it is briefly comprehended in this saying, namely, thou shalt love thy neighbor as thyself. Love worketh no ill to his neighbor: therefore love is the fulfilling of the law. (Romans 13:9–10)**

Make loving others your highest priority. First Corinthians, Chapter 13 is called the Love Chapter. It explains how to love other people.

> Though I speak with the tongues of men and of angels, and have not charity, I am become as sounding brass, or a tinkling cymbal. And though I have the gift of prophecy, and understand all mysteries, and all knowledge; and though I have all faith, so that I could remove mountains, and have not charity, I am nothing. (1 Corinthians 13:1–3)

In this passage, God explains what he means by the term "love." It is behavior that is based on a particular attitude of the heart. It is the opposite of fear and sin. "Charity" is the ancient word for this kind of love.

> Charity suffereth long, and is kind; charity envieth not; charity vaunteth not itself, is not puffed up, doth not behave itself unseemly, seeketh not her own, is not easily provoked, thinketh no evil; rejoiceth not in iniquity, but rejoiceth in the truth; beareth all things, believeth all things, hopeth all things, endureth all things. Charity never faileth. (1 Corinthians 13:4–8)

Love is the secret handshake that believers in Christ can use to recognize each other.

> Beloved, let us love one another: for love is of God; and every one that loveth is born of God, and knoweth God. He that loveth not knoweth not God; for God is love. (1 John 4:7–8)

This is how you know that you are in Christ and he is in you. You will find yourself loving other people in spite of their shortcomings.

> If we love one another, God dwelleth in us, and his love is perfected in us. Hereby know we that we dwell in him, and

> he in us, because he hath given us of his Spirit. (1 John 4:12–13)

The Holy Spirit causes you to change from the inside out. He supplies the love, and you supply the willingness to apply it.

> Seeing ye have purified your souls in obeying the truth through the Spirit unto unfeigned love of the brethren, see that ye love one another with a pure heart fervently, being born again, not of corruptible seed, but of incorruptible, by the word of God, which liveth and abideth for ever. (1 Peter 1:22–23)

## PATIENCE

God is never in a hurry, but he is always on time. You have to wait on his timing without giving up and quitting. Sometimes that takes a long time. You have to keep hoping and trusting in Jesus. Patience is one of the elements of God's love. Jesus is very patient. He is seated at the right hand of the Father waiting for his enemies to be made his footstool. He has patience for the precious fruit of the earth. He is patient toward us, not willing that any should perish, but that all should come to repentance.

Just as lifting weights develops your muscles, overcoming opposition develops your patience. I used to be overly assertive, irritable, and impatient. I made life unpleasant for everyone around me. I was ruining my health and shortening my life. But God changed me. He gave me much more patience. The more patience you have, the happier you will be.

Tribulation is trouble. It is a part of life. You develop patience by overcoming your problems.

> But we glory in tribulations also: knowing that tribulation worketh patience; and patience, experience; and experience hope. (Romans 5:3–4)

"In due season" means according to God's timing. "Fainting not" means that you don't quit.

> And let us not be weary in well doing: for in due season we shall reap, if we faint not. (Galatians 6:9)

When you are meeting the needs of others, you are demonstrating your faith in God. It takes both faith and patience to receive what God has promised.

> For God is not unrighteous to forget your work and labor of love, which ye have showed toward his name, in that ye have ministered to the saints, and do minister. And we desire that every one of you do show the same diligence to the full assurance of hope unto the end: that ye be not slothful, but followers of them who through faith and patience inherit the promises. (Hebrews 6:9–12)

God always delivers what he has promised, but it is always according to his timing. Continue to work while you are waiting on God.

> For ye have need of patience, that, after ye have done the will of God, ye might receive the promise. (Hebrews 10:36)

Get rid of every sin you have. Live the Christian life as if you are running in a race.

> Wherefore seeing we also are compassed about with so great a cloud of witnesses, let us lay aside every weight, and the sin which doth so easily beset us, and let us run with patience the race that is set before us, looking unto Jesus, the author and finisher of our faith; who for the joy that was set before him endured the cross, despising the shame, and is set down at the right hand of the throne of God. For consider him that endured such contradiction of

**sinners against himself, lest ye be wearied and faint in your minds. Ye have not yet resisted unto blood, striving against sin. (Hebrews 12:1–4)**

Patience is an essential part of receiving what God has for you.

**Knowing this, that the trying of your faith worketh patience. But let patience have her perfect work, that ye may be perfect and entire, wanting nothing. (James 1:3–4)**

## PEACE

Peace comes from the Lord. It is the absence of conflict in your heart and mind. When you are at peace with God, you will be at peace within yourself, and you will be able to live in peace with others. If you follow the Golden Rule, you will get along well with most people. You won't be bickering with them over trivial matters. You cannot buy peace of mind with money. You can only get it from God.

Aaron was Moses' brother and God's priest. God told him to speak this blessing to God's people. Men of God still speak this same blessing to God's people today.

**And the Lord spake unto Moses, saying, Speak unto Aaron and unto his sons, saying, On this wise ye shall bless the children of Israel, saying unto them, The Lord bless thee, and keep thee: the Lord make his face shine upon thee, and be gracious unto thee: the Lord lift up his countenance upon thee, and give thee peace. And they shall put my name upon the children of Israel; and I will bless them. (Numbers 6:22–27)**

Focus your mind on God and he will give you peace.

**Thou wilt keep him in perfect peace, whose mind is stayed on thee: because he trusteth in thee. (Isaiah 26:3)**

There will always be people who will be rude to you. If you are offended by them, then you are giving up your peace.

> Great peace have they which love thy law: and nothing shall offend them. (Psalms 119:165)

This is one of the fringe benefits that result from pleasing God.

> When a man's ways please the Lord, he maketh even his enemies to be at peace with him. (Proverbs 16:7)

Nothing can compare to the peace that Jesus provides.

> Peace I leave with you, my peace I give unto you: not as the world giveth, give I unto you. Let not your heart be troubled, neither let it be afraid. (John 14:27)

If you are in the midst of confusion, it does not come from God.

> For God is not the author of confusion, but of peace, as in all churches of the saints. (1 Corinthians 14:33)

Follow God's instructions and his peace will follow. "Be careful for nothing" means not to take anxious thought about anything. God knows what you need. He invites you to ask him for these things, and he will give them to you.

> Be careful for nothing; but in every thing by prayer and supplication with thanksgiving let your requests be made known unto God. And the peace of God, which passeth all understanding, shall keep your hearts and minds through Christ Jesus. (Philippians 4:6–7)

## A PURE HEART

Your heart is where you keep the things that you treasure. Everything in your heart will affect your life. The thoughts and intents of your heart create the circumstances of your life. The things that you believe determine your future and your health. That is why you must meditate on the word of God. Fill your heart so full of God's word that there is no room for anything else. God's Spirit will be like a fire within you that consumes the evil that is in your heart, including the desire to sin.

Men base their judgments on what they see, but everything is open and exposed to God.

> **For the Lord seeth not as man seeth; for man looketh on the outward appearance, but the Lord looketh on the heart. (1 Samuel 16:7)**

King David tried to cover up his adultery with Bathsheba, but God sent Nathan, the prophet, to tell David that God saw what he had done. This is David's response to God.

> **Create in me a clean heart, O God; and renew a right spirit within me. (Psalm 51:10)**

"Iniquity" is sin. Sin in your heart prevents the Lord from hearing your prayer.

> **If I regard iniquity in my heart, the Lord will not hear me. (Psalm 66:18)**

This passage tells you how to keep yourself from sin. "Hiding God's word in your heart" means reading it until you remember it.

> **Wherewithal shall a young man cleanse his way? By taking heed thereto according to thy word. With my whole**

> heart have I sought thee: O let me not wander from thy commandments. Thy word have I hid in mine heart, that I might not sin against thee. (Psalm 119:9–11)

God's word is essential to your life. You have to pay attention to what it says to enjoy good health.

> My son, attend to my words; incline thine ear unto my sayings. Let them not depart from thine eyes; keep them in the midst of thine heart. For they are life unto those that find them, and health to all their flesh. Keep thy heart with all diligence; for out of it are the issues of life. (Proverbs 4:20–23)

This word from the Lord explains how things work. What you think about is what you become. If you think about negative things, you will get negative results. If you focus your attention on the word of God, you will get what it says. You will become like Jesus and receive the blessing of the Lord.

> For as he thinketh in his heart, so is he. (Proverbs 23:7)

God promised he would give you a new heart, one that has a desire to please him. When you are not sure what to do, follow your heart.

> And I will give them one heart, and I will put a new spirit within you; and I will take the stony heart out of their flesh, and will give them a heart of flesh: that they may walk in my statutes, and keep mine ordinances, and do them: and they shall be my people, and I will be their God. But as for them whose heart walketh after the heart of their detestable things and their abominations, I will recompense their way upon their own heads, saith the Lord God. (Ezekiel 11:19–21)

Your attention is focused on the things you value the most, whether it is the things of God or the things of this world.

> For where your treasure is, there will your heart be also. (Matthew 6:21)

During a dispute with the Pharisees, Jesus revealed this valuable information.

> Out of the abundance of the heart the mouth speaketh. A good man out of the good treasure of the heart bringeth forth good things: and an evil man out of the evil treasure bringeth forth evil things. (Matthew 12:34–35)

When you practice the things that are mentioned in the following passage, you are qualified to teach others to do the same.

> Now the end of the commandment is charity out of a pure heart, and of a good conscience, and of faith unfeigned: from which some having swerved have turned aside unto vain jangling; desiring to be teachers of the law; understanding neither what they say, nor whereof they affirm. (1 Timothy 1:5–7)

When your mind is renewed, you think differently. Your old inappropriate thoughts will be replaced by these Christian virtues. You used to be driven by your lusts. Now you have power over them. The best way to overcome lust is to remove yourself from the situation, like Joseph did when he ran away from Potiphar's wife.

> Flee also youthful lusts: but follow righteousness, faith, charity, peace, with them that call on the Lord out of a pure heart. (2 Timothy 2:22)

Sin hardens people's hearts. The "provocation" is the time when the Children of Israel provoked God so severely that he considered destroying them all.

> But exhort one another daily, while it is called Today; lest any of you be hardened through the deceitfulness of sin.... While it is said, today, if ye will hear his voice, harden not your hearts, as in the provocation. (Hebrews 3:13, 15)

Stop flip-flopping back and forth between serving God and serving yourself. You cannot give your heart to the Lord and withhold part of it for yourself. He wants your whole heart. The commandment is to love God with all your heart, all your soul, all your strength, and all your mind.

> Draw nigh to God, and he will draw nigh to you. Cleanse your hands, ye sinners; and purify your hearts, ye double-minded. (James 4:8)

## A RENEWED MIND

You are accustomed to thinking like the world thinks. But now that you are in Christ, you have to think like Jesus. Exposure to God's word will renew your mind. The Holy Spirit will enable you to think like Jesus. The world is opposed to God and his Word. They say that there is no such thing as God or truth. But you know that Jesus is the truth. They think that truth is constantly changing. You know that truth is something that never changes. Jesus Christ is the same yesterday, today, and forever. They think that God is a creation of man. You know that God created the heavens and the Earth.

In order to follow the Lord, you must renew your mind. You do that by studying and meditating on the Bible daily.

> I beseech you therefore, brethren, by the mercies of God, that ye present your bodies a living sacrifice, holy,

> acceptable unto God, which is your reasonable service. And be not conformed to this world: but be ye transformed by the renewing of your mind, that ye may prove what is that good, and acceptable, and perfect, will of God. (Romans 12:1–2)

Make it your goal to demonstrate God's love to other people. That will require that you change the way you think. Instead of thinking, "what can this person do to help me?" Now you have to think, "what can I do to help this person?" That is having the mindset of Christ.

> But we have the mind of Christ. (1 Corinthians 2:16)

Your renewed mind understands what God is doing. He provides you with resources. He expects you to use them for the benefit of others. They will recognize the goodness of God, and thank him for his help. Your acts of love will strengthen the inner man of your heart.

> For all things are for your sakes, that the abundant grace might through the thanksgiving of many redound to the glory of God. For which cause we faint not; but though our outward man perish, yet the inward man is renewed day by day. (2 Corinthians 4:15–16)

Jesus changes you from the inside out. He gives you a new life and a fresh start.

> Therefore if any man be in Christ, he is a new creature: old things are passed away; behold, all things are become new. (2 Corinthians 5:17)

The "old man" is your old world-based self. The "new man" is your renewed spiritual self.

> If so be that ye have heard him, and have been taught by him, as the truth is in Jesus: that ye put off concerning the former conversation the old man, which is corrupt according to the deceitful lusts; and be renewed in the spirit of your mind; and that ye put on the new man, which after God is created in righteousness and true holiness. (Ephesians 4:21–23)

Be motivated by love. When it is your intention is to love other people, you have the mind of Christ.

> Look not every man on his own things, but every man also on the things of others. Let this mind be in you, which was also in Christ Jesus. (Philippians 2:4–5)

You must stop doing what your carnal (fleshy) mind desires and do the things your new spiritual mind tells you.

> But now ye also put off all these; anger, wrath, malice, blasphemy, filthy communication out of your mouth. Lie not one to another, seeing that ye have put off the old man with his deeds; and have put on the new man, which is renewed in knowledge after the image of him that created him. (Colossians 3:8–10)

## REWARDS

It is not generally known, but God rewards you for obeying his word. There is a reward for you in heaven, and there are additional rewards for you in this life. These rewards are not for everyone. There is a built-in safeguard that keeps them from those who haven't earned them. You will receive what God promised when you meet his requirements. "By humility and the fear of the Lord are riches, and honor, and life" (Proverbs 22:4). God cannot reward you if you will not obey his rules. That wouldn't be fair to the ones who do obey him. If you think that he should reward you anyway, then you do not understand the meaning of the word "humility."

This Psalm is talking about the written word of God and all of its benefits.

> The law of the Lord is perfect, converting the soul: the testimony of the Lord is sure, making wise the simple. The statutes of the Lord are right, rejoicing the heart: the commandment of the Lord is pure, enlightening the eyes. The fear of the Lord is clean, enduring for ever: the judgments of the Lord are true and righteous altogether. More to be desired are they than gold, yea, than much fine gold: sweeter also than honey and the honeycomb. Moreover by them is thy servant warned: and in keeping of them there is great reward. (Psalm 19:7–11)

You will always benefit by doing what is right.

> To him that soweth righteousness shall be a sure reward. (Proverbs 11:8)

God rewards you for "being good."

> For God giveth to a man that is good in his sight wisdom, and knowledge, and joy; but to the sinner he giveth travail, to gather and to heap up, that he may give to him that is good before God. This also is vanity and vexation of spirit. (Ecclesiastes 2:26)

You will be rewarded for even a small kindness.

> And whosoever shall give to drink unto one of these little ones a cup of cold water only in the name of a disciple, verily I say unto you, he shall in no wise lose his reward. (Matthew 10:42)

The Lord will reward you in this life for the sacrifices you have made.

> And Jesus answered and said, Verily I say unto you, there is no man that hath left house, or brethren, or sisters, or father, or mother, or wife, or children, or lands, for my sake, and the gospel's, but he shall receive an hundredfold now in this time, houses, and brethren, and sisters, and mothers, and children, and lands, with persecutions; and in the world to come eternal life. (Mark 10:29–30)

The Lord will repay you for everything you spend on others.

> Knowing that whatsoever good thing any man doeth, the same shall he receive of the Lord, whether he be bond or free. (Ephesians 6:8)

You please God by placing your faith in him. When you seek him diligently, he will reward you.

> But without faith, it is impossible to please him: for he that cometh to God must believe that he is, and that he is a rewarder of them that diligently seek him. (Hebrews 11:6)

## SALVATION

The word "gospel" literally means good news. God's good news is that salvation is a free gift. Jesus has already paid for your salvation. You do not have to do anything to earn it or deserve it. If you receive Jesus as your Lord and Savior, you will be saved from death and hell. As long as you are alive, you can take this deal. It is not too late for you. It does not matter how bad you have been. The following scriptures contain everything you need to know in order to be saved.

Jesus came to Earth to save people from death and hell.

> For God so loved the world, that he gave his only begotten Son, that whosoever believeth in him should not perish, but have everlasting life. For God sent not his Son into the world to condemn the world; but that the world through him might be saved. (John 3:16–17)

In Jerusalem, on the day of Pentecost, the Holy Spirit came to live in the hearts of believers in Jesus. He caused those believers to speak the word of God with great boldness. Peter preached this sermon to the men who caused Jesus to be put to death. Peter told them the truth. Salvation can only be obtained though Jesus, the Son of God.

> Be it known unto you all, and to all the people of Israel, that by the name of Jesus Christ of Nazareth, whom ye crucified, whom God raised from the dead, even by him doth this man stand here before you whole....Neither is there salvation in any other: for there is none other name under heaven given among men, whereby we must be saved. (Acts 4:10, 12)

This passage explains how to go about being saved.

> That if thou shalt confess with thy mouth the Lord Jesus, and shalt believe in thine heart that God hath raised him from the dead, thou shalt be saved. For with the heart man believeth unto righteousness; and with the mouth confession is made unto salvation. (Romans 10:9–10)

As a descendent of Adam you were under a sentence of death, but Jesus died on your behalf. God raised him from the dead and gave you the gift of eternal life.

> For the wages of sin is death; but the gift of God is eternal life through Jesus Christ our Lord. (Romans 6:23)

You receive salvation by faith, which is accepting God's word as true. Just as gold is purified by fire, your faith will be tested by the trials that you face.

> That the trial of your faith, being much more precious than of gold that perisheth, though it be tried with fire, might be found unto praise and honor and glory at the appearing of Jesus Christ: whom having not seen, ye love; in whom, though now ye see him not, yet believing, ye rejoice with joy unspeakable and full of glory: receiving the end of your faith, even the salvation of your souls. (1 Peter 1:7–9)

## STRENGTH

When you sing praises to God, you access his strength. That is an offering that he desires. Don't wait until you have a problem before you contact God. Make it a habit to pray and sing to him on a daily basis. When a crisis comes along, you will be prepared for it. The following Bible passages reveal a plan of action for believers to assist each other. When you need God's help, get together with other believers and sing praises to him. If you try to fight life's battles by yourself, you will probably lose. That is because you did not follow God's battle plan.

This is from Hannah's song of thanksgiving to the Lord for giving her a child. It reveals a surprising truth. It is not God's will for you to prevail in your own strength.

> He will keep the feet of his saints, and the wicked shall be silent in darkness; for by strength shall no man prevail. (1 Samuel 2:9)

The following passage shows you what to do in a crisis. An overwhelming military force was coming to destroy Judah. King Jehosaphat assembled the whole nation together. All of them asked God to deliver them. Then, they gave him an offering of praise. God answered their prayer immediately. He spoke to them through his prophet and told them exactly what to do. The next day they followed his instructions. Their army went on offense and set out to meet the enemy, and the praisers went before the army. God fought for them and defeated their enemy.

> Thus saith the Lord unto you, Be not afraid nor dismayed by reason of this great multitude; for the battle is not yours, but God's. . . .Ye shall not need to fight in this battle: set yourselves, stand ye still, and see the salvation of the Lord with you, O Judah and Jerusalem: fear not, nor be dismayed; tomorrow go out against them: for the Lord will be with you. And Jehosaphat bowed his head with his face to the ground: and all Judah and the inhabitants of Jerusalem fell before the Lord, worshipping the Lord. And the Levites, of the children of the Kohathites, and of the children of the Korhites, stood up to praise the Lord God of Israel with a loud voice on high....And when he had consulted with the people, he appointed singers unto the Lord, and that should praise the beauty of holiness, as they went out before the army, and to say, Praise the Lord; for his mercy endureth forever. And when they began to sing and to praise, the Lord set ambushments against the children of Ammon, Moab, and Mount Seir, which were come against Judah; and they were smitten. (2 Chronicles 20:15, 17–19, 21–22)

The Holy Spirit supplies you with joy. Expressing this joy will enable you to overcome adversity.

> The joy of the Lord is your strength. (Nehemiah 8:10)

When you praise God, you release his strength into your situation. God stills the enemy and the avenger. Your praise authorizes him to intervene on your behalf. Praise equals God's strength.

> **Out of the mouth of babes and sucklings hast thou ordained strength because of thine enemies, that thou mightest still the enemy and the avenger. (Psalm 8:2)**

The Lord provides you the moral and spiritual strength you need. "Waiting upon the Lord," is serving him. Having your strength renewed is another benefit of being a servant of God.

> **Hast thou not known? hast thou not heard, that the everlasting God, the Lord, the Creator of the ends of the earth, fainteth not, neither is weary? There is no searching of his understanding. He giveth power to the faint; and to them that have no might he increaseth strength. Even the youths shall faint and be weary, and the young men shall utterly fall: but they that wait upon the Lord shall renew their strength; they shall mount up with wings as eagles; they shall run, and not be weary; and they shall walk, and not faint. (Isaiah 40:28–31)**

The Holy Spirit does things that are impossible for you to do alone.

> **Not by might, nor by power, but by my spirit, saith the Lord of hosts. (Zechariah 4:6)**

Compare this verse with Psalm 8:2 above. It seems that the words "praise" and "strength" are interchangeable. When you praise God, you release his strength into your situation.

> **And Jesus saith unto them, Yea; have ye never read, Out of the mouth of babes and sucklings thou hast perfected praise? (Matthew 21:16)**

Jesus explained that you are connected to him. You cannot succeed apart from him.

> I am the vine, ye are the branches: he that abideth in me, and I in him, the same bringeth forth much fruit: for without me ye can do nothing. (John 15:5)

In Philippi, Paul and Silas were beaten and thrown into prison. They could have complained about their situation. But they were thankful to be alive. They expressed the joy of the Lord that was within them by praying and singing praises to God. God responded to their praise and intervened to deliver them.

> And when they had laid many stripes upon them, they cast them into prison, charging the jailer to keep them safely: who, having received such a charge, thrust them into the inner prison, and made their feet fast in the stocks. And at midnight Paul and Silas prayed, and sang praises unto God: and the prisoners heard them. And suddenly there was a great earthquake, so that the foundations of the prison were shaken: and immediately all the doors were opened, and every one's bands were loosed. (Acts 16:23–26)

In this passage the Apostle Paul explained an important fact about God's strength. God's strength is triggered after you have exhausted all the strength that you have. That will keep you from being filled with pride, thinking that you don't need God.

> And lest I should be exalted above measure through the abundance of the revelations, there was given to me a thorn in the flesh, the messenger of Satan to buffet me, lest I should be exalted above measure. For this thing I besought the Lord thrice, that it might depart from me. And he said unto me, My grace is sufficient for thee: for my strength is made perfect in weakness. Most gladly therefore will I rather glory in my infirmities, that the power of Christ may rest upon me. Therefore I take pleasure in infirmities, in reproaches, in necessities, in persecutions, in

> distresses for Christ's sake: for when I am weak, then am I strong. (2 Corinthians 12:7–10)

Learn to depend on the Lord's strength instead of your own.

> Finally, my brethren, be strong in the Lord, and in the power of his might. (Ephesians 6:10)

The Lord will empower you to do the things that he commands you to do.

> I can do all things through Christ which strengtheneth me. (Philippians 4:13)

## THE TRUTH

The truth is something that never changes. The Bible says that Jesus is the same yesterday, today and forever. He is the Truth. The Bible is all about him. It is the written word of God. He is the Living Word of God. God defines truth, and there is no truth apart from him. The world thinks they determine what is true, but their "truths" are always changing. To them, there is no absolute truth and no right or wrong. Their lives are empty and have no meaning because there is no truth in them. They are looking for something to fill the emptiness in their lives. They are on a quest to find something beautiful and true. They don't know that what they are seeking can only be found in Jesus.

Jesus is the Son of God. He is alive, and he continues to set people free today. These are his words to you. Disciples are "disciplined ones." You are a disciple of Jesus when you follow his teachings.

> Then said Jesus to those Jews which believed on him, If you continue in my word, then are ye my disciples indeed; and ye shall know the truth, and the truth shall make you free....If the Son therefore shall make you free, ye shall be free indeed. (John 8:31–32, 36)

No other religious leader compares to Jesus. His credentials are unique. He was sent to Earth by his Father, who is God. He taught us how to live. He died on the cross for us, and God raised him from the dead. He ascended to heaven and sent the Holy Spirit to guide us.

> Jesus saith unto him, I am the way, the truth, and the life: no man cometh unto the Father, but by me. (John 14:6)

Since the Bible is the word of God, it has to be the truth because God cannot lie.

> Sanctify them through thy truth: thy word is truth. (John 17:17)

Pontius Pilate was the Roman Governor of Palestine. He gave the order to crucify Jesus. Jesus said that everyone who is of the truth hears his voice. Pilate met the Truth face-to-face and did not know it.

> Pilate therefore said unto him, Art thou a king then? Jesus answered, Thou sayest that I am a king. To this end was I born, and for this cause came I into the world, that I should bear witness unto the truth. Every one that is of the truth heareth my voice. Pilate saith unto him, What is truth? And when he had said this, he went out again unto the Jews, and saith unto them, I find in him no fault at all. (John 18:37–38)

Jesus is not merely one of several ways to God. He is the only way to God.

> Neither is there salvation in any other: for there is none other name under heaven given among men, whereby we must be saved. (Acts 4:12)

You are preparing yourself for a successful life when you study God's word.

> **Study to show thyself approved unto God, a workman that needeth not to be ashamed, rightly dividing the word of truth. (2 Timothy 2:15)**

When you know the Lord, you will desire to please him and keep his commandments.

> **He that saith, I know him, and keepeth not his commandments, is a liar, and the truth is not in him. (1 John 2:4)**

If you catch someone in a lie, you know they are not speaking for the Lord.

> **I have not written unto you because ye know not the truth, but because ye know it, and that no lie is of the truth. (1 John 2:21)**

Jesus is truth. He is also the Holy Spirit.

> **And it is the Spirit that beareth witness, because the Spirit is truth. (1 John 5:6)**

## TRUE RELIGION

God explains true religion in the following verses. Basically, it is obeying his word. Many people are Christians in name only. They are from a Christian culture, and they believe that Jesus exists. But they do not know him personally. They call him Lord, but they are not doing the things he said. They are not practicing God's love toward others. They are not attracting people to the Lord, but repelling them instead.

You can fool people, but you cannot fool the Lord. He knows what is in your heart. That is why you have to be completely honest with him.

> But the hour cometh, and now is, when the true worshippers shall worship the Father in spirit and in truth: for the Father seeketh such to worship him. God is a Spirit: and they that worship him must worship him in spirit and in truth. (John 4:23–24)

Men use religion to serve themselves, but God gets the blame for their evil works. God defines true religion in the following passage.

> If any man among you seem to be religious, and bridleth not his tongue, but deceiveth his own heart, this man's religion is vain. Pure religion and undefiled before God and the Father is this, to visit the fatherless and widows in their affliction, and to keep himself unspotted from the world. (James 1:26–27)

You know you belong to Jesus when keeping the Golden Rule is a way of life for you.

> My little children, let us not love in word, neither in tongue; but in deed and in truth. And hereby we know that we are of the truth, and shall assure our hearts before him. For if our heart condemn us, God is greater than our heart, and knoweth all things. Beloved, if our heart condemn us not, then have we confidence toward God. And whatsoever we ask, we receive of him, because we keep his commandments, and do those things that are pleasing in his sight. And this is his commandment, That we should believe on the name of his Son Jesus Christ, and love one another, as he gave us commandment. And he that keepeth his commandments dwelleth in him, and he in him. And hereby we know that he abideth in us, by the Spirit which he hath given us. (1 John 3:18–24)

## UNDERSTANDING

When you understand the Bible, you will do what it says. When you understand that God rewards you for following his commandments, you will want those rewards. Every time you disobey him, you lose a reward. Wisdom is incorporating God's word into your life. Understanding is eliminating the things that God hates, such as lying.

Wisdom is adding the positive things of God. Understanding is eliminating the negative things of the flesh.

> **And unto man he said, Behold, the fear of the Lord, that is wisdom; and to depart from evil is understanding. (Job 28:28)**

In the Bible, God has told you what he expects you to do. He is watching you to see if you will obey him or not.

> **The Lord looked down from heaven upon the children of men, to see if there were any that did understand, and seek God. (Psalm 14:2)**

If you are willing to do whatever the Lord tells you, that is the attitude that pleases God.

> **Give me understanding, and I shall keep thy law; yea, I shall observe it with my whole heart. (Psalm 119:34)**

The Bible causes you to understand God's ways.

> **How sweet are thy words unto my taste! Yea, sweeter than honey to my mouth. Through thy precepts I get understanding: therefore I hate every false way. (Psalm 119:103–104)**

The Holy Spirit will explain what God is saying to you.

**I am thy servant; give me understanding, that I may know thy testimonies. (Psalm 119:125)**

Understanding the Bible will keep you from being naïve.

**The entrance of thy words giveth light; it giveth understanding unto the simple. (Psalm 119:130)**

Do everything God's way instead of your own way.

**Trust in the Lord with all thine heart; and lean not unto thine own understanding. In all thy ways acknowledge him, and he shall direct thy paths. (Proverbs 3:5–6)**

This is what King Solomon taught his son about wisdom and understanding.

**Hear, ye children, the instruction of a father, and attend to know understanding. For I give you good doctrine, forsake ye not my law. For I was my father's son, tender and only beloved in the sight of my mother. He taught me also, and said unto me, Let thine heart retain my words: keep my commandments, and live. Get wisdom, get understanding: forget it not; neither decline from the words of my mouth. Forsake her not, and she shall preserve thee: love her, and she shall keep thee. Wisdom is the principal thing; therefore get wisdom: and with all thy getting get understanding. (Proverbs 4:1–7)**

Fools have no interest in the Bible. They love the world and the things of the world. Understanding causes a craving for God's word.

> The heart of him that hath understanding seeketh knowledge: but the mouth of fools feedeth on foolishness. (Proverbs 15:14)

People who understand God's word always try to do what is right. Fools enjoy doing things that are wrong.

> Folly is joy to him that is destitute of wisdom: but a man of understanding walketh uprightly. (Proverbs 15:21)

Understanding is paying attention to what God is saying to you.

> Hear now this, O foolish people, and without understanding; which have eyes, and see not; which have ears, and hear not. (Jeremiah 5:21)

The Lord gives you the answers to life's important questions. You can ask him anything.

> Evil men understand not judgment: but they that seek the Lord understand all things. (Proverbs 28:5)

## WEALTH

There are people who have money, but nothing else. They have traded their souls for their money. They think that it is the most important thing in life. Do not seek riches apart from God. If you manage to get rich without him, your wealth will bring you sorrow. You won't have peace of mind or the time to enjoy your riches. The true riches of life come from God. A believer might not have any money, but will still be rich in faith, love, joy, peace and hope. Applying the Bible to your life will cause you to be wise. Wealth follows wisdom.

Your ability to earn money is based on the talents and gifts God has given you.

> **But thou shalt remember the Lord thy God: for it is he that giveth thee power to get wealth, that he may establish his covenant which he sware unto thy fathers, as it is this day. (Deuteronomy 8:18)**

The Lord can make you rich just as easily as he can make you poor. He considers your attitude, your intentions, and your humility.

> **The Lord maketh poor, and maketh rich: he bringeth low, and lifteth up. (1 Samuel 2:7)**

Make it your highest priority to fear the Lord, and you will eventually become rich.

> **Praise ye the Lord. Blessed is the man that feareth the Lord, that delighteth greatly in his commandments. His seed shall be mighty upon earth: the generation of the upright shall be blessed. Wealth and riches shall be in his house: and his righteousness endureth for ever. (Psalm 112:1–3)**

There are two ways to obtain riches, either with God or without him. Go for the blessing of the Lord. It is the one with no sorrow attached to it.

> **Treasures of wickedness profit nothing: . . .The blessing of the Lord, it maketh rich, and he addeth no sorrow with it. (Proverbs 10:2,22)**

Trust in God instead of money.

> **He that trusteth in his riches shall fall. (Proverbs 11:28)**

Some people think they are rich, but they are poor in the things of God. Others think they are poor, but they are spiritual millionaires.

> There is that maketh himself rich, yet hath nothing: there is that maketh himself poor, yet hath great riches. (Proverbs 13:7)

When you mature in wisdom, riches will follow.

> The crown of the wise is their riches. (Proverbs 14:24)

If you always do the right thing, you will grow rich. The wicked have problems connected with their income.

> In the house of the righteous is much treasure: but in the revenues of the wicked is trouble. (Proverbs 15:6)

The Bible says not to work to make yourself rich.

> Labor not to be rich: cease from thine own wisdom. Wilt thou set thine eyes upon that which is not? For riches certainly make themselves wings; they fly away as an eagle toward heaven. (Proverbs 23:4–5)

God makes people rich. He is very generous. He is a giver, not a taker.

> Every man also to whom God hath given riches and wealth, and hath given him power to eat thereof, and to take his portion, and to rejoice in his labor; this is the gift of God. (Ecclesiastes 5:19)

This is one of Jesus' parables. It is about a man who only thought of what he could get for himself. He cared nothing for the people around him. He was rich in things, but he was not rich toward God.

> And he spake a parable unto them saying, The ground of a certain rich man brought forth plentifully: and he thought

> within himself, saying, What shall I do, because I have no room where to bestow my fruits? And he said, This will I do: I will pull down my barns, and build greater; and there will I bestow all my fruits and my goods. And I will say to my soul, Soul, thou hast much goods laid up for many years; take thine ease, eat, drink, and be merry. But God said unto him, Thou fool, this night thy soul shall be required of thee: then whose shall those things be, which thou hast provided? So is he that layeth up treasure for himself, and is not rich toward God. (Luke 12:16–21)

## WISDOM

God's wisdom is found throughout the Bible. All true wisdom is derived from God's word. What the world thinks is wisdom contradicts the Bible. God's wisdom is foolishness to them, but man's wisdom is foolishness to God. Wisdom consists of taking God's teachings and applying them to your life. The more of God's wisdom you incorporate, the more successful you will be. Man's wisdom is useless to you, since it is the opposite of God's word. God's wisdom is more valuable than gold. It will get you everything, including good health and riches.

Everything that's worth knowing comes from the Lord.

> For the Lord giveth wisdom: out of his mouth cometh knowledge and understanding. (Proverbs 2:6)

Here wisdom is represented as a lovely wife. You desire her company. She gives you peace and pleasantness in life. She also helps you to become rich and live a long happy life.

> Happy is the man that findeth wisdom, and the man that getteth understanding: for the merchandise of it is better than the merchandise of silver, and the gain thereof than fine gold. She is more precious than rubies: and all the things thou canst desire are not to be compared unto her.

> Length of days is in her right hand; and in her left hand riches and honor. Her ways are ways of pleasantness, and all her paths are peace. She is a tree of life to them that lay hold upon her: and happy is every one that retaineth her. (Proverbs 3:13–18)

Solomon was the wisest man who ever lived except for Jesus. God inspired him to write these words about wisdom.

> Wisdom is the principal thing; therefore get wisdom: and with all thy getting get understanding. Exalt her, and she shall promote thee: she shall bring thee to honor, when thou dost embrace her. She shall give to thine head an ornament of grace: a crown of glory shall she deliver to thee. Hear, O my son, and receive my sayings; and the years of thy life shall be many. I have taught thee in the way of wisdom; I have led thee in right paths. When thou goest, thy steps shall not be straitened; and when thou runnest, thou shalt not stumble. Take fast hold of instruction; let her not go: keep her; for she is thy life. (Proverbs 4:7–13)

In Chapter Eight of Proverbs, wisdom is personified as a woman.

> I lead in the way of righteousness, in the midst of the paths of judgment: that I may cause those that love me to inherit substance; and I will fill their treasures. (Proverbs 8:20–21)

Wisdom adds years to your life. The first step to wisdom is to fear the Lord. To know the Lord is understanding.

> The fear of the Lord is the beginning of wisdom: and the knowledge of the Holy is understanding. For by me thy days shall be multiplied, and the years of thy life shall be increased. (Proverbs 9:10–11)

On your journey to wisdom, you might have to terminate some old friendships.

> He that walketh with wise men shall be wise: but a companion of fools shall be destroyed. (Proverbs 13:20)

God gives wisdom to everyone who asks him for it. When you ask God a specific question, he will answer that question. You will find his answer somewhere. It is usually in the Bible, but it might show up on the radio, the television, in a sermon, or even in a personal conversation.

> If any of you lack wisdom, let him ask of God, that giveth to all men liberally, and upbraideth not; and it shall be given him. But let him ask in faith, nothing wavering. For he that wavereth is like a wave of the sea driven with the wind and tossed. For let not that man think that he shall receive any thing of the Lord. (James 1:5–7)

You can recognize God's wisdom by the following characteristics.

> But the wisdom that is from above is first pure, then peaceable, gentle, and easy to be entreated, full of mercy and good fruits, without partiality, and without hypocrisy. And the fruit of righteousness is sown in peace of them that make peace. (James 3:17–18)

God uses people who have been rejected by the world. The preaching of the cross is foolishness to those who perish.

> For ye see your calling, brethren, how that not many wise men after the flesh, not many mighty, not many noble, are called: but God hath chosen the foolish things of the world to confound the wise; and God hath chosen the weak things of the world to confound the things which are mighty. (1 Corinthians 1:26–27)

God's people can quickly tell the difference between God's wisdom and the wisdom of men.

> And my speech and my preaching was not with enticing words of man's wisdom, but in demonstration of the Spirit and of power: that your faith should not stand in the wisdom of men, but in the power of God. (1 Corinthians 2:4–5)

## WORKS OF FAITH

God does not require you to work your way to heaven. Your salvation is a gift from God. You are saved by a combination of grace and faith. Grace is God's part and faith is yours. Placing your faith in Jesus is easy enough that anyone can do it, even the old, the sick, and those who are not very smart. When you have been born again, there will be some evidence of it. Your words and actions will show God's influence on you. You will do things that show your love for others. Feeding the hungry, clothing the naked, and visiting those in prison, these things are works of faith.

It is your mission in life is to show people how excellent God is.

> Let your light so shine before men, that they may see your good works, and glorify your Father who is in heaven. (Matthew 5:16)

Salvation does not depend on your own efforts. You will be rewarded for everything you do that contributes to the cause of Christ.

> For other foundation can no man lay than that is laid, which is Jesus Christ. Now if any man build upon this foundation gold, silver, precious stones, wood, hay, stubble; every man's work shall be made manifest: for the day shall declare it, because it shall be revealed by fire; and the fire shall try every man's work of what sort it is. If

> any man's work abide which he hath built thereupon, he shall receive a reward. If any man's work shall be burned, he shall suffer loss: but he himself shall be saved; yet so as by fire. (1 Corinthians 3:11–15)

Faith works. It rolls up its sleeves and goes to work. Loving people is that work.

> For in Jesus Christ neither circumcision availeth any thing, nor uncircumcision; but faith which worketh by love. (Galatians 5:6)

Make sure that everything you say and do is consistent with the word of God.

> And whatsoever ye do in word or deed, do all in the name of the Lord Jesus, giving thanks to God and the Father by him. (Colossians 3:17)

When you are living by faith, the fruit of the Spirit will be apparent.

> We give thanks to God always for you all, making mention of you in our prayers; remembering without ceasing your work of faith, and labor of love, and patience of hope in our Lord Jesus Christ, in the sight of God and our Father. (1 Thessalonians 1:3)

You are not working to earn your salvation. You are keeping the Lord's commandment.

> This is a faithful saying, and these things I will that thou affirm constantly, that they which have believed in God might be careful to maintain good works. These things are good and profitable unto men. (Titus 3:8)

When you sincerely believe that Jesus is God, you will want to do what he says. Your lifestyle is evidence of your faith in him, or the lack of it.

> **Even so faith, if it hath not works, is dead, being alone. Yea, a man may say, Thou hast faith and I have works: show me thy faith without thy works, and I will show thee my faith by my works. Thou believest that there is one God; thou doest well: the devils also believe, and tremble. But wilt thou know, O vain man, that faith without works is dead? (James 2:17–20)**

## YOUR FAITH

God calls things into existence before they exist. He calls you the righteousness of Christ before you have begun to do any righteousness. Over time, you will become what he says you are. He wants you to be like Jesus. He wants you to use your faith to create things that are good. Faith is the substance of things hoped for, the evidence of things not seen. This is not a religion because religion involves external things. Faith is internal. It is choosing to believe what God says, even when it makes no sense to your natural mind. This is an example of what faith is. God changed Abram's name to Abraham, which means "father of many nations." This defied logic because he had no children and his wife, Sarah, was barren. But Abraham believed it anyway. He honored God by believing his word, and what God said was true. Abraham became the father of many nations. Nothing is too hard for God. He specializes in doing the impossible. He invites you to be like him. He operates in faith just as he expects you to do.

The principle is the same throughout the Bible and in life as we know it today. The people who receive healing are the ones who believe that he will heal them.

> **And when Jesus departed thence, two blind men followed him, crying, and saying, Thou Son of David, have mercy on**

> us. And when he was come into the house, the blind men came to him: and Jesus saith unto them, Believe ye that I am able to do this? They said unto him, Yea, Lord. Then touched he their eyes, saying, According to your faith be it unto you. And their eyes were opened; and Jesus straitly charged them, saying, See that no man know it. But they, when they were departed, spread abroad his fame in all that country. (Matthew 9:27–31)

The following verse explains that hearing the Word of God will cause you to have faith in God.

> So then faith cometh by hearing, and hearing by the word of God. (Romans 10:17)

Living by faith is based on this truth. Your salvation is assured because of Jesus' finished work on the cross. You receive salvation by faith, not by works.

> But that no man is justified by the law in the sight of God, it is evident: for, the just shall live by faith. And the law is not of faith: but, the man that doeth them shall live in them. Christ hath redeemed us from the curse of the law, being made a curse for us: for it is written, Cursed is every one that hangeth on a tree: that the blessing of Abraham might come on the Gentiles through Jesus Christ; that we might receive the promise of the Spirit through faith. (Galatians 3:11–14)

The law explains that all have sinned, and that the wages of sin is death. Under the New Testament we learn that there is a way to escape from this predicament. It is through our Savior, Jesus Christ.

> But the scripture hath concluded all under sin, that the promise by faith of Jesus Christ might be given to them

> that believe. But before faith came, we were kept under the law, shut up unto the faith which should afterwards be revealed. Wherefore the law was our schoolmaster to bring us unto Christ, that we might be justified by faith. But after that faith is come, we are no longer under a schoolmaster. For ye are all the children of God by faith in Christ Jesus. (Galatians 3:22–26)

When you have God's word, you have something of value, something of substance. You can be certain that what he says is true. God created everything that exists. He spoke it into existence. That is how things are created, by faith. God speaks, and whatever he says will come to pass.

> Now faith is the substance of things hoped for, the evidence of things not seen....Through faith we understand that the worlds were framed by the word of God, so that things which are seen were not made of things which do appear. (Hebrews 11:1, 3)

Jesus is the author and the finisher of your faith. He will finish the good work that he started in you.

> Wherefore seeing we also are compassed about with so great a cloud of witnesses, let us lay aside every weight, and the sin which doth so easily beset us, and let us run with patience the race that is set before us, looking unto Jesus the author and finisher of our faith; who for the joy that was set before him endured the cross, despising the shame, and is set down at the right hand of the throne of God. (Hebrews 12:1–2)

# PART FOUR
# Evil Things

**An evil man out of the evil treasure of his heart bringeth forth that which is evil: for of the abundance of the heart his mouth speaketh. (Luke 6:45)**

The ideas that you accept as your own become a part of you. God's ideas always produce good things. Ideas that disagree with God's word create evil things. These evil things have the capacity to steal, kill, and destroy everything you have. Those who reject God and the Bible put their faith in the things of the world. Instead of being blessed by God, they are living under the curse of sin and death.

In the Garden of Eden, Adam and Eve accepted one of Satan's ideas. They thought that God was holding out on them. That lie still causes trouble for everyone who believes it. When you go against God's word, you will cause evil things to happen. When you hurt somebody else, you are hurting yourself. Retaliating against others causes evil things to come your way. What you give out is what you will get back, both good and evil. You have to eat the fruit of everything you do. You are eating the fruit of the tree of the knowledge of good and evil. That is why you should make it your goal to only do that which is right and good.

## AFFLICTION

God expects you to follow his rules. You will be rewarded if you do, and afflicted if you do not. Adam and Eve had just one rule to follow. That was not to eat from the tree of the knowledge of good and evil. Because they rebelled against God, all of mankind has to suffer affliction. When you rebel against God, you bring affliction on yourself. God uses everything that happens to you for your benefit. He uses affliction to correct you. Most people will not touch a hot stove again after being burned by it. Always do what is right and you will minimize your affliction.

God watched his people gather manna to see who would follow his rules. He watches you to see if you will obey him or not.

> **Then said the Lord unto Moses, Behold I will rain bread from heaven for you; and the people shall go out and gather a certain rate every day, that I may prove them, whether they will walk in my law, or no. (Exodus 16:4)**

God is very merciful. Your punishment will always be less than you deserve.

> **And after all that is come upon us for our evil deeds, and for our great trespass, seeing that thou our God hast punished us less than our iniquities deserve, and hast given us such deliverance as this. (Ezra 9:13)**

The Lord will deliver you out of all your afflictions.

> **Many are the afflictions of the righteous: but the Lord delivereth him out of them all. (Psalm 34:19)**

Do not blame God when things go wrong. You are responsible for the things that happen to you. You are not a victim of circumstance.

> Also unto thee, O Lord, belongeth mercy: for thou renderest to every man according to his work. (Psalm 62:12)

When you get tired of being afflicted, stop rebelling against God. Get in fellowship with him, ask him to rescue you and he will.

> Such as sit in darkness and in the shadow of death, being bound in affliction and iron because they rebelled against the words of God, and contemned the counsel of the most High: therefore he brought down their heart with labor; they fell down and there was none to help. Then they cried unto the Lord in their trouble, and he saved them out of their distresses. (Psalm 107:10–14)

A "fool" is someone who intentionally rebels against God, and brings affliction upon himself.

> Fools because of their transgression, and because of their iniquities, are afflicted. Their soul abhorreth all manner of meat; and they draw unto the gates of death. Then they cry unto the Lord in their trouble, and he saveth them out of their distresses. He sent his word, and healed them, and delivered them from their destructions. (Psalm 107:17–20)

After you have endured affliction, this should be the attitude of your heart: "Thank you, Lord, for teaching me the things I needed to learn."

> Before I was afflicted I went astray: but now have I kept thy word....It is good for me that I have been afflicted; that I might learn thy statutes. (Psalm 119:67, 71)

While you were in the furnace of affliction, God chose you to serve him.

> **Behold, I have refined thee, but not with silver; I have chosen thee in the furnace of affliction. (Isaiah 48:10)**

Shadrach, Meshach, and Abednego were the three Hebrew children who were thrown into the fiery furnace of King Nebuchadnezzar. The fourth man in the fiery furnace had to be Jesus. You will go through a furnace of affliction in your own life. Jesus will be there with you. He will protect you and help you through it, and you will come forth as gold.

> **Then Nebuchadnezzar the king was astonished, and rose up in haste, and spake, and said unto his counsellors, Did not we cast three men bound into the midst of the fire? They answered and said unto the king, True, O king. He answered and said, Lo, I see four men loose, walking in the midst of the fire, and they have no hurt; and the form of the fourth is like the Son of God. (Daniel 3:24–25)**

This verse proves that men are punished for their sins in this life.

> **Wherefore doth a living man complain, a man for the punishment of his sins? (Lamentations 3:39)**

Bible believers care more about spiritual things than they do material things. You may be temporarily inconvenienced by your afflictions. But you are gaining eternal possessions.

> **For our light affliction, which is but for a moment, worketh for us a far more exceeding and eternal weight of glory; while we look not at the things which are seen, but at the things which are not seen: for the things which are seen are temporal; but the things which are not seen are eternal. (2 Corinthians 4:17–18)**

You are going to be afflicted. Satan will see this as an opportunity to seize control of your mind and your emotions. If he gains control of these elements of your soul, he is in control of your life.

> **Be sober, be vigilant; because your adversary the devil, as a roaring lion, walketh about, seeking whom he may devour: whom resist steadfast in the faith, knowing that the same afflictions are accomplished in your brethren that are in the world. But the God of all grace, who hath called us unto his eternal glory by Christ Jesus, after that ye have suffered a while, make you perfect, stablish, strengthen, settle you. (1 Peter 5:8–10)**

## ANGER

Anger affects your thinking and your emotions at the same time. It will steal your peace and your joy. It will steal your energy and your strength. It will destroy your relationships with the people you love. It opens the door of your life to Satan. Suppressed anger manifests itself in both physical and mental disorders. I learned anger from my dad. I thought that I had the right to punish others when I was frustrated or disappointed.

I was enraged by the way I was treated on my job at the Postal Service. I suppressed this anger. But it was always present, just below the surface, ready to erupt. I had an attitude of anger, a spirit of anger. I was angry when I went to sleep at night and angry when I got up in the morning. I was completely blinded to the fact that anger is a sin that is based on pride. I was angry at the supervisors who were abusing me, and I wanted to punish them for it. Jesus delivered me from the sin of anger. He was beaten, and tortured, and put to death when he had done nothing wrong, but he did not respond in anger. He kept the commandment to love his neighbor. He prayed for the men who crucified him saying, "Father, forgive them. They know not what they do." I thank God everyday for delivering me from anger.

Do not even think about punishing people who have mistreated you. This is what God says about anger.

> **Cease from anger, and forsake wrath: fret not thyself in any wise to do evil. (Psalm 37:8)**

Quick-tempered people make bad decisions.

> **He that is soon angry dealeth foolishly:… He that is slow to wrath is of great understanding: but he that is hasty of spirit exalteth folly. (Proverbs 14:17, 29)**

Angry people expect that you will respond to them in anger. It disarms them when you don't.

> **A soft answer turneth away wrath: but grievous words stir up anger. (Proverbs 15:1)**

It is a difficult challenge to control your own mind and emotions.

> **He that is slow to anger is better than the mighty; and he that ruleth his spirit than he that taketh a city. (Proverbs 16:32)**

A "scorner" is a smart-aleck. He gets mad when people don't show him the respect he thinks he deserves.

> **Proud and haughty scorner is his name, who dealeth in proud wrath. (Proverbs 21:24)**

You will become like your friends, and anger is contagious.

> **Make no friendship with an angry man; and with a furious man thou shalt not go; Lest thou learn his ways, and get a snare to thy soul. (Proverbs 22:24–25)**

When you're overcome by anger, you're vulnerable to loss.

**He that hath no rule over his own spirit is like a city that is broken down, and without walls. (Proverbs 25:28)**

A "fool" is someone who rebels against the Lord. Never argue with a fool. You won't be able to communicate with him.

**If a wise man contendeth with a foolish man, whether he rage or laugh, there is no rest....An angry man stirreth up strife, and a furious man aboundeth in transgression. (Proverbs 29:9, 22)**

If you allow the spirit of anger to take up residence in you, then you will become a fool.

**Be not hasty in thy spirit to be angry: for anger resteth in the bosom of fools. (Ecclesiastes 7:9)**

## ARROGANCE

Arrogance is evidence of pride. It is the attitude that says, "I am better than you," or, "I am smarter than you." An arrogant man thinks God's rules don't apply to him. He thinks of himself as being on the same level as God. He cannot see his arrogance, but it is obvious to everyone around him. He has no idea that he is sabotaging himself with his own pride. If you will humble yourself before God, you won't be arrogant. Submit yourself to God's authority by doing everything he says in his word.

Hannah was barren. She asked God to give her a child, and he answered her prayer. This is part of her song of thanksgiving to God. She says that none of us has any reason to be arrogant. There is nothing we have that did not come from God.

**Talk no more so exceeding proudly; let not arrogancy come out of your mouth: for the Lord is a God of knowledge,**

> and by him actions are weighed. The bows of the mighty men are broken, and they that stumbled are girded with strength. They that were full have hired out themselves for bread; and they that were hungry ceased: so that the barren hath born seven; and she that hath many children is waxed feeble. The Lord killeth and maketh alive: he bringeth down to the grave, and bringeth up. The Lord maketh poor, and maketh rich: he bringeth low, and lifteth up. (1 Samuel 2:3–7)

There is a curse on people who are proud.

> Thou hast rebuked the proud that are cursed, which do err from thy commandments. (Psalm 119:21)

The Lord does not associate with the proud.

> Though the Lord be high, yet hath he respect unto the lowly: but the proud he knoweth afar off. (Psalm 138:6)

This is how the Bible defines "the fear of the Lord." It is the opposite of arrogance and pride.

> The fear of the Lord is to hate evil: pride, and arrogancy, and the evil way, and the froward mouth, do I hate. (Proverbs 8:13)

## BITTERNESS

Attitude is everything with God. When he does something for you, thank him for it and act like you appreciate it. Bitterness is the opposite of thankfulness. It is the opposite of praising God. It prevents him from intervening in your life. If you become bitter and resentful when things go wrong, that will keep God's blessing away from you. When you are full of joy, the blessing of God will overtake you.

The Children of Israel had a bad attitude. They did not thank God for what they had. They just complained about what they did not have. They were bitter about their living conditions. Marah symbolizes a place of spiritual bitterness. There is a connection between bitterness and sickness. Protect your heart with all diligence by keeping the right attitude. Attend to God's word and do what it says. It will keep you in perfect health.

> And when they came to Marah, they could not drink of the waters of Marah, for they were bitter: therefore the name of it was called Marah. And the people murmured against Moses, saying, What shall we drink? And he cried unto the Lord; and the Lord showed him a tree, which when he had cast into the waters, the waters were made sweet: there he made for them a statute and an ordinance, and there he proved them and said, If thou wilt diligently hearken to the voice of the Lord thy God, and wilt do that which is right in his sight, and wilt give ear to his commandments, and keep all his statutes, I will put none of these diseases upon thee, which I have brought upon the Egyptians: for I am the Lord that healeth thee. (Exodus 15:23–26)

In this passage Jesus was addressing the religious leaders of his day. He told them that because they were evil, they caused evil things to happen. The condition of your heart determines the circumstances of your life.

> Either make the tree good, and his fruit good; or else make the tree corrupt, and his fruit corrupt: for the tree is known by his fruit. O generation of vipers, how can ye, being evil, speak good things? For out of the abundance of the heart the mouth speaketh. A good man out of the good treasure of the heart bringeth forth good things: and an evil man out of the evil treasure bringeth forth evil things. (Matthew 12:33–35)

According to Jesus, the things that you say are a picture of what is in your heart. Everything that you believe will be revealed.

> But those things which proceed out of the mouth come forth from the heart; and they defile the man. For out of the heart proceed evil thoughts, murders, adulteries, fornications, thefts, false witness, blasphemies: these are the things which defile a man: but to eat with unwashen hands defileth not a man. (Matthew 15:18–20)

To the people around you, you are a church. The Spirit of God has a chance to minister to them through you.

> Know ye not that ye are the temple of God, and that the Spirit of God dwelleth in you? If any man defile the temple of God, him shall God destroy; for the temple of God is holy, which temple ye are. (1 Corinthians 3:16–17)

These are God's rules for you as a member of his family.

> Let all bitterness, and wrath, and anger, and clamor, and evil speaking, be put away from you, with all malice: and be ye kind one to another, tenderhearted, forgiving one another, even as God for Christ's sake hath forgiven you. (Ephesians 4:31–32)

Bitterness, resentfulness and unforgiveness defile you and cause you to be sick.

> Wherefore lift up the hands which hang down, and the feeble knees; and make straight paths for your feet, lest that which is lame be turned out of the way; but let it rather be healed. Follow peace with all men, and holiness, without which no man shall see the Lord: looking diligently lest any man fail of the grace of God; lest any root of

> bitterness springing up trouble you, and thereby many be defiled. (Hebrews 12:12–15)

Your words reveal what is in your heart. My old country preacher said it like this: "What's down in the well will come up in the bucket."

> Out of the same mouth proceedeth blessing and cursing. My brethren, these things ought not to be. Doth a fountain send forth at the same place sweet water and bitter? Can the fig tree, my brethren, bear olive berries? Either a vine figs? So can no fountain both yield salt water and fresh. Who is a wise man and endued with knowledge among you? Let him show out of a good conversation his works with meekness of wisdom. But if you have bitter envying and strife in your hearts, glory not and lie not against the truth. This wisdom descended not from above, but is earthly, sensual, devilish. For where envying and strife is, there is confusion and every evil work. But the wisdom that is from above is first pure, then peaceable, gentle, and easy to be entreated, full of mercy and good fruits, without partiality, and without hypocrisy. And the fruit of righteousness is sown in peace of them that make peace. (James 3:10–18)

## CALAMITIES

These calamities are personal disasters like bankruptcy or divorce. They are caused by a lack of diligence, so they are preventable. When you fail to apply God's word to your life, you will suffer calamities. This is due to a lack of knowledge. Focus your attention on Jesus. Do not allow anything else to take his place in your heart. Communicate with him daily. He will advise you and instruct you. When you do what he says, you won't have so many calamities.

This is part of a song that Moses gave God's people. It refers to people who worship other "gods." Their idolatry causes them personal calamities.

> To me belongeth vengeance, and recompense; their foot shall slide in due time: for the day of their calamity is at hand, and the things that shall come upon them make haste. (Deuteronomy 32:35)

Wisdom is applying God's word to your life. It will keep calamities away from you. Naïve people don't have any idea how much their sins are costing them. Fools will not change their ways. Mockers are never serious about anything.

> Wisdom crieth without; she uttereth her voice in the streets: she crieth in the chief place of concourse, in the openings of the gates: in the city, she uttereth her words, saying, How long, ye simple ones, will ye love simplicity? and the scorners delight in their scorning, and fools hate knowledge? Turn you at my reproof: behold, I will pour out my spirit unto you, I will make known my words unto you. Because I have called, and ye refused; I have stretched out my hand, and no man regarded; but ye have set at nought all my counsel, and would none of my reproof: I also will laugh at your calamity; I will mock when your fear cometh. (Proverbs 1:20–26)

In this passage, Wisdom is personified, and she describes those who have rejected her. People who rebel against God are destroyed by their own success. Wisdom will save those who embrace her.

> They would none of my counsel: they despised all my reproof. Therefore shall they eat of the fruit of their own way, and be filled with their own devices. For the turning away of the simple shall slay them, and the prosperity of fools shall destroy them. But whoso hearkeneth unto me shall dwell safely, and shall be quiet from fear of evil. (Proverbs 1:30–33)

A "froward" man refuses to do right. His word is not any good. He deceives others and causes trouble for them. He will eventually experience a calamity that will destroy him.

> **A naughty person, a wicked man, walketh with a froward mouth. He winketh with his eyes, he speaketh with his feet, he teacheth with his fingers; frowardness is in his heart, he deviseth mischief continually; he soweth discord. Therefore shall his calamity come suddenly; suddenly shall he be broken without remedy. (Proverbs 6:12–15)**

## CAPTIVITY

The Children of Israel eventually became two nations, Israel and Judah. Both prospered for a while. Then, they forgot God, and worshipped idols. The Assyrians defeated Israel and took them into captivity. Then, the Babylonians did the same to Judah. They didn't stop being God's people because they were captives, but they were physically removed from their place of protection and blessing. If you go into captivity spiritually, you don't stop being part of God's family. Don't leave the place where God can bless you and be a captive to sin. Don't limit what God can do for you. When you don't do things God's way, you are vulnerable to the enemy. Satan takes you captive in your mind, your emotions, and your will. He is the original control freak. He wants to control your life. The good news is that you escape from his captivity whenever you want. Get back in fellowship with the Lord and he will deliver you.

This passage refers to people who have been taken captive by the devil. They can return to the Lord and enjoy a new life of prosperity.

> **And if they be bound in fetters, and be holden in cords of affliction; then he showeth them their work and their transgressions that they have exceeded. He openeth also their ear to discipline, and commandeth that they return from iniquity. If they obey and serve him, they shall spend**

> their days in prosperity, and their years in pleasures. (Job 36:8–11)

God helps those who help others. When Job prayed for his friends, God released him from his captivity. He will reward you when you express your love for others.

> And the Lord turned the captivity of Job, when he prayed for his friends: also the Lord gave Job twice as much as he had before. (Job 42:10)

God's people go into captivity because they don't know any better. They hunger and thirst for the knowledge of God, but they are unable to find it on their own.

> Therefore my people are gone into captivity, because they have no knowledge: and their honorable men are famished, and their multitude dried up with thirst. (Isaiah 5:13)

God told his prophets to tell his children exactly what he said, whether they would listen, or not.

> Moreover he said unto me, Son of man, all my words that I shall speak unto thee receive in thine heart, and hear with thine ears. And go, get thee to them of the captivity, unto the children of thy people, and speak unto them, and tell them, Thus saith the Lord God; whether they will hear, or whether they will forbear. (Ezekiel 3:10–11)

Worldly people are easily offended. They are constantly involved in strife. These are two of the devil's snares. God has provided a way for you to escape from them.

> But foolish and unlearned questions avoid, knowing that they do gender strifes. And the servant of the Lord must

> not strive; but be gentle unto all men, apt to teach, patient, in meekness instructing those that oppose themselves; if God peradventure will give them repentance to the acknowledging of the truth; and that they may recover themselves out of the snare of the devil, who are taken captive by him at his will. (2 Timothy 2:23–26)

## CONFUSION

God's word is truth. Truth is always clear and plain. Everything God does is consistent with the Bible. His word leaves no room for confusion. Men cause confusion for their own selfish motives. The devil uses confusion to take advantage of you. God never causes confusion. He creates order out of chaos, not chaos out of order. Where confusion reigns, God doesn't.

This is from one of David's Psalms. He makes a prayer request for his enemies in it. He asks God to let them be ashamed and confused.

> Let them be ashamed and brought to confusion together that rejoice at mine hurt: let them be clothed with shame and dishonor that magnify themselves against me. (Psalm 35:26)

When people worship idols instead of God, they become confused.

> They shall be ashamed, and also confounded, all of them: they shall go to confusion together that are makers of idols. (Isaiah 45:16)

God's ways are ways of pleasantness. His paths are paths of peace. If something is taking away your peace, you know that God is not involved in it.

> Happy is the man that findeth wisdom, and the man that getteth understanding. For the merchandise of it is better

> than the merchandise of silver, and the gain thereof than fine gold. She is more precious than rubies: and all the things thou canst desire are not to be compared unto her. Length of days is in her right hand; and in her left hand riches and honor. Her ways are ways of pleasantness, and all her paths are peace. She is a tree of life to them that lay hold upon her: and happy is every one that retaineth her. (Proverbs 3:13–18)

Demetrius was a silversmith in Ephesus. He made his living selling silver shrines to worshippers of the goddess Diana. Paul's preaching was a threat to his livelihood. He caused a riot to keep the Ephesians from hearing about Jesus.

> Some therefore cried one thing, and some another: for the assembly was confused; and the more part knew not wherefore they were come together. (Acts 19:32)

God does not ever cause confusion.

> For God is not the author of confusion, but of peace, as in all churches of the saints. (1 Corinthians 14:33)

The causes of confusion are envy and strife.

> For where envying and strife is, there is confusion and every evil work. (James 3:16)

## CONTENTION

Contention is business as usual for people of the world. They love to argue. Don't let them draw you into an argument. Do not become offended by their disrespect for you. Don't take the bait and become angry with them. The devil uses contention to control you. He uses it to steal your joy and your peace. Getting along with people is your job. When you are in agreement with God's word, you know that you are right. God knows that you are right. You don't have to prove it to anyone else.

Pride is the cause of all contention.

**Only by pride cometh contention. (Proverbs 13:10)**

A man who rebels against God will be in constant disagreement with other people.

**A fool's lips enter into contention, and his mouth calleth for strokes. (Proverbs 18:6)**

People who reject the Bible idolize the devil's children. They dislike anyone who stands up for God. They will certainly never agree with you.

**They that forsake the law praise the wicked: but such as keep the law contend with them. (Proverbs 28:4)**

The Lord will deal with the people who give you a hard time.

**For I will contend with him that contendeth with thee. (Isaiah 49:25)**

"Contentious" people are those who like to argue. God rewards everyone who does right and punishes everyone who does wrong.

**But unto them that are contentious, and do not obey the truth, but obey unrighteousness, indignation and wrath, tribulation and anguish, upon every soul of man that doeth evil, of the Jew first, and also of the Gentile; but glory, honor and peace, to every man that worketh good, to the Jew first, and also to the Gentile: For there is no respect of persons with God. (Romans 2:8–11)**

It is easy for Bible believers to agree with each other. You are to "speak as the oracles of God," which is the Bible. Make sure everything you say agrees with it.

> Now I beseech you, brethren, by the name of our Lord Jesus Christ, that ye all speak the same thing, and that there be no divisions among you; but that ye be perfectly joined together in the same mind and in the same judgment. For it hath been declared unto me of you, my brethren, by them which are of the house of Chloe, that there are contentions among you. (1 Corinthians 1:10–11)

Whenever the word of God is preached, someone will take a stand against it. This is what happened when Paul preached the gospel at Philippi.

> But even after that we had suffered before, and were shamefully entreated, as ye know, at Philippi, we were bold in our God to speak unto you the gospel of God with much contention. For our exhortation was not of deceit, nor of uncleanness, nor in guile: but as we were allowed of God to be put in trust with the gospel, even so we speak: not as pleasing men, but God, which trieth our hearts. (1 Thessalonians 2:2–4)

Your good works are worth more than your words. People don't listen to what you say, but they do watch everything you do.

> This is a faithful saying, and these things I will that thou affirm constantly, that they which have believed in God might be careful to maintain good works. These things are good and profitable unto men. But avoid foolish questions, and genealogies, and contentions, and strivings about the law; for they are unprofitable and vain. (Titus 3:8–9)

## COVETOUSNESS

Covetousness is constantly grasping for personal gain. Most of the time, it is for money, but it could also be lusting for someone else's wife or his property. Money is the god of the covetous. They are obsessed with it. It is the object of their fascination and desire. Every decision they make is based on what effect it would have on their own finances. Their minds are so filled with thoughts of money, that there is no room for anything else. That's why it is a form of idolatry. A covetous man has given money the place in his heart that rightfully belongs to God.

Moses received the Ten Commandments from God and delivered them to the people. These words were written on tablets of stone by the finger of God, (which is the actually the Spirit of God.)

> **Thou shalt not covet thy neighbor's house, thou shalt not covet thy neighbor's wife, nor his manservant, nor his maidservant, nor his ox, nor his ass, nor anything that is thy neighbor's. (Exodus 20:17)**

It is better to be righteous and poor, than wicked and rich.

> **A little that a righteous man hath is better than the riches of many wicked. (Psalm 37:16)**

Greediness consumes the life of the greedy.

> **So are the ways of every one that is greedy of gain; which taketh away the life of the owners thereof. (Proverbs 1:19)**

Having the fear of the Lord is better than having a lot of money.

> **Better is little with the fear of the Lord, than great treasure and trouble therewith. (Proverbs 15:16)**

Righteous people are generous. Lazy people are covetous.

> The desire of the slothful killeth him; for his hands refuse to labor. He coveteth greedily all the day long: but the righteous giveth and spareth not. (Proverbs 21:25–26)

This is an important word from the Lord. It will help you to live a longer life.

> But he that hateth covetousness shall prolong his days. (Proverbs 28:16)

People are the same today as they were in Ezekiel's day. They love to hear God's word but they have no intention of basing their lives on it.

> Also, thou son of man, the children of thy people still are talking against thee by the walls and in the doors of the houses, and speak one to another, every one to his brother, saying, Come, I pray you, and hear what is the word that cometh forth from the Lord. And they come unto thee as the people cometh, and they sit before thee as my people, and they hear thy words, but they will not do them: for with their mouth they show much love, but their heart goeth after their covetousness. And, lo, thou art unto them as a very lovely song of one that hath a pleasant voice, and can play well on an instrument: for they hear thy words, but they do them not. (Ezekiel 33:30–32)

"Mammon" is money. It is an idol that takes the place of God.

> No man can serve two masters: for either he will hate the one, and love the other; or else he will hold to the one, and despise the other. Ye cannot serve God and mammon. (Matthew 6:24)

Jesus said that there is more to life than money. Do not measure your success by the amount of money you have.

**And he said unto them, Take heed, and beware of covetousness: for a man's life consisteth not in the abundance of the things which he possesseth. (Luke 12:15)**

## DEATH

Your relationship with Jesus is the most important part of your life. Because of him, you do not have to be afraid to die. Your soul and your spirit immediately go to be with Jesus. Your physical body will "sleep" until the resurrection. Then, you will receive a new body that lasts forever. Death is not as bad as you imagine it to be. To the cancer patient in terrible pain, it is a welcome relief. Death is not the end of your existence, but is a transition to a place where you will live forever. Death is the last enemy that Jesus will destroy.

There has always been a place for the righteous dead. It used to be a place called "Abraham's Bosom." Now it is with Jesus in Heaven.

**For I know that thou wilt bring me to death, and to the house appointed for all living. (Job 30:23)**

The Lord cares about you. He pays attention to your life and your death.

**Precious in the sight of the Lord is the death of his saints. (Psalm 116:15)**

Keep your name good by doing what is right. Death is the beginning of a new adventure.

**A good name is better than precious ointment; and the day of death than the day of one's birth. (Ecclesiastes 7:1)**

When you die, your spirit returns to God. Your body has to stay behind.

Then shall the dust return to the earth as it was: and the spirit shall return unto God who gave it. (Ecclesiastes 12:7)

Here Jesus quoted the words that God spoke to Moses at the burning bush. He pointed out that even though the Patriarchs had died physically, spiritually they were still alive.

But as touching the resurrection of the dead, have ye not read that which was spoken unto you by God, saying, I am the God of Abraham, and the God of Isaac, and the God of Jacob? God is not the God of the dead, but of the living. (Matthew 22:31–32)

These are Jesus' words to everyone who believes in him.

Let not your heart be troubled: ye believe in God, believe also in me. In my Father's house are many mansions: if it were not so, I would have told you. I go to prepare a place for you. And if I go and prepare a place for you, I will come again, and receive you unto myself; that where I am, there ye may be also. (John 14:1–3)

This is part of the prayer that Jesus prayed for you just before he was crucified.

Neither pray I for these alone, but for them also which shall believe on me through their word; . . .Father, I will that they also, whom thou hast given me, be with me where I am. (John 17:20,24)

This passage tells us that one day there will be no more death.

But now is Christ risen from the dead, and become the firstfruits of them that slept. For since by man came death, by man came also the resurrection of the dead. For as in

Adam all die, even so in Christ shall all be made alive. But every man in his own order: Christ the firstfruits; afterward they that are Christ's at his coming. Then cometh the end, when he shall have delivered up the kingdom to God, even the Father; when he shall have put down all rule and all authority and power. For he must reign, till he hath put all enemies under his feet. The last enemy that shall be destroyed is death. (1 Corinthians 15:20–26)

When you die, you will immediately go to be with the Lord.

Therefore we are always confident, knowing that, whilst we are at home in the body, we are absent from the Lord: (for we walk by faith, not by sight:) we are confident, I say, and willing rather to be absent from the body, and to be present with the Lord. (2 Corinthians 5:6–8)

The Apostle Paul wrote these words just before he died. They summarize the proper attitude to have toward life and death.

For me to live is Christ, and to die is gain. (Philippians 1:21)

This passage is a description of the "catching away," or Rapture of the Church. That is when Jesus returns and evacuates every believer from the Earth. Those who are alive at that time will go off into eternity without experiencing death.

But I would not have you to be ignorant, brethren, concerning them which are asleep, that ye sorrow not, even as others which have no hope. For if we believe that Jesus died and rose again, even so them also which sleep in Jesus will God bring with him. For this we say unto you by the word of the Lord, that we which are alive and remain unto the coming of the Lord shall not prevent them which

> are asleep. For the Lord himself shall descend from heaven with a shout, with the voice of the archangel, and with the trump of God: and the dead in Christ shall rise first: then we which are alive and remain shall be caught up together with them in the clouds, to meet the Lord in the air: and so shall we ever be with the Lord. Wherefore comfort one another with these words. (1 Thessalonians 4:13–1)

This is what you can look forward to in the future. You will continue to live with God forever.

> And God shall wipe away all tears from their eyes; and there shall be no more death, neither sorrow, nor crying, neither shall there be any more pain: for the former things are passed away. (Revelation 21:4)

## DECEPTION

Wicked people deceive others to take advantage of them. Most of the time, there is money involved. To understand why people behave as they do, follow the flow of the money. See where the money is going and who is receiving it. Knowing God's word makes you wise. It will keep you from being deceived. You will be able to tell when people are lying, and when they are telling the truth. Knowing the Bible will keep you from being deceived by false doctrines.

Jesus overturned the tables of the moneychangers and drove them out of the Temple. His words to them were based on this passage of scripture.

> Behold, ye trust in lying words, that cannot profit. Will ye steal, murder and commit adultery, and swear falsely, and burn incense unto Baal, and walk after other gods whom ye know not; and come and stand before me in this house, which is called by my name, and say, We are delivered to

> do all these abominations? Is this house, which is called by my name, become a den of robbers in your eyes? Behold, even I have seen it, saith the Lord. (Jeremiah 7:8–11)

You are either confessing or denying Jesus by the way that you live your life.

> Also I say unto you, Whosoever shall confess me before men, him shall the Son of man also confess before the angels of God: but he that denieth me before men shall be denied before the angels of God. (Luke 12:8–9)

The things that you do reveal the condition of your heart.

> Unto the pure all things are pure: but unto them that are defiled and unbelieving is nothing pure; but even their mind and conscience is defiled. They profess that they know God; but in works they deny him, being abominable, and disobedient, and unto every good work reprobate. (Titus 1:15–16)

You have to obey God before you can receive what he promised.

> But be ye doers of the word, and not hearers only, deceiving your own selves. (James 1:22)

The world is totally deceived. They think that man is basically good, and that there is no right or wrong. God's way of doing things is completely different from theirs. Even though you are still committing sins, God loves you anyway.

> If we say that we have no sin, we deceive ourselves, and the truth is not in us. (1 John 1:8)

## DEFEAT

The Children of Israel would not listen to God. When he told them to fight, they would not do it. When they decided they would fight, they lost. They did not know that obedience to God is the prerequisite to victory. They were relying on their own efforts. If they had gone when he sent them, they would have won. But they did not put their trust in God. When they fought the enemy without him, they had no chance of winning on their own. It is the same way in the personal battles in your life. When you express your faith in God by obeying him, he will fight for you. When you humble yourself before God, he will exalt you. When you honor him, he will honor you. With God all things are possible, but without him you can do nothing.

God explained to his people why they were defeated. It was because they did not obey him.

> Then ye answered and said unto me, We have sinned against the Lord, we will go up and fight, according to all that the Lord our God commanded us. And when ye had girded on every man his weapons of war, ye were ready to go up into the hill. And the Lord said unto me, Say unto them, Go not up, neither fight; for I am not among you; lest ye be smitten before your enemies. So I spake unto you; and ye would not hear, but rebelled against the commandment of the Lord, and went presumptuously up into the hill. And the Amorites, which dwelt in that mountain, came out against you, and chased you, as bees do, and destroyed you in Seir, even unto Hormah. (Deuteronomy 1:42–44)

No one who turns away from God can continue to prosper.

> And the Spirit of God came upon Zechariah the son of Jehoida the priest, which stood above the people, and said unto them, thus saith God, Why transgress ye the

> **commandments of the Lord, that ye cannot prosper? Because ye have forsaken the Lord, he hath also forsaken you. (2 Chronicles 24:20)**

God calls Israel "my glory." He explains that his people went into captivity because of their sin. They were out of touch with God, and did not even know that he had left them. You can go into captivity because of your sin. Their captivity was literal. Yours is spiritual.

> **And I will set my glory among the heathen, and all the heathen shall see my judgment that I have executed, and my hand that I have laid upon them. So the house of Israel shall know that I am the Lord their God from that day and forward. And the heathen shall know that the house of Israel went into captivity for their iniquity: because they trespassed against me, therefore hid I my face from them, and gave them into the hand of their enemies: so fell they all by the sword. According to their uncleanness and according to their transgressions have I done unto them, and hid my face from them. (Ezekiel 39:21–24)**

## ENVY

Envy surfaces when you focus your attention on what your neighbor has. Let's say your neighbor has a high-paying job, a loving wife and a new house. You have a menial job, are divorced and live in an apartment. As long as you envy that other man, you cannot enjoy the things you have. Envy affects your mind and your heart, keeping you from doing things to improve your own situation. You're not thankful for the things that you have. You forget that a man's life doesn't consist of his material possessions. Envy makes you vulnerable to the enemy. It's one of the most effective roadblocks on the road to success. The good news is that envy is just another sin. You can overcome it with God's help.

The devil uses your own envy and anger against you.

> For wrath killeth the foolish man, and envy slayeth the silly one. (Job 5:2)

This is the voice of a man who envied the ungodly. They had everything they desired, and did whatever they pleased.

> For I was envious at the foolish, when I saw the prosperity of the wicked. For there are no bands in their death: but their strength is firm. They are not in trouble as other men; neither are they plagued like other men. Therefore pride compasseth them about as a chain; violence covereth them as a garment. Their eyes stand out with fatness: they have more than heart could wish. They are corrupt, and speak wickedly concerning oppression: they speak loftily. They set their mouth against the heavens, and their tongue walketh through the earth....Behold, these are the ungodly, who prosper in the world; they increase in riches. Verily I have cleansed my heart in vain, and washed my hands in innocency. For all the day long have I been plagued, and chastened every morning. (Psalm 73:3–9, 12–14)

The story ends when the psalmist realized the horrors that awaited these people in hell. He also realized that God had saved him from it.

> When I thought to know this, it was too painful for me; until I went into the sanctuary of God; then understood I their end. Surely thou didst set them in slippery places: thou castedst them down into destruction. How are they brought into desolation, as in a moment! They are utterly consumed with terrors. (Psalm 73:16–19)

Envy destroys your physical health.

> A sound heart is the life of the flesh: but envy the rottenness of the bones. (Proverbs 14:30)

Replace envy with the fear of the Lord. Then God can give you the things you desire.

> Let not thine heart envy sinners; but be thou in the fear of the Lord all the day long. For surely there is an end; and thine expectation shall not be cut off. (Proverbs 23:17–18)

Do not underestimate the destructive power of envy. The chief priests and elders had Jesus killed because they envied him. He had power they didn't have. He could do miracles and they could not. The people loved him. He made the rulers look bad, and he reduced their income.

> Therefore when they were gathered together, Pilate said unto them, Whom will ye that I release unto you? Barabbas, or Jesus which is called Christ? For he knew that for envy they had delivered him....But the chief priests and elders persuaded the multitude that they should ask Barabbas, and destroy Jesus. (Matthew 27:17–18, 20)

The Bible says to be content with the things that you have. You have the Lord. Not everyone does. He is more valuable than anything on Earth.

> Let your conversation be without covetousness; and be content with such things as ye have: for he hath said, I will never leave thee, nor forsake thee. So that we may boldly say, the Lord is my helper, and I will not fear what man shall do unto me. (Hebrews 13:5–6)

If you want your circumstances to change, apply God's wisdom to your life and allow the Holy Spirit to lead you. Stop being controlled by your emotions.

> But if you have bitter envying and strife in your hearts,

> glory not, and lie not against the truth. This wisdom descendeth not from above, but is earthly, sensual, devilish. For where envying and strife is, there is confusion and every evil work. (James 3:14–16)

## ERROR

God's word defines reality and truth. You can't change the truth into what you want it to be. God never intended for man to change his word, but people do it anyway. They use the Bible to support their own doctrines. They ignore the parts of the Bible that contradict what they believe, saying that the men who wrote it were expressing their own points of view. They say that the Bible is outdated, and has to be adjusted to fit our modern times. Error is departing from the truth of what God has said in the Bible.

God said not to listen to any teaching that contradicts his word.

> Cease, my son, to hear the instruction that causeth to err from the words of knowledge. (Proverbs 19:27 )

Worldly people hate the things of God. They are motivated by the love of money in everything they do. They prey on the poor. "Vile" means offensive. A "churl" is a miser.

> The vile person shall be no more called liberal, nor the churl said to be bountiful. For the vile person will speak villany, and his heart will work iniquity, to practice hypocrisy, and to utter error against the Lord, to make empty the soul of the hungry, and he will cause the drink of the thirsty to fail. The instruments also of the churl are evil: he deviseth devices to destroy the poor with lying words, even when the needy speaketh right. But the liberal deviseth liberal things; and by liberal things shall he stand. (Isaiah 32:5–8)

The Sadducees did not believe in the resurrection of the dead. They questioned Jesus' interpretation of the scriptures. The Holy Spirit is the power of God. He wrote the scriptures, and he reveals their meaning.

> **Jesus answered and said unto them, Ye do err, not knowing the scriptures, nor the power of God. (Matthew 22:29 )**

Everything that is good comes from God. There is nothing good apart from him.

> **Do not err, my beloved brethren. Every good gift and every perfect gift is from above, and cometh down from the Father of lights, with whom is no variableness, neither shadow of turning. (James 1:16–17)**

Do not be swayed by error. "Steadfastness" is standing firm without changing.

> **Ye therefore, beloved, seeing ye know these things before, beware lest ye also, being led away with the error of the wicked, fall from your own stedfastness. (2 Peter 3:17)**

This is how to tell the truth from an error. An idea that is consistent with the word of God, is true. Ideas that contradict the Bible are errors.

> **Ye are of God, little children, and have overcome them: because greater is he that is in you, than he that is in the world. They are of the world: therefore speak they of the world, and the world heareth them. We are of God: he that knoweth God heareth us; he that is not of God heareth not us. Hereby know we the spirit of truth, and the spirit of error. (1 John 4:4–6 )**

## EVIL

"Evil" is like a street with traffic flowing in two directions. Evil is the harm that you do to others; and it is also the harm that comes back to you. When you do evil, you will be repaid with evil. Evil is a malevolent force that seeks out those who do evil. Robbers get robbed. Cheaters get cheated. Killers get killed. That is reason enough to never do anything that is evil. If all your works are evil, you will have nothing but evil coming to you. Wicked people die because of their own evil works.

> Evil shall slay the wicked: and they that hate the righteous shall be desolate. (Psalm 34:21)

Evildoers attract evil. The righteous do what is right. They are repaid with good.

> Evil pursueth sinners: but to the righteous good shall be repaid. (Proverbs 13:21)

If you mistreat someone who has treated you well, you will be plagued with evil.

> Whoso rewardeth evil for good, evil shall not depart from his house. (Proverbs 17:13 )

If you will walk with God, you do not have to be afraid of anything.

> Yea, thou I walk through the valley of the shadow of death, I will fear no evil: for thou art with me; thy rod and thy staff they comfort me. (Psalm 23:4)

When you are in fellowship with God, he will keep evil away from you.

Because thou hast made the Lord, which is my refuge, even the most High, thy habitation; there shall no evil befall thee, neither shall any plague come nigh thy dwelling. (Psalm 91:9–10)

God has promised to protect you from evil.

The Lord shall preserve thee from all evil: he shall preserve thy soul. (Psalm 121:7)

If you persist in doing evil, you are choosing death instead of life.

As righteousness tendeth to life: so he that pursueth evil pursueth it to his own death. (Proverbs 11:19)

Evil stays away from those who fear the Lord.

The fear of the Lord tendeth to life: and he that hath it shall abide satisfied; he shall not be visited with evil. (Proverbs 19:23)

God does not preserve the life of the wicked. Without his protection, they are dead.

Fret not thyself because of evil men, neither be thou envious at the wicked; for there shall be no reward to the evil man; the candle of the wicked shall be put out. (Proverbs 24:19–20)

Worldly people do not understand that there is a penalty for every evil work.

Because sentence against an evil work is not executed speedily, therefore the heart of the sons of men is fully set in them to do evil. (Ecclesiastes 8:11)

God told his people that evil came their way because of their disobedience to God.

> **Because ye have burned incense, and because ye have sinned against the Lord, and have not obeyed the voice of the Lord, nor walked in his law, nor in his statutes, nor in his testimonies; therefore this evil is happened unto you, as at this day. (Jeremiah 44:23)**

## FALSE GOSPEL

"Gospel" means good news. The good news of the Bible is that Jesus came to save you from sin and death. His sacrifice for your sins is the only one that God accepts. He died so that you can live. Your salvation is a free gift. You do not have to do anything to earn it or deserve it. You receive it by faith alone, because you believe in Jesus. He is real, and he is alive today. Ask him to be your Savior and your Lord. And you will live with him forever.

A false prophet only tells people things they want to hear. A true prophet of God will never contradict the Bible. The Bible says that those who despise God will have no peace, and those who break God's rules shall be visited with evil. This passage gives two examples of how a false prophet could contradict God's word.

> **Thus saith the Lord of hosts, Hearken not unto the words of the prophets that prophesy unto you: they make you vain: they speak a vision of their own heart, and not out of the mouth of the Lord. They say still unto them that despise me, The Lord hath said, Ye shall have peace; and they say unto every one that walketh after the imagination of his own heart, No evil shall come upon you. (Jeremiah 23:16–17)**

There is only one true gospel. It is the gospel of Jesus Christ as recorded in the Bible. Anyone who preaches a different gospel is a deceiver.

> **But though we, or an angel from heaven, preach any other gospel unto you than that which we have preached unto you, let him be accursed. (Galatians 1:8)**

Worldly people love fables more than they love the truth. They enjoy believing in pagan religions. Reincarnation, astrology, and talking to the dead are ideas they enjoy. They refuse to accept the idea that Jesus is the only way to God. They want a religion that allows them to commit their favorite sins.

> **For the time will come when they will not endure sound doctrine; but after their own lusts shall they heap to themselves teachers, having itching ears; and they shall turn away their ears from the truth, and shall be turned unto fables. (2 Timothy 4:3–4)**

Do not believe anything that does not agree with the Bible. Do not support anyone who promotes a false gospel.

> **Whosoever transgresseth, and abideth not in the doctrine of Christ, hath not God. He that abideth in the doctrine of Christ, he hath both the Father and the Son. If there come any unto you, and bring not this doctrine, receive him not into your house, neither bid him Godspeed: for he that biddeth him Godspeed is partaker of his evil deeds. (2 John 9–10)**

## FEAR

Most people are afraid of what will happen in the future. Fear is the opposite of faith and actually causes bad things to happen. You must replace all your fears with faith. Faith in God causes good things to happen. Expect God to answer your prayers and to watch out for you. Anticipate the good things that are coming your way. Fearing the Lord is showing him the respect he deserves. It is obeying him. It is having a relationship with him. You bring obedience to the relationship. That obedience is a demonstration of your faith. It causes God to protect you, help you, and bless you.

This is what Moses told God's people just before they went into the Promised Land.

> **Be strong and of a good courage, fear not, nor be afraid of them: for the Lord thy God, he it is that doth go with thee; he will not fail thee, nor forsake thee. (Deuteronomy 31:6)**

Job was afraid something bad would happen, and it did. He received the thing he feared.

> **For the thing which I greatly feared is come upon me, and that which I was afraid of is come unto me. (Job 3:25)**

The Lord will deliver you from your fears.

> **I sought the Lord, and he heard me, and delivered me from all my fears. (Psalm 34:4)**

Memorize these verses. Say them aloud whenever you are afraid.

> **What time I am afraid, I will trust in thee. In God I will praise his word, in God I have put my trust; I will not fear what flesh can do unto me. (Psalm 56:3–4)**

The wicked live in fear, and receive the things they fear. You can live in faith and receive the things you desire.

> **The fear of the wicked, it shall come upon him: but the desire of the righteous shall be granted. (Proverbs 10:24)**

Your enemies are afraid of God. They are afraid of what he might do to them. Jesus is God. And he is always present with you.

> **When I cry unto thee, then shall mine enemies turn back: this I know; for God is for me. (Psalm 56:9)**

Fear is a spirit. It does not come from God. It is not God's will for you to be afraid of anything.

> **For God hath not given us the spirit of fear; but of power, and of love, and of a sound mind. (2 Timothy 1:7)**

"Conversation" means lifestyle. You are part of God's family. When you have Jesus to assist you, he is all you need. His resources are unlimited.

> **Let your conversation be without covetousness; and be content with such things as ye have: for he hath said, I will never leave thee, nor forsake thee. So that we may boldly say, The Lord is my helper, and I will not fear what man shall do unto me. (Hebrews 13:5–6)**

This verse explains that love is the cure for fear. "Perfect" love is love that has been practiced until it is perfect.

> **There is no fear in love; but perfect love casteth out fear: because fear hath torment. He that feareth is not made perfect in love. (1 John 4:18)**

## FIERY DARTS

Fiery darts are words that cause pain to others. People who have been hurt by fiery darts tend to use them on others. What they are really saying is this: "Someone has hurt me, so I'm going to hurt you." You have had fiery darts thrown at you, and you have thrown them at others. You cannot control other peoples' mouths, but you can control your own. You always get back what you give out. When you stop lashing out at others, you will reduce the number of fiery darts coming back on you.

In this Psalm, David asked God to keep him from being afraid of his enemy. They were using their words as weapons against him.

> Hear my voice, O God, in my prayer: preserve my life from fear of the enemy. Hide me from the secret counsel of the wicked; from the insurrection of the workers of iniquity: who whet their tongue like a sword, and bend their bows to shoot their arrows, even bitter words: that they may shoot in secret at the perfect: suddenly do they shoot at him, and fear not. (Psalm 64:1–4)

"Froward things" are things that are reversed, things that are contrary to what is right.

> An ungodly man diggeth up evil: and in his lips there is as a burning fire....He shutteth his eyes to devise froward things: moving his lips he bringeth evil to pass. (Proverbs 16:27, 30)

Contentious people love to argue. Their hurtful words cause spiritual wounds.

> Where no wood is, there the fire goeth out: so where there is no talebearer, the strife ceaseth. As coals are to burning coals, and wood to fire; so is a contentious man to kindle strife. The words of a talebearer are as wounds and they go down into the innermost parts of the belly. (Proverbs 26:20–22)

Your faith is like a shield that deflects all the fiery darts of your enemy.

> Above all, taking the shield of faith, wherewith ye shall be able to quench all the fiery darts of the wicked. (Ephesians 6:16)

Your words determine the course of your life. When they are consistent with the Bible, your life will reflect it. If you do not control your words, you are inviting the devil into your life.

> Even so the tongue is a little member, and boasteth great things. Behold, how great a matter a little fire kindleth! And the tongue is a fire, a world of iniquity: so is the tongue among our members, that it defileth the whole body, and setteth on fire the course of nature; and it is set on fire of hell. (James 3:5–6)

## FINANCIAL OPPRESSION

Do you feel like a slave to the people you owe? The Bible says that the borrower is servant to the lender. It is normal to feel beaten down by financial needs and bills you cannot pay. Most financial oppression is self-inflicted. Another form of it is making others feel bad about their lack of money. Consider the Golden Rule. You don't like to feel poor, so don't make others feel that way. Don't flaunt your money in front of people who are poor. It makes them feel worthless and small. To overcome financial oppression, focus on the things of God. Do not think about what you do not have. Be thankful to God for what he has given you.

If you hire someone to work for you, be sure and pay him promptly.

> Thou shalt not oppress an hired servant that is poor and needy, whether he be of thy brethren, or of thy strangers that are in thy land within thy gates: at his day thou shalt give him his hire, neither shall the sun go down upon it; for he is poor, and setteth his heart upon it: lest he cry against thee unto the Lord, and it be sin unto thee. (Deuteronomy 24:14–15)

Demanding that people pay you money that they do not have is financial oppression.

> The wicked in his pride doth persecute the poor. (Psalm 10:2)

God says not to oppress the poor. He will avenge them. "To spoil" someone means to take something away from them.

> Rob not the poor, because he is poor: neither oppress the afflicted in the gate: for the Lord will plead their cause, and spoil the soul of those that spoiled them. (Proverbs 22:22–23)

This passage describes people who are financially oppressed.

> But this is a people robbed and spoiled; they are all of them snared in holes, and they are hid in prison houses: they are for a prey, and none delivereth; for a spoil, and none saith, Restore. (Isaiah 42:22)

The best advice my Dad ever gave me is to never borrow money. But I did not follow his advice. I did feel like a slave to those who loaned me the money.

> The rich ruleth over the poor, and the borrower is servant to the lender. (Proverbs 22:7)

If you want your circumstances to be different, you will have to be different. Before God blesses you financially, he requires that you keep his commandment to love your neighbor.

> Now therefore thus saith the Lord of hosts; consider your ways. Ye have sown much, and bring in little; ye eat, but ye have not enough; ye drink, but ye are not filled with drink; ye clothe you, but there is none warm; and he that earneth wages earneth wages to put it into a bag with holes. (Haggai 1:5–6)

## FOOLISHNESS

We know from the Bible that God created us. We know from the Bible that Jesus is the Son of God. But these ideas are foolishness to the people of the world. They are horribly prejudiced against the Bible. They do not have this same reaction to any other book. For example, the writings of Josephus are accepted as true, but the Bible is considered to be a collection of myths. The world is familiar with the prophecies of Nostradamus, but they know nothing about the Old Testament Prophets. The world does not ridicule those who believe in reincarnation or talking to the dead. But the Bible is just too weird for them. It is foolishness to them. The truth is that anything that contradicts the word of God is foolishness.

Do not associate with those who rebel against God. Their opinions will affect you.

> Go from the presence of a foolish man, when thou perceivest not in him the lips of knowledge. (Proverbs 14:7)

Your words reveal whether you are wise, or whether you are a fool.

> The tongue of the wise useth knowledge aright: but the mouth of fools poureth out foolishness. (Proverbs 15:2)

Fools can only speak foolishness. Because it is all they know. They are not interested in wisdom and truth.

> The heart of him that hath understanding seeketh knowledge: but the mouth of fools feedeth on foolishness. (Proverbs 15:14)

Discipline is necessary to keep your children from acting foolishly.

> Foolishness is bound in the heart of a child; but the rod of correction will drive it far from him. (Proverbs 22:15)

The cross of Christ is foolishness to the people of the world. They cannot see how it affects them. All you can do is to tell them about Jesus. The Holy Spirit will do the rest.

> For Christ sent me not to baptize, but to preach the gospel: not with wisdom of words, lest the cross of Christ should be made of none effect. For the preaching of the cross is to them that perish foolishness; but unto us which are saved it is the power of God. (1 Corinthians 1:17–18)

Worldly people depend entirely on their intellect. They reject everything they cannot understand. The things of God and the preaching of the cross do not make sense to them.

> Where is the wise? Where is the scribe? Where is the disputer of this world? Hath not God made foolish the wisdom of this world? For after that in the wisdom of God the world by wisdom knew not God, it pleased God by the foolishness of preaching to save them that believe. For the Jews require a sign, and the Greeks seek after wisdom: but we preach Christ crucified, unto the Jews a stumbling block, and unto the Greeks foolishness; but unto them which are called, both Jews and Greeks, Christ the power of God, and the wisdom of God. Because the foolishness of God is wiser than men; and the weakness of God is stronger than men. (1 Corinthians 1:20–25)

The wisdom of God does not appeal to the world, but it is not for them. It is for the children of God.

> But God hath chosen the foolish things of this world to confound the wise; and God hath chosen the weak things of the world to confound the things which are mighty. (Corinthians 1:27)

God's wisdom is the only true wisdom.

> **Let no man deceive himself. If any man among you seemeth to be wise in this world, let him become a fool, that he may be wise. For the wisdom of this world is foolishness with God. For it is written, He taketh the wise in their own craftiness. And again, The Lord knoweth the thoughts of the wise, that they are vain. (Corinthians 3:18–20)**

## FORNICATION

Adultery is the generic term for all sexual activity outside of marriage. Technically, adultery involves at least one cheating spouse. Fornication is sexual activity between unmarried people. It is perfectly acceptable to worldly people. God says it is sin, and there is always a price to pay for it. Like all sin, it has the power to take you captive and destroy your life. Anything that is pleasurable can become an addiction. Fornication is man's favorite sin. It is probably the most powerful weapon the devil has. He is selling the idea that your life is not worth living unless you are participating in some form of illicit sex. For some people, sex is the most important thing in life. To others, it hardly matters. Fornication is just another sin. When you decide to turn away from it, the Holy Spirit will enable you to do so. It is important to God that you abstain from fornication.

> **For it seemed good to the Holy Ghost, and to us, to lay upon you no greater burden than these necessary things; that ye abstain from meats offered to idols, and from blood, and from things strangled, and from fornication: from which if ye keep yourselves, ye do well. (Acts 15:29)**

The best way to deal with fornication is to run away from it. This verse says that it is harmful to your body.

> **Flee fornication. Every sin that a man doeth is without the body; but he that committeth fornication sinneth against his own body. (1 Corinthians 6:18)**

God provides wives and husbands to satisfy each others' sexual desires.

> **Nevertheless, to avoid fornication, let every man have his own wife, and let every woman have her own husband. (1 Corinthians 7:2)**

"Sanctification" means being set apart to serve God. Abstaining from fornication is a part of being sanctified.

> **For this is the will of God, even your sanctification, that ye should abstain from fornication. (1 Thessalonians 4:3)**

A "whoremonger" is a man who has sex with prostitutes.

> **Marriage is honorable in all, and the bed undefiled: but whoremongers and adulterers God will judge. (Hebrews 13:4)**

Jude was Jesus' half-brother. He wrote this about men who turned away from the Lord. They followed their own lust and taught others to do the same. That is a popular idea in our society, but there is nothing new about immorality.

> **For there are certain men crept in unawares, who were before of old ordained to this condemnation, ungodly men, turning the grace of our God into lasciviousness, and denying the only Lord God, and our Lord Jesus Christ. I will therefore put you in remembrance, though ye once knew this, how that the Lord, having saved the people out of the land of Egypt, afterward destroyed them that believed**

> **not....Even as Sodom and Gomorrah, and the cities about them in like manner, giving themselves over to fornication, and going after strange flesh, are set forth for an example suffering the vengeance of eternal fire. Likewise also these filthy dreamers defile the flesh, despise dominion, and speak evil of dignities. (Jude 4–5,7–9)**

## THE GRAVE

The grave is only temporary, not permanent. It is a place for your physical body to "sleep" for a while. Those who are "asleep in Jesus" will continue to live with him forever. One day, your physical body will be resurrected from the dead along with everyone else's. As a believer in Christ, you share in the Lord's victory over death, and you will reign with him as a king and a priest forever.

The grave has no power over you. Jesus has redeemed you from death and hell.

> **But God will redeem my soul from the power of the grave: for he shall receive me. (Psalm 49:15)**

At the time of the resurrection, the dead will hear Jesus' voice.

> **Marvel not at this: for the hour is coming, in the which all that are in the graves shall hear his voice, and shall come forth; they that have done good unto the resurrection of life; and they that have done evil, unto the resurrection of damnation. (John 5:28–29)**

Jesus' bodily resurrection proves that there is a resurrection of the dead.

> **Now if Christ be preached that he rose from the dead, how say some among you that there is no resurrection of the dead? (1 Corinthians 15:12)**

Jesus is called the Second Adam. The First Adam caused you to die. The Second Adam caused you to live forever.

> But now is Christ risen from the dead, and become the firstfruits of them that slept. For since by man came death, by man came also the resurrection of the dead. For as in Adam all die, even so in Christ shall all be made alive. (1 Corinthians 15:20–22)

Your physical body is perishable, but you will receive a new body that will last forever.

> The first man is of the earth, earthy: the second man is the Lord from heaven. As is the earthy, such are they also that are earthy; and as is the heavenly, such are they also that are heavenly. And as we have borne the image of the earthy, we shall also bear the image of the heavenly. (1 Corinthians 15:47–49)

This is a description of the Rapture of the church. Believers in Jesus will meet him in the air. If you are alive during the Rapture, you will never know death.

> Behold, I show you a mystery; we shall not all sleep, but we shall all be changed, in a moment, in the twinkling of an eye, at the last trump: for the trumpet shall sound, and the dead shall be raised incorruptible, and we shall be changed. For the corruptible must put on incorruption, and this mortal must put on immortality. So when this corruptible shall have put on incorruption, and this mortal shall have put on immortality, then shall be brought to pass the saying that is written, Death is swallowed up in victory. O death, where is thy sting? O grave, where is thy victory? (1 Corinthians 15:51–55)

For you, death is merely "sleep." Your hope for the future is based on what Jesus has already done.

> **But I would not have you to be ignorant, brethren, concerning them which are asleep, that ye sorrow not, even as others which have no hope. For if we believe that Jesus died and rose again, even so them also which sleep in Jesus will God bring with him. (1 Thessalonians 4:13–14)**

This is another description of the Rapture of the church. You'll be "caught away" together with all other believers. The Lord will evacuate you from the Earth, before he pours out his judgment upon it.

> **For the Lord himself shall descend from heaven with a shout, with the voice of the archangel, and with the trump of God: and the dead in Christ shall rise first: then we which are alive and remain shall be caught up together with them in the clouds, to meet the Lord in the air: and so shall we ever be with the Lord. Wherefore comfort one another with these words. (Thessalonians 4:16–18)**

## HATRED

Hatred is the opposite of love. It can easily destroy your life. It prevents God from blessing you. Accept people the way they are. Jesus hates sin, but he loves the sinner. You can hate the things that people do and not hate the people. Refuse to hate those who hate you. Follow the example Jesus set for you. He prayed for those who crucified him, saying, "Father, forgive them, they know not what they do." When you develop the habit of obeying God by loving others, you will receive the blessing of the Lord. If you do not do this, you will miss the life God has planned for you. You and your family will suffer because of your negativity and selfishness.

Overlooking the shortcomings of others is a part of loving them. Let God deal with those who constantly oppose you and slander you.

> Hatred stirreth up strifes: but love covereth all sins....He that hideth hatred with lying lips, and he that uttereth a slander is a fool. (Proverbs 10:12,18)

These are Jesus' words to everyone who believes in him.

> And ye shall be hated of all men for my name's sake: but he that endureth to the end shall be saved. (Matthew 10:22)

The Christ-rejecting world hates you because you belong to Jesus.

> If the world hate you, ye know that it hated me before it hated you. If ye were of the world, the world would love his own; but because ye are not of the world, but I have chosen you out of the world, therefore the world hateth you. (John 15:18–19)

In this passage, Jesus was referring to the religious leaders of his day. They loved their traditions more than they loved God.

> He that hateth me hateth my Father also. If I had not done among them the works which none other man did, they had not had sin: but now have they both seen and hated both me and my Father. But this cometh to pass, that the word might be fulfilled that is written in their law, They hated me without a cause. (John 15:23–25)

Just before Jesus was crucified, he prayed this prayer for you.

> I have given them thy word; and the world hath hated them, because they are not of the world, even as I am not of the world. I pray not that thou shouldest take them out of the world, but that thou shouldest keep them from the evil. They are not of the world, even as I am not of the

> world. Sanctify them though thy truth: thy word is truth.... Neither pray I for these alone, but for them also which shall believe on me through their word. (John 17:14–17,20)

Children of God love one another. Children of the devil hate other people. To God there is little difference between hatred and murder. Both are symptoms of a lack of love.

> In this the children of God are manifest, and the children of the devil: whosoever doeth not righteousness is not of God, neither he that loveth not his brother. For this is the message that ye heard from the beginning, that we should love one another. Not as Cain, who was of that wicked one, and slew his brother. And wherefore slew he him? Because his own works were evil, and his brother's righteous. Marvel not, my brethren, if the world hate you. We know that we have passed from death unto life, because we love the brethren. He that loveth not his brother abideth in death. Whosoever hateth his brother is a murderer: and ye know that no murderer hath eternal life abiding in him. (1 John 3:14–15)

## HELL

How can a loving God allow people to go to hell? That is a problem to the people who do not know God. Hell was prepared for the devil and his angels. People go to hell because they choose to go there, not because it is God's will. "God is not willing that any should perish but that all should come to repentance." But when people reject Jesus, they are choosing death and hell. God has already done everything that is necessary to save you from hell. Salvation is free to you, but Jesus died to pay your death penalty. You do not have to try and earn it on your own. It is available to everyone who asks God for it. You receive it by faith alone. Do not allow yourself to go to hell.

Hell is a real place. Unsaved people go there when they die.

> **The wicked shall be turned into hell, and all the nations that forget God. (Psalm 9:17)**

So many people are in hell that it has had to be expanded.

> **Therefore hell hath enlarged herself, and opened her mouth without measure; and their glory, and their multitude, and their pomp, and he that rejoiceth, shall descend into it. (Isaiah 5:14)**

This is what the Lord will say to those who have rejected him.

> **Then shall he say also unto them on the left hand, Depart from me, ye cursed, into everlasting fire, prepared for the devil and his angels. (Matthew 25:41)**

In this passage, Jesus gives us a glimpse of what Hell is like. It involves Lazarus and a rich man who knew him. This is not the same Lazarus that Jesus raised from the dead. "Abraham's Bosom" was the place of the righteous dead. Lazarus died and went there. The rich man also died and went to a place called "Torments." "The law and the prophets" means the written word of God. Those who refuse to believe the Bible are not going to believe a man, even if he returned from the dead.

> **And it came to pass, that the beggar died, and was carried by the angels into Abraham's bosom: the rich man also died, and was buried; and in hell he lifted up his eyes, being in torments, and seeth Abraham afar off, and Lazarus in his bosom. And he cried and said, Father Abraham, have mercy on me, and send Lazarus, that he may dip the tip of his finger in water, and cool my tongue; for I am tormented in this flame. But Abraham said, Son, remember that thou in thy lifetime receivedst thy good things, and likewise Lazarus evil things: but now he is**

> comforted, and thou art tormented. And beside all this, between us and you, there is a great gulf fixed: so that they which would pass from hence to you cannot; neither can they pass to us, that would come from thence. Then he said, I pray thee therefore, father, that thou wouldest send him to my father's house: for I have five brethren; that he may testify unto them, lest they also come into this place of torment. Abraham saith unto him, They have Moses and the prophets; let them hear them. And he said, Nay, father Abraham, but if one went unto them from the dead, they will repent. And he said unto him, If they hear not Moses and the prophets, neither will they be persuaded, though one rose from the dead. (Luke 16:22–31)

This passage tells what happens to those who reject Jesus. They are not covered by Jesus' perfect work on the cross. They are judged according to their own works.

> And I saw the dead, small and great, stand before God; and the books were opened: and another book was opened, which is the book of life: and the dead were judged out of those things which were written in the books, according to their works. And the sea gave up the dead which were in it; and death and hell delivered up the dead which were in them: and they were judged every man according to their works. And death and hell were cast into the lake of fire. This is the second death. And whosoever was not found written in the book of life was cast into the lake of fire. (Revelation 20:11–15)

## HOMOSEXUALITY

Homosexuality is just another sin that people get caught up in, like adultery. God calls it an abomination, and says it causes death. Who is able to refute God's word, and "correct" him? The only people who attempt it have to be filled with pride. The Bible is God's word, and is not open for debate. It doesn't need to be updated to adapt to our popular culture. You cannot select which parts of the Bible you want to believe and disregard the rest.

God created two sexes, not three or four. It is an insult to God when his created beings change themselves into something else.

> So God created man in his own image, in the image of God created he him; male and female created he them. (Genesis 1:27)

God says homosexuality is an abomination. That means he really hates it. Homosexual clergymen say this is acceptable to God. Choose for yourself whom you will believe.

> If a man also lie with mankind, as he lieth with a woman, both of them have committed an abomination: they shall surely be put to death; their blood shall be upon them. (Leviticus 20:13)

Cross-dressers and transvestites are also abominations to God.

> The woman shall not wear that which pertaineth unto a man, neither shall a man put on a woman's garment: for all that do so are abomination unto the Lord thy God. (Deuteronomy 22:5)

Here God challenges those who commit abominations and then stand before him in his house and expect him to accept them.

> Behold, ye trust in lying words, that cannot profit. Will ye steal, murder, and commit adultery, and swear falsely, and burn incense unto Baal, and walk after other gods whom

> ye know not; and come and stand before me in this house, which is called by my name, and say, We are delivered to do all these abominations? (Jeremiah 7:9–10)

These are God's words to the nation of Israel. He said that her sins were worse than those of her sister Sodom. God said that he destroyed the Sodomites for their idleness, stinginess and pride, as well as for their abomination.

> Behold, this was the iniquity of thy sister Sodom, pride, fullness of bread, and abundance of idleness was in her and in her daughters, neither did she strengthen the hand of the poor and needy. And they were haughty, and committed abomination before me: therefore I took them away as I saw good. (Ezekiel 16:49–50)

God allows people to do whatever they choose. If you choose homosexuality, you have to take everything that goes along with it. It will cost you everything you have and everything you could have had. You will miss the good things of God. You will forfeit the blessing of the Lord, and you will remove yourself from God's protection.

> Wherefore God also gave them up to uncleanness through the lusts of their own hearts, to dishonor their own bodies between themselves; who changed the truth of God into a lie, and worshipped and served the creature more than the Creator, who is blessed for ever. Amen. For this cause God gave them up unto vile affections: for even their women did change the natural use into that which is against nature: and likewise also the men, leaving the natural use of the woman, burned in their lust one toward another; men with men working that which is unseemly, and receiving in themselves that recompense of their error which was meet. (Romans 1:24–27)

We call them gays. God calls them "the abominable." According to this verse, they are one of the groups of people who will be thrown into the lake of fire.

> **But the fearful, and unbelieving, and the abominable, and murderers, and whoremongers, and sorcerers, and idolaters, and all liars, shall have their part in the lake which burneth with fire and brimstone: which is the second death. (Revelation 21:8)**

## IDOLATRY

An idol is something that occupies God's place in your heart. Anything can become an idol. People become obsessed with money, sex, power, alcohol, and drugs and devote their lives to these things. These God-substitutes take everything they have. Idolaters are actually worshipping themselves. They are filled with pride and think of themselves as equal to God. They think that they can get away with breaking God's law. They think that they can sin now and get forgiveness later. Why should they deprive themselves of pleasure?

Rebellion against God is to know what he wants and refuse to do it.

> **For rebellion is as the sin of witchcraft, and stubbornness is as iniquity and idolatry. (1 Samuel 15:23)**

The God of the Bible is unique. He is the only true God. He is the Creator of heaven and earth. He is the Father of our Lord, Jesus Christ. All other gods are idols.

> **For the Lord is great, and greatly to be praised: he is to be feared above all gods. For all the gods of the nations are idols: but the Lord made the heavens. (Psalm 96:4–5)**

Idols and the people who worship them are alike. They have eyes that do not see and ears that do not hear. Idols are physically dead. Their worshippers are dead spiritually.

> The idols of the heathen are silver and gold, the work of men's hands. They have mouths, but they speak not; eyes have they, but they see not; they have ears, but they hear not; neither is there any breath in their mouths. They that make them are like unto them: so is every one that trusteth in them. (Psalm 135:15–18)

While Moses was receiving the Ten Commandments, the people were worshipping a golden calf. The "host of heaven" refers to the angels who were thrown out of heaven with Satan.

> And they made a calf in those days, and offered sacrifice unto the idol, and rejoiced in the work of their own hands. Then God turned, and gave them up to worship the host of heaven. (Acts 7:41)

If you are an idolater, you are going to experience the wrath of God.

> For this ye know, that no whoremonger, nor unclean person, nor covetous man, who is an idolater, hath any inheritance in the kingdom of Christ and of God. Let no man deceive you with vain words: for because of these things cometh the wrath of God upon the children of disobedience. Be not ye therefore partakers with them. (Ephesians 5:5–7)

An "inordinate affection" is an inappropriate romantic relationship. "Evil concupiscence" is longing for sex outside of marriage. These are all sexual sins.

> Mortify therefore your members which are upon the earth: fornication, uncleanness, inordinate affection, evil concupiscence, and covetousness, which is idolatry: for which things' sake the wrath of God cometh on the children of disobedience. (Colossians 3:5–6)

## THE LAKE OF FIRE

Hell is not a permanent place. It is a holding area for the future. The inhabitants of hell will eventually be thrown into the lake of fire. This is their ultimate destiny. Unsaved people do not like to hear about the fire and brimstone, but one day they will experience it.

John saw a vision of the end of the world. He described the last battle on Earth. The Anti-Christ will fight against the Lord in one great last battle. Jesus will, of course, defeat him. Then, the Anti-Christ and the False Prophet will be cast alive into the lake of fire.

> And I saw the beast, and the kings of the earth, and their armies, gathered together to make war against him that sat on the horse, and against his army. And the beast was taken, and with him the false prophet that wrought miracles before him, with which he deceived them that had received the mark of the beast, and them that worshipped his image. These both were cast alive into a lake of fire burning with brimstone. (Revelation 19:19–20)

This passage is a description of what is known as the great white throne judgment. Those who reject Jesus will be judged according to their works. Then, they will be thrown into the lake of fire. As a believer in Christ, you will not be present at this judgment. Your name is written in the Lamb's Book of Life. It contains the name of everyone who will live forever with the Lord.

> And the devil that deceived them was cast into the lake of fire and brimstone, where the beast and the false prophet

> are, and shall be tormented day and night for ever and ever. And I saw a great white throne, and him that sat on it, from whose face the earth and the heaven fled away; and there was found no place for them. And I saw the dead, small and great, stand before God; and the books were opened: and another book was opened, which is the book of life: and the dead were judged out of those things which were written in the books, according to their works. And the sea gave up the dead which were in it; and death and hell delivered up the dead which were in them: and they were judged every man according to their works. And death and hell were cast into the lake of fire. This is the second death. And whosoever was not found written in the book of life was cast into the lake of fire. (Revelation 20:10–15)

Those who reject Jesus are in bad company. These are the kind of people who spit in Jesus' face and tortured him before they crucified him.

> He that overcometh shall inherit all things; and I will be his God, and he shall be my son. But the fearful, and unbelieving, and the abominable, and murderers, and whoremongers, and sorcerers, and idolaters, and all liars, shall have their part in the lake which burneth with fire and brimstone: which is the second death. (Revelation 21:7–8)

## LASCIVIOUSNESS

Lasciviousness is the tendency to commit sexual sins. Some sexual sins are gateways to fornication and adultery, such as uncleanness, inordinate affection, and evil concupiscence. "Uncleanness" is impure thinking. "Inordinate affection" is depraved passion, and "evil concupiscence" is wicked craving. Sins are attitudes. They strongly affect your heart and mind. How can you overcome them? By using the self-control the Holy

Spirit provides. In order to maintain it, you must immerse yourself in the Bible. Fill yourself so full of the word of God that there is no room for anything else. Then your thoughts will be the same as God's.

The Bible says to stay away from those who would lead you astray. They do not care if they destroy your life by causing you to sin.

> For the commandment is a lamp; and the law is light; and reproofs of instruction are the way of life: to keep thee from the evil woman, from the flattery of the tongue of a strange woman. Lust not after her beauty in thine heart; neither let her take thee with her eyelids. For by means of a whorish woman a man is brought to a piece of bread: and the adulteress will hunt for the precious life. (Proverbs 6:23–26)

These are Jesus' words concerning lasciviousness. He has set a high standard of purity. The sin you allow in your heart will show up in your life. Imaginary adultery always precedes actual adultery.

> But I say unto you, That whosoever looketh on a woman to lust after her hath committed adultery with her already in his heart. (Matthew 5:28)

The sins that you commit originate within your heart.

> For from within, out of the heart of men, proceed evil thoughts, adulteries, fornications, murders, thefts, covetousness, wickedness, deceit, lasciviousness, an evil eye, blasphemy, pride, foolishness: all these evil things come from within, and defile the man. (Mark 7:21–23)

You cannot focus on two thoughts at the same time. Focus your attention on the Bible. God's word will replace negative ideas. To "mortify" something is to put it to death.

> If ye then be risen with Christ, seek those things which are above, where Christ sitteth on the right hand of God. Set your affection on things above, not on things on the earth. For ye are dead, and your life is hid with Christ in God. When Christ, who is our life, shall appear, then shall ye also appear with him in glory. Mortify therefore your members which are upon the earth; fornication, uncleanness, inordinate affection, evil concupiscence, and covetousness, which is idolatry: for which things' sake the wrath of God cometh on the children of disobedience: (Colossians 3:1–6)

Worldly people make no effort to control their minds. Don't be like them. Be like Jesus.

> This I say therefore, and testify in the Lord, that ye henceforth walk not as other Gentiles walk, in the vanity of their mind, having the understanding darkened, being alienated from the life of God through the ignorance that is in them, because of the blindness of their heart: who being past feeling have given themselves over unto lasciviousness, to work all uncleanness with greediness. (Ephesians 4:17–19)

Sin is not a collection of individual acts so much as it is an attitude of the heart. Being under God's law of liberty does not give you a license to sin. If you get caught up in these sexual sins, God will chasten you.

> For there are certain men crept in unawares, who were before of old ordained to this condemnation, ungodly men, turning the grace of our God into lasciviousness, and denying the only Lord God, and our Lord Jesus Christ. I will therefore put you in remembrance, though ye once knew this, how that the Lord, having saved the people

> out of the land of Egypt, afterward destroyed them that believed not. (Jude 4–5)

## LAZINESS

Laziness and diligence are opposites. Each of them is a state of mind that determines how much you will exert yourself. Because God rewards the diligent, he cannot bless the lazy. You cannot afford to be lazy. Lazy people lose the rewards they could have had. God expects every man to earn his own way. It is a matter of morality. If you are an employee and you don't give your employer full value for his money, you are cheating him and yourself.

God cursed Adam by commanding him to earn his bread by the sweat of his brow. This curse still applies to all of us as his descendants.

> And unto Adam he said, Because thou hast hearkened unto the voice of thy wife, and hast eaten of the tree, of which I commanded thee, saying, Thou shalt not eat of it: cursed is the ground for thy sake; in sorrow shalt thou eat of it all the days of thy life; thorns also and thistles shall it bring forth to thee: and thou shalt eat the herb of the field; in the sweat of thy face shalt thou eat bread, till thou return unto the ground; for out of it wast thou taken: for dust thou art, and unto dust shalt thou return. (Genesis 3:17–19)

Lazy people complain about what they do not have. But they are not willing to earn the money to buy these things.

> The soul of the sluggard desireth, and hath nothing. (Proverbs 13:4)

Work at a low-paying job is better than doing nothing. "Penury" is extreme poverty.

**In all labor there is profit; but the talk of the lips tendeth only to penury. (Proverbs 14:23)**

Lazy people spend most of their time sleeping instead of working.

**Slothfulness casteth into a deep sleep; and an idle soul shall suffer hunger. (Proverbs 19:15)**

God has an incentive plan. You can be lazy and live in poverty; or, you can work and have the money to buy the things you need.

**I went by the field of the slothful, and by the vineyard of the man void of understanding; and, lo, it was all grown over with thorns, and nettles had covered the face thereof, and the stone wall thereof was broken down. Then I saw, and considered it well: I looked upon it, and received instruction. Yet a little sleep, a little slumber, a little folding of the hands to sleep: so shall thy poverty come as one that traveleth; and thy want as an armed man. (Proverbs 24:30–34)**

Idolaters never stop serving their idols. They spend most of their time eating, drinking, and amusing themselves.

**Neither be ye idolaters, as were some of them; as it is written, The people sat down to eat and drink, and rose up to play. (1 Corinthians 10:7)**

Do not take advantage of other people by being a freeloader. Earn your own way in life.

**And that you study to be quiet, and to do your own business, and to work with your own hands, as we commanded you; that ye may walk honestly toward them**

> that are without, and that ye may have lack of nothing. (1 Thessalonians 4:11–12)

If you are taking a free ride, it is on somebody else's back. It is morally wrong for you to take someone else's money, and give them nothing in return.

> Now we command you, brethren, in the name of our Lord Jesus Christ, that ye withdraw yourselves from every brother that walketh disorderly, and not after the tradition which he received of us. For yourselves know how ye ought to follow us: for we behaved not ourselves disorderly among you; neither did we eat any man's bread for nought; but wrought with labor and travail night and day, that we might not be chargeable to any of you: for even when we were with you, this we commanded you, that if any would not work, neither should he eat. For we hear that there are some which walk among you disorderly, working not at all, but are busybodies. Now them that are such we command and exhort by our Lord Jesus Christ, that with quietness they work, and eat their own bread. But ye, brethren, be not weary in well doing. And if any man obey not our word by this epistle, note that man, and have no company with him, that he may be ashamed. Yet count him not as an enemy, but admonish him as a brother. (2 Thessalonians 3:10–15)

Paul wrote this to Timothy concerning some young women in his church who were being lazy.

> And withal they learn to be idle, wandering about from house to house; and not only idle, but tattlers also and busybodies, speaking things which they ought not. (1 Timothy 5:13)

When you are a blessing to others, God will bless you. Your highest priority should be to love your neighbor as yourself. You have to work to provide for yourself and your own family; and also to provide for the needs of others.

> **For God is not unrighteous to forget your work and labor of love, which ye have shown toward his name, in that ye have ministered to the saints, and do minister. And we desire that every one of you show the same diligence to the full assurance of hope unto the end. That ye be not slothful, but followers of them who through faith and patience inherit the promises. (Hebrews 6:12)**

## LUST OF THE EYE

Sexual sins begin with the lust of the eye. David decided to commit adultery with Bathsheba after he saw her when she was bathing. Sexual sins always bring God's judgment. Lust of the eye is a strong temptation. You can overcome it with the self-control the Holy Spirit supplies. The power of God can keep you clean and pure. Your new way of life will make you feel good about yourself.

You face the same decision every day. Are you going to sabotage your whole life for a very small reward? Will you present yourself a living sacrifice, holy and acceptable to God? Or, are you going to sell out to the devil and let him run your life?

If you are a man, you cannot look at women as sexual objects. They are people just like you. Prevent trouble before it starts.

> **I made a covenant with mine eyes; why then should I think upon a maid? . . .For it is a fire that consumeth to destruction, and would root out all my increase. (Job 31:1, 12)**

Millions of men have destroyed their marriages, their families, and their lives by falling into adultery. God says to have nothing to do with the ungodly woman. She is motivated by money. "Honor" is money, as in the word, "honorarium."

> For the lips of a strange woman drop as a honeycomb, and her mouth is smoother than oil: but her end is bitter as wormwood, sharp as a two edged sword. Her feet go down to death; her steps take hold on hell. Lest thou shouldest ponder the path of life, her ways are moveable, that thou canst not know them. Hear me now therefore, O ye children, and depart not from the words of my mouth. Remove thy way far from her, and come not nigh the door of her house: lest thou give thine honor unto others, and thy years unto the cruel: lest strangers be filled with thy wealth; and thy labors be in the house of a stranger; and thou mourn at the last, when thy flesh and thy body are consumed, and say, How have I hated instruction, and my heart despised reproof; and have not obeyed the voice of my teachers, nor inclined mine ear to them that instructed me! I was almost in all evil in the midst of the congregation and assembly. (Proverbs 5:3–14)

No amount of excess will ever satisfy the lust of the eye.

> Hell and destruction are never full; so the eyes of man are never satisfied. (Proverbs 27:20)

Jesus said that looking at a woman lustfully constitutes adultery. God looks at the thoughts and the intentions of your heart. Your heart cannot tell the difference between things you have imagined and things you have actually done.

> But I say unto you, That whosoever looketh on a woman to lust after her hath committed adultery with her already in his heart. (Matthew 5:28)

It's better to bring your thoughts into captivity than it is to be taken captive yourself.

> **Casting down imaginations, and every high thing that exalteth itself against the knowledge of God, and bringing into captivity every thought to the obedience of Christ; and having in a readiness to revenge all disobedience, when your obedience is fulfilled. (2 Corinthians 10:5–6)**

"The world" is everything that opposes God and his word. Satan is the ruler of it. Even though you are in the world, you are not part of it. You are part of God's kingdom.

> **Love not the world, neither the things that are in the world. If any man love the world, the love of the Father is not in him. For all that is in the world, the lust of the flesh, and the lust of the eyes, and the pride of life, is not of the Father, but is of the world. And the world passeth away, and the lust thereof: but he that doeth the will of God abideth for ever. (1 John 2:15–17)**

This passage applies to some people you know. They do whatever they please. All they care about is what they can get for themselves.

> **Spots they are and blemishes, sporting themselves with their own deceivings while they feast with you; having eyes full of adultery, and that cannot cease from sin; beguiling unstable souls; an heart they have exercised with covetous practices; cursed children: which have forsaken the right way, and are gone astray, following the way of Balaam the son of Bosor, who loved the wages of unrighteousness;... These are wells without water, clouds that are carried with a tempest; to whom the mist of darkness is reserved for ever. For when they speak great swelling words of vanity,**

> they allure through the lusts of the flesh, through much wantonness, those that were clean escaped from them who live in error. While they promise them liberty, they themselves are the servants of corruption: for of whom a man is overcome, of the same is he brought in bondage. (2 Peter 2:13–15, 17–19)

## MADNESS

Madness is a mental and emotional illness. It is caused by failing to follow God's instruction. Being mad is the result of getting mad and staying mad. I was extremely angry about the Viet Nam war ever since I participated in it. My doctors told me I had post-traumatic stress disorder, but they did not tell me how to get over it. But I was angry all the time, and I was always in a bad mood. I had anger like a volcano. It was ready to erupt at the slightest provocation. While I was working on this book, God reached down and healed me. I was so fully immersed in the word of God, that it replaced my usual thought life. I woke up one morning and the rage was gone. I have been in a good mood ever since that day. God gave me a gift of healing and I thank him for it. But I had to humble myself before God first. I had submitted myself to his authority by keeping his commandments. God does not love me any more than he loves you. I believe that he will heal you just as he healed me.

This verse explains one of the causes of madness.

> So that thou shalt be mad for the sight of thine eyes which thou shalt see. (Deuteronomy 28:34)

The Bible makes people wise; oppressing the wise will cause them to go mad.

> Surely oppression maketh a wise man mad; and a gift destroyeth the heart. (Ecclesiastes 7:7)

The people of the world experience both evil and madness. Then they die. There is not much quality of life without God.

> This is an evil among all things that are done under the sun, that there is one event unto all: yea, also the heart of the sons of men is full of evil, and madness is in their heart while they live, and after that they go to the dead. (Ecclesiastes 9:3)

Fools are full of words. They say things that they do not mean and things that do not make sense.

> The words of a wise man's mouth are gracious; but the lips of a fool will swallow up himself. The beginning of the words of his mouth is foolishness: and the end of his talk is mischievous madness. A fool also is full of words: a man cannot tell what shall be; and what shall be after him, who can tell him? (Ecclesiastes 10:12–14)

The scribes and Pharisees hated Jesus. They were obsessed with finding a way to destroy him. They did not care about this man who had a withered hand. But Jesus did.

> And it came to pass also on another Sabbath, that he entered into the synagogue and taught: and there was a man whose right hand was withered. And the scribes and Pharisees watched him, whether he would heal on the Sabbath day; that they might find an accusation against him. But he knew their thoughts, and said to the man which had the withered hand, Rise up, and stand forth in the midst. And he arose and stood forth. Then said Jesus unto them, I will ask you one thing; is it lawful on the Sabbath days to do good, or to do evil? To save life, or to destroy it? And looking round about upon them all, he said

> **unto the man, Stretch forth thy hand. And he did so: and his hand was restored whole as the other. And they were filled with madness; and communed one with another what they might do to Jesus. (Luke 6:6–12)**

## OPPRESSION

Pharaoh physically oppressed God's people in Egypt. Satan oppresses God's people in this world. Oppression is pressuring people, causing them unnecessary stress. The devil uses other people to stress you, and he uses you to stress other people. You can easily oppress someone and not even know it. You can be hurting God's people and not even know it. Do not focus your attention entirely on yourself and your own problems. Take time to be nice to other people. They have hopes and dreams just as you do. Find a way to do something good for others. While you are helping them, God will be helping you.

When other people mistreat you, do not mistreat them in return. If you repay anyone with evil, it will come back on you. Do not try to get even. Treat others the way you want to be treated. That is what the Lord has commanded you. When you honor him, he will honor you.

> **Thou shalt neither vex a stranger, nor oppress him: for ye were strangers in the land of Egypt. (Exodus 22:21)**

When you are being oppressed, do not think about your situation. Think about God and his word instead. That is how to avoid the devil's snare.

> **Let the proud be ashamed; for they dealt perversely with me without a cause: but I will meditate in thy precepts. (Psalm 119:78)**

A "froward" man is a man who intentionally does what is wrong.

> Envy thou not the oppressor, and choose none of his ways. For the froward is abomination to the Lord: but his secret is with the righteous. (Proverbs 3:31–32)

The way you treat others shows what you think of God. He loves poor people, and expects you to help them.

> He that oppresseth the poor reproacheth his Maker: but he that honoreth him hath mercy on the poor. (Proverbs 14:31)

God says, do not oppress the poor. "The gate" is a court of law. God's judgment extends beyond the courts. If you take money from the poor, God will take something from you.

> Rob not the poor, because he is poor: neither oppress the afflicted in the gate: for the Lord will plead their cause, and spoil the soul of those that spoiled them. (Proverbs 22:22–23)

The relationship between borrower and lender is like that of a servant and his master.

> The rich ruleth over the poor, and the borrower is servant to the lender. (Proverbs 22:7)

This was God's judgment on his people when they turned away from him. They had no respect for God, and they were disrespected by their own children.

> And I will give children to be their princes, and babes shall rule over them. And the people shall be oppressed, every one by another, and every one by his neighbor: the child shall behave himself proudly against the ancient, and the base against the honorable. (Isaiah 3:4–5)

Some people are afraid of everything. They are afraid of what might happen. They are afraid of losing something—their mates, their health, their jobs, or their money. They are afraid of being punished for the things they have done wrong. Fear causes oppression.

> **In righteousness shalt thou be established: thou shalt be far from oppression; for thou shalt not fear: and from terror; for it shall not come near thee. (Isaiah 54:14)**

This is part of Peter's sermon to the first Gentiles to believe in Jesus. He told them that Jesus delivers people from the oppression of the devil.

> **The word which God sent unto the children of Israel, preaching peace by Jesus Christ: (he is Lord of all:) that word, I say, ye know, which was published throughout all Judea, and began from Galilee, after the baptism which John preached; how God anointed Jesus of Nazareth with the Holy Ghost and with power: who went about doing good, and healing all that were oppressed of the devil; for God was with him. (Acts 10:36–38)**

## PERSECUTION

The devil will persecute you for living right, because that makes you a threat to him. When others see your prosperity, they will want to prosper too. The devil will incite people to give you a hard time. If you let yourself be offended, then you are caught in the devil's snare. If you are angry at someone, that puts you under the control of the spirit of anger. If you are motivated by anger instead of love, then God cannot use you. The devil will have accomplished his mission, and you will no longer be a threat to him. You must be led by the Spirit of God, and God is love.

This part of the "Parable of the Sower" is about a person who is not rooted and grounded in love. The devil uses persecution to offend that person and steal the word of God.

> But he that received the seed into stony places, the same is he that heareth the word, and anon with joy receiveth it; yet hath he not root in himself, but dureth for a while: for when tribulation or persecution ariseth because of the word, by and by he is offended. (Matthew 13:20–21)

When you give up something for the cause of Christ, God will repay you for it a hundredfold. The devil tries to keep you from receiving God's rewards, by increasing the persecution.

> And Jesus answered and said, Verily I say unto you, There is no man that hath left house, or brethren, or sisters, or father, or mother, or wife, or children, or lands, for my sake, and the gospel's, but he shall receive a hundredfold now in this time, houses, and brethren, and sisters, and mothers, and children, and lands, with persecutions; and in the world to come eternal life. (Mark 10:29–30)

Jesus said you will be persecuted because you belong to him. The fact that you are being persecuted confirms the fact that you are his.

> Remember the word that I said unto you, The servant is not greater than his lord. If they have persecuted me, they will also persecute you;…But all these things will they do unto you for my name's sake, because they know not him that sent me. (John 15:20–21)

You know that you are living right when you are being persecuted by the devil. He is trying to keep you from being like Jesus. Everyone who lives a godly life will be persecuted.

> But thou hast fully known my doctrine, manner of life, purpose, faith, longsuffering, charity, patience, persecutions, afflictions, which came unto me at Antioch, at Iconium, at Lystra; what persecutions I endured: but out

> of them all the Lord delivered me. Yea, and all that will live godly in Christ Jesus shall suffer persecution. (2 Timothy 3:10–12)

When you are being persecuted, take comfort in the fact that the Lord will reward you for your suffering.

> Beloved, think it not strange concerning the fiery trial which is to try you, as though some strange thing happened unto you: but rejoice, inasmuch as ye are partakers of Christ's sufferings; that, when his glory shall be revealed, ye may be glad also with exceeding joy. (1 Peter 4:12–13)

## POVERTY

My wife and I came from poor families, and our own family knows what being poor is like. It is not because we did not work. We were part of the working poor. We had three children and were overwhelmed with living expenses, taxes, and loan repayments. We know how disheartening it is to work really hard and to never have enough money.

The War on Poverty was based on the idea that government could put an end to poverty. Jesus said that we would always have the poor with us. You can win your own personal war against poverty. But you will have to rely on God, and on yourself. The government is not going to help you. Do not expect anyone else to pay your way through life. Our government has become one massive Ponzi scheme. Politicians buy votes from the poor with their own money. "Vote for us," they say, "we will take money from the rich and give it to you." After they are elected, they take money from everyone and spend it on whatever they please. That is how the world works.

The poor spend everything they have on survival.

> The strong man's wealth is his strong city: the destruction of the poor is their poverty. (Proverbs 10:15)

You can escape poverty by applying God's word to your life.

**Poverty and shame shall be to him that refuseth instruction:.... (Proverbs 13:18)**

Every job produces an income. A small paycheck is better than no paycheck.

**In all labor there is profit: but the talk of the lips tendeth only to penury. (Proverbs 14:23)**

God-fearing people have a better quality of life. Wealth without God brings trouble.

**Better is little with the fear of the Lord, than great treasure and trouble therewith. (Proverbs 15:16)**

No amount of money is worth leaving God behind.

**Better is a little with righteousness, than great revenues without right. (Proverbs 16:8)**

Everyone wants to be friends with the rich. It will cost you money to befriend the poor.

**Wealth maketh many friends; but the poor is separated from his neighbor. . . .All the brethren of the poor do hate him: how much more do his friends go far from him? He pursueth them with words, yet they are wanting to him. (Proverbs 19:4,7)**

A leading cause of poverty is sleeping instead of working.

**Love not sleep, lest thou come to poverty: open thine eyes, and thou shalt be satisfied with bread. (Proverbs 20:13)**

Lazy people spend more time sleeping than they do working.

> Yet a little sleep, a little slumber, a little folding of the hands to sleep: So shall thy poverty come as one that travelleth; and thy want as an armed man. (Proverbs 24:33–34)

Pursuing pleasure will keep you poor.

> He that loveth pleasure shall be a poor man: he that loveth wine and oil shall not be rich. (Proverbs 21:17)

Overindulging in food, drink, and sleep will consume all of your resources.

> For the drunkard and the glutton shall come to poverty: and drowsiness shall clothe a man with rags. (Proverbs 23:21)

The best way to increase your income is to work hard at the job you have.

> He that tilleth his land shall have plenty of bread: but he that followeth after vain persons shall have poverty enough. (Proverbs 28:19)

God is willing to provide you everything you need. Everything certainly includes money.

> He that spareth not his own Son, but delivered him up for us all, how shall he not with him also freely give us all things? (Romans 8:32)

## PRIDE

You cannot see your own pride, even though it is obvious to everyone around you. When I was full of pride, I didn't know it. God gives grace to the humble, not the proud. I expected God to deliver me from trouble on my job at the Post Office, but I was limiting what God could do for me by not obeying his commandment to love others. He did not leave me, but I went off on my own to fight a battle without him. I lost that battle. This was before I learned about humility. I had to recognize the fact that God makes all the rules. I could either follow them or not. I had to find out the hard way that I was full of pride. Nobody could tell me anything. Judge yourself to see if you are full of pride. Here are some of the symptoms: Do you think that you're better than other people? Do you think that you're smarter than other people? Do you try to force other people to do what you want? Do you think that it is okay for you to break God's rules? Do you think that you can get along without God's help? If you have answered "yes" to any of these questions, you are full of pride. You must humble yourself before God.

God gives you the power to get wealth. He wants you to acknowledge his contribution to your success. It is a big mistake to think that you succeeded without God's help.

> **Beware that thou forget not the Lord thy God, in not keeping his commandments, and his judgments, and his statutes, which I command thee this day: . . .And thou say in thine heart, My power and the might of my hand hath gotten me this wealth. But thou shalt remember the Lord thy God: for it is he that giveth thee power to get wealth, that he may establish his covenant which he sware unto thy fathers, as it is this day. (Deuteronomy 8:11, 17–18)**

Some people think that they can remain anonymous with God, and if they don't bother him, he won't bother them. They think they can do whatever they please, but God sees everything. They do not know how merciful he is, and that they cannot live without him.

> The wicked, through the pride of his countenance, will not seek after God: God is not in all his thoughts. His ways are always grievous; thy judgments are far above out of his sight: as for all his enemies, he puffeth at them. He hath said in his heart, I shall not be moved: for I shall never be in adversity....He hath said in his heart, God hath forgotten: he hideth his face; he will never see it. (Psalm 10:4–6,11)

If you continue to be full of pride, God will bring you down to nothing.

> The Lord will destroy the house of the proud: . . .(Proverbs 15:25)

God really hates pride. There is nothing a proud man can do to prevent being punished by God.

> Every one that is proud in heart is an abomination to the Lord: though hand join in hand, he shall not be unpunished. (Proverbs 16:5)

Everyone who continues to live his life in pride will be destroyed.

> Pride goeth before destruction, and a haughty spirit before a fall. Better it is to be of a humble spirit with the lowly, than to divide the spoil with the proud. (Proverbs 16:18–19)

God spoke to Satan through his prophet Isaiah. He told him that it was his pride that caused him to fall. Satan thought that he was equal to God.

> How art thou fallen from heaven, O Lucifer, son of the morning! How art thou cut down to the ground, which didst weaken the nations! For thou hast said in thine heart, I will ascend into heaven, I will exalt my throne above the stars

> of God: I will sit also upon the mount of the congregation, in the sides of the north: I will ascend above the heights of the clouds: I will be like the most High. Yet thou shalt be brought down to hell, to the sides of the pit. They that see thee shall narrowly look upon there, and consider thee, saying, Is this the man that made the earth to tremble, that did shake kingdoms; that made the world as a wilderness; and destroyed the cities thereof; that opened not the house of his prisoners. (Isaiah 14:6–7)

Here Paul summarizes the attitude of humility: Never think of yourself as being better than anyone else. Follow Jesus' example of serving others and building them up.

> Let nothing be done through strife or vainglory; but in lowliness of mind let each esteem other better than themselves. (Philippians 2:3)

Here is another test for pride. Have you replaced the Lord's doctrine with your own? Have you modified God's word to fit your own agenda? Presuming to change God's word is attempting to making yourself equal to him.

> If any man teach otherwise, and consent not to wholesome words, even the words of our Lord Jesus Christ, and to the doctrine which is according to godliness; he is proud, knowing nothing. (1 Timothy 6:3–4)

## REBELLION

Rebelling against God's word is the same as defying him. God always punishes rebellion. A third of the angels joined Satan in his rebellion. They were thrown out of heaven with him. Adam and Eve were thrown out of the Garden of Eden because of their rebellion against God. Do not let Satan deceive you into rebellion. Stay in fellowship with God and obey him.

Cain was angry because God accepted his brother's sacrifice. He knew what God expected, but he refused to do it. God warned Cain that if he did not rule over sin, sin would rule over him. He ignored God's warning and committed the world's first murder.

> **And the Lord said unto Cain, Why art thou wroth? And why is thou countenance fallen? If thou doest well, shalt thou not be accepted? And if thou doest not well, sin lieth at the door. And unto thee shall be his desire, and thou shalt rule over him. (Genesis 4:6–7)**

God's people sent ten spies into the land of Canaan. Joshua and Caleb were the only ones who encouraged the people to have faith in God. The others were afraid of the Canaanites and gave a negative report. The Children of Israel chose to be motivated by fear instead of faith and rejected the word of the Lord. All of this took place at a place called Kadesh-barnea.

> **If the Lord delight in us, then he will bring us into this land, and give it us; a land which floweth with milk and honey. Only rebel not ye against the Lord, neither fear ye the people of the land; for they are bread for us: their defense is departed from them, and the Lord is with us: fear them not. But all the congregation bade stone them with stones. (Numbers 14:8–10)**

Years later, just before they entered the Promised Land, Moses told the Children of Israel about the time their fathers rebelled against God at Kadesh-barnea.

> **Likewise when the Lord sent you from Kadesh-barnea, saying, Go up and possess the land which I have given**

> you; then ye rebelled against the commandment of the Lord your God, and ye believed him not, nor hearkened to his voice. Ye have been rebellious against the Lord from the day that I knew you. (Deuteronomy 9:23–24)

God said not to consult any practitioner of the occult. He requires his people to communicate with him instead of some other spirit. This passage describes what happened when Saul, the King of Israel, consulted the Witch of Endor. This was an act of rebellion against God, because Saul knew that God prohibited his people from consulting anyone who communicates with familiar spirits.

> And Samuel said, Hath the Lord as great delight in burnt offerings and sacrifices, as in obeying the voice of the Lord? Behold, to obey is better than sacrifice, and to hearken than the fat of rams. For rebellion is as the sin of witchcraft, and stubbornness is as iniquity and idolatry. (1 Samuel 15:22–23)

Evil people love to rebel against authority, but it brings God's judgment upon them.

> An evil man seeketh only rebellion: therefore a cruel messenger shall be sent against him. (Proverbs 17:11)

## RESPECT OF PERSONS

The world is full of big shots—kings, presidents, billionaires, CEO's, senators, generals, admirals, judges, movie stars and other celebrities. And rank does have its privileges. These people are treated like gods in our society, but they do not receive any special treatment from God. He is no respecter of persons. He expects you to be like Jesus. That is the standard of success in the kingdom of God.

The Jews did not associate with Gentiles, but God revealed to

Peter in a vision that the good news of Jesus Christ is for everyone. God will accept everyone who believes in Jesus.

> Then Peter opened his mouth, and said, Of a truth I perceive that God is no respecter of persons: but in every nation he that feareth him, and worketh righteousness, is accepted with him. (Acts 10:34)

People who refuse to do what is right go from one problem to another. If you do what is right, you will have peace.

> But unto them that are contentious, and do not obey the truth, but obey unrighteousness, indignation and wrath, Tribulation and anguish, upon every soul of man that doeth evil, of the Jew first, and also of the Gentile; but glory, honor, and peace, to every man that worketh good, to the Jew first, and also to the Gentile: for there is no respect of persons with God. (Romans 2:8–11)

Everyone gets the same deal. You reap what you sow, no matter who you are.

> But he that doeth wrong shall receive for the wrong which he hath done: and there is no respect of persons. (Colossians 3:25)

Be like Jesus and treat everyone the same, whether they are rich or poor.

> My brethren, have not the faith of our Lord Jesus Christ, the Lord of glory, with respect of persons. For if there come unto your assembly a man with a gold ring, in goodly apparel, and there come in also a poor man in vile raiment; and ye have respect to him that weareth the gay clothing,

> and say unto him, Sit thou here in a good place; and say to the poor, Stand thou there, or sit here under my footstool: are ye not then partial in yourselves and are become judges of evil thoughts? (James 2:1–4)

When you are keeping the Love Commandment, do not exclude anyone. They are all people for whom Jesus died.

> If ye fulfill the royal law according to the scripture, Thou shalt love thy neighbor as thyself, ye do well: but if ye have respect to persons, ye commit sin, and are convinced of the law as transgressors. (James 2:8–9)

The people of the world will fawn over everyone who has money.

> These are murmurers, complainers, walking after their own lusts; and their mouth speaketh great swelling words, having men's person in admiration because of advantage. (Jude 16)

## SIN

Satan's main strategy is to dispute the word of God. If you buy one of his ideas, you are agreeing with him that God is a liar. Specific acts of rebellion against God are only a reflection of the sin that is in your heart. Before you were born again, you had the heart of a sinner. The Lord gave you a new heart, one that desires to please him. He will not bless you if you are rebelling against him. The Holy Spirit in you is more powerful than your flesh, but he will not violate your will. He will reveal your sins to you. As soon as you become aware of a specific sin, confess it to God. Repent of it and ask him to forgive you. Receive your forgiveness and cleansing from all unrighteousness.

God warned Cain not to let sin to rule over him. If you don't control your urge to sin, it will control you.

> If thou doest well, shalt thou not be accepted? And if thou doest not well, sin lieth at the door. And unto thee shall be his desire, and thou shalt rule over him. (Genesis 4:7)

You probably have at least one sin in your life that you would like to keep. But keeping it will cost you more than you want to pay.

> And be sure your sin will find you out. (Numbers 32:23)

God expects you to do what is right. Everything that a wicked man does is sin.

> To do justice and judgment is more acceptable to the Lord than sacrifice. A high look, and a proud heart, and the plowing of the wicked, is sin. (Proverbs 21:3–4)

Sin stops the flow of good things from God.

> But this people hath a revolting and a rebellious heart; they are revolted and gone. Neither say they in their heart, Let us now fear the Lord our God, that giveth rain, both the former and the latter, in his season: he reserveth unto us the appointed weeks of the harvest. Your iniquities have turned away these things, and your sins have withholden good things from you. (Jeremiah 5:23–25)

Do not allow sin to rule over you. The Spirit of God will empower you to overcome temptations.

> Let not sin therefore reign in your mortal body, that ye should obey it in the lusts thereof. Neither yield ye your members as instruments of unrighteousness unto sin: but yield yourselves unto God, as those that are alive from the dead, and your members as instruments of righteousness

unto God. For sin shall not have dominion over you: for ye are not under the law, but under grace. (Romans 6:12–14)

If you knowingly commit a sin, you become a servant to that sin.

Know ye not, that to whom ye yield yourselves servants to obey, his servants ye are to whom ye obey; whether of sin unto death, or of obedience unto righteousness? (Romans 6:16)

Now that you are a servant of righteousness, you have to keep yourself free from sin.

For when ye were the servants of sin, ye were free from righteousness. (Romans 6:20)

Because of Jesus, you have eternal life.

For the wages of sin is death; but the gift of God is eternal life through Jesus Christ our Lord. (Romans 6:23)

Base your life on what the word of God says, and not by the way that things appear.

For whatsoever is not of faith is sin. (Romans 14:23)

Your own lust within is what causes you to sin.

Let no man say when he is tempted, I am tempted of God: for God cannot be tempted with evil, neither tempteth he any man: but every man is tempted, when he is drawn away of his own lust, and enticed. Then when lust hath conceived, it bringeth forth sin: and sin, when it is finished, bringeth forth death. (James 1:15)

These verses explain how to receive forgiveness for sin. To "confess your sin" is to agree with God that what you are doing is a sin. When you confess your sins to him, he will forgive you and cleanse you from all unrighteousness. That is how great God is, and how merciful he is to you.

> **If we say that we have no sin, we deceive ourselves, and the truth is not in us. If we confess our sins, he is faithful and just to forgive us our sins, and to cleanse us from all unrighteousness. (1 John 1:8–9)**

The following verse is the best definition of sin. It is failing to do what you know is right.

> **Therefore to him that knoweth to do good, and doeth it not, to him it is sin. (James 4:17)**

## SNARES

Satan uses such things as anger, envy, pride, and lust as snares. They are also sins. He tries to get you to sin so that he can take you captive to do his will. He takes advantage of circumstances and "inspires" people to manipulate you through your emotions. He makes it easy for you to sin because when you sin, he can control you. People are constantly doing things to offend you. If you become offended, then you are caught in the devil's snare. If you become angry, you might retaliate against your neighbor. Then you would be operating in a lack of love toward him. Practicing negative faith produces negative events in your life.

You cannot compromise with the people of the world. Their god is the devil, and they have a different value system. They are not interested in helping you, they are trying to take advantage of you.

> **Thou shalt make no covenant with them, nor with their gods. They shall not dwell in thy land, lest they make thee**

> **sin against me: for if thou serve their gods, it will surely be a snare unto thee. (Exodus 23:32–33)**

Being in fellowship with God will keep you out of the devil's snares. The Holy Spirit will guide you away from them.

> **When my spirit was overwhelmed within me, then thou knewest my path. In the way wherein I walked have they privily laid a snare for me. (Psalm 142:3)**

Your words reveal what you believe in your heart. Your own words can ensnare you if they are inconsistent with the Bible. The things that you talk about are the things that you will get.

> **Thou art snared with the words of thy mouth, thou art taken with the words of thy mouth. (Proverbs 6:2)**

A fool is anyone who rebels against God's word. His mouth is his own worst enemy.

> **A fool's mouth is his destruction, and his lips are the snare of his soul. (Proverbs 18:7)**

Fear of what others think is another one of the devil's snares. Live your life in such a way that pleases God.

> **The fear of man bringeth a snare: but whoso putteth his trust in the Lord shall be safe. (Proverbs 29:25)**

A man who is obsessed with personal gain cannot think of anything else. He is not concerned with God or family. He is thinking about how to use others to get what he wants. God's word says to do just the opposite, to focus your attention on helping others.

> But they that will be rich fall into temptation and a snare, and into many foolish and hurtful lusts, which drown men in destruction and perdition. (1 Timothy 6:9)

Allow God's spirit to control your tongue. Say things that are positive. Say what the Bible says. Do not complain. Do not say negative things about others. Do not gossip or use profane language. Do not become involved in arguments and strife.

> For in many things we offend all. If any man offend not in word, the same is a perfect man, and able also to bridle the whole body. Behold we put bits in the horses' mouths, that they may obey us; and we turn about their whole body. Behold also the ships, which though they be so great, and are driven of fierce winds, yet are they turned about with a very small helm, whithersoever the governor listeth. Even so the tongue is a little member, and boasteth great things. Behold, how great a matter a little fire kindleth! And the tongue is a fire, a world of iniquity: so is the tongue among our members, that it defileth the whole body, and setteth on fire the course of nature; and it is set on fire of hell. (James 3:2–6)

## STRIFE

Strife is the result of the exchange of negative words. Wherever there is a lack of love, there will be strife. Worldly people are constantly arguing with each other. There are many benefits that result from seeking peace and avoiding strife. Strife is deadly. It causes many illnesses, such as high blood pressure, heart disease and stroke. It is also expensive. Our legal and political systems exist to solve problems caused by strife.

The Lord requires that you love other people. Refusing to fight with them is a way of loving them.

> **Hatred stirreth up strifes: but love covereth all sins. (Proverbs 10:12)**

The Bible says that a soft answer turns away anger. Do not answer an angry man in anger.

> **A wrathful man stirreth up strife: but he that is slow to anger appeaseth strife. (Proverbs 15:18)**

Strife is caused by people intentionally doing what is wrong. Gossiping causes strife among friends.

> **A froward man soweth strife: and a whisperer separateth chief friends. (Proverbs 16:28)**

People who are filled with pride start arguments with others.

> **He that is of a proud heart stirreth up strife. (Proverbs 28:25)**

A proud man thinks that he knows everything. He thinks that he is smarter than everyone else.

> **If any man teach otherwise, and consent not to wholesome words, even the words of our Lord Jesus Christ, and to the doctrine which is according to godliness; he is proud, knowing nothing, but doting about questions and strifes of words, whereof cometh envy, strife, railings, evil surmisings, perverse disputings of men of corrupt minds, and destitute of the truth, supposing that gain is godliness: from such withdraw thyself. (1 Timothy 6:3–5)**

Don't argue over different interpretations of the Bible in front of others. It might undermine their faith.

> Of these things put them in remembrance, charging them before the Lord that they strive not about words to no profit but to the subverting of the hearers. (2 Timothy 2:14)

God's servants must not argue with anyone about what God's word says. You are not going to promote the cause of Christ through strife.

> But foolish and unlearned questions avoid, knowing that they do gender strifes. And the servant of the Lord must not strive; but be gentle unto all men, apt to teach, patient, in meekness instructing those that oppose themselves; if God peradventure will give them repentance to the acknowledging of the truth; and that they may recover themselves out of the snare of the devil, who are taken captive by him at his will. (2 Timothy 2:23–26)

Envy and strife come from a heart that is not right toward God. God says to eliminate them from your life.

> But if ye have bitter envying and strife in your hearts, glory not, and lie not against the truth. This wisdom descendeth not from above, but is earthly, sensual, devilish. For where envying and strife is, there is confusion and every evil work. (James 3:14–16)

## SUFFERING

Suffering is part of being a Christian. It is the bad that you have to take along with the good. Jesus did not say, "Take up your bed and lie in it." He said, "Take up your cross and follow me." The suffering you will experience is nothing when compared to that of the Apostles and other Christian martyrs. They were tortured to death because of their belief in Jesus.

You will forget about your suffering when you receive part of the greatest inheritance of all time.

> The Spirit itself beareth witness with our spirit, that we are the children of God: and if children, then heirs; heirs of God, and joint-heirs with Christ; if so be that we suffer with him, that we may be also glorified together. For I reckon that the sufferings of this present time are not worthy to be compared with the glory which shall be revealed in us. (Romans 8:16–18)

The Lord will comfort you when you need it. He will provide you so much comfort that it will overflow to others.

> Blessed be God, even the Father of our Lord Jesus Christ, the Father of mercies, and the God of all comfort; who comforteth us in all our tribulation, that we may be able to comfort them which are in any trouble, by the comfort wherewith we are comforted of God. For as the sufferings of Christ abound in us, so our consolation also aboundeth by Christ. And whether we be afflicted, it is for your consolation and salvation, which is effectual in the enduring of the same sufferings which we also suffer: or whether we be comforted, it is for your consolation and salvation. And our hope of you is stedfast, knowing, that as ye are partakers of the sufferings, so shall ye be also of the consolation. (2 Corinthians 1:3–7)

Because you are a believer in Christ, you will have to experience some amount of suffering.

> For unto you it is given in the behalf of Christ, not only to believe on him, but also to suffer for his sake. (Philippians 1:29)

Suffering is something that you and Jesus have in common. Your suffering is very slight in comparison to his.

> That I might know him, and the power of his resurrection, and the fellowship of his sufferings, being made conformable unto his death. (Philippians 3:10)

The fact that you have suffered for the Lord is proof that you belong to him and that you will rule and reign with him forever.

> If we suffer, we shall also reign with him. (2 Timothy 2:12)

You might have to suffer undeservedly just as Jesus did.

> For it is better, if the will of God be so, that ye suffer for well doing, than for evil doing. (1 Peter 3:17)

When you are suffering for being a Christian, you know you are a threat to the enemy.

> But let none of you suffer as a murderer, or as a thief, or as an evildoer, or as a busybody in other men's matters. Yet if any man suffer as a Christian, let him not be ashamed; but let him glorify God on this behalf. (1 Peter 4:15–16)

The devil will use your suffering as an opportunity to defeat you. If you become offended and angry over it, he will control you, but God will relieve your suffering.

> Be sober, be vigilant; because your adversary the devil, as a roaring lion, walketh about, seeking whom he may devour: whom resist steadfast in the faith, knowing that the same afflictions are accomplished in your brethren that are in the world. But the God of all grace, who hath called us unto his eternal glory by Christ Jesus, after that ye have suffered a while, make you perfect, stablish, strengthen, settle you. (1 Peter 5:8–10)

## TEMPTATION

Jesus dealt with temptation by saying what God said on that same subject. When the Lord was hungry, Satan tempted him with bread. This is what Jesus told him: "It is written, that man shall not live by bread alone but by every word that proceedeth out of the mouth of God." You can do the same thing when you are thoroughly familiar with the Bible. You will be able to think God's thoughts and to speak his word. The Holy Spirit will bring God's word to your mind. He will strengthen you and enable you to overcome any temptation. He will provide a way for you to escape. You become a disciple of Jesus, "a disciplined one," by learning how to resist temptation.

Your old nature is predisposed to sin. That is your "flesh." Jesus said that in order to overcome temptation, you will have to pray. That is how you strengthen your spirit. Your spirit will prevail over your flesh when it is stronger than your flesh.

> **Watch and pray, that ye enter not into temptation: the spirit indeed is willing, but the flesh is weak. (Matthew 26:41)**

This is part of the Parable of the Sower. Jesus talked about people who hear the word of God but do not hold on to it. They are overcome by temptation before it has time to take root in their hearts.

> **They on the rock are they, which, when they hear, receive the word with joy; and these have no root, which for a while believe, and in time of temptation fall away. (Luke 8:13)**

You cannot resist temptation with your own will power. You must have the self-control that comes from the Holy Spirit. God will help you overcome temptation because of his great mercy.

> **There hath no temptation taken you but such as is common to man: but God is faithful, who will not suffer**

> you to be tempted above that ye are able; but will with the temptation also make a way to escape, that ye may be able to bear it. (1 Corinthians 10:13)

When you start thinking that you are invincible, you are headed for a fall because that is pride. Nobody is immune to temptation. In order to overcome it, you must have the power of God.

> Brethren, if a man be overtaken in a fault, ye which are spiritual, restore such an one in the spirit of meekness; considering thyself, lest thou also be tempted. (Galatians 6:1)

Be on guard against temptations that involve money. The power of God is not available to anyone who loves money more than God.

> But they that will be rich fall into temptation and a snare, and into many foolish and hurtful lusts, which drown men in destruction and perdition. For the love of money is the root of all evil: which while some coveted after, they have erred from the faith, and pierced themselves through with many sorrows. (1 Timothy 6:9–10)

This refers to Jesus. He is your high priest, and he is accessible to you. To "succour" means to aid or assist.

> For in that he himself hath suffered being tempted, he is able to succour them that are tempted. (Hebrews 2:18)

Jesus knows what it is like to be tempted. He has faced every temptation and overcome them all.

> For we have not an high priest which cannot be touched with the feeling of our infirmities; but was in all points tempted like as we are, yet without sin. (Hebrews 4:15)

Overcoming temptation teaches you patience. Patience is an essential part of loving your neighbor. Patience combined with faith causes you to receive what God has promised.

> **My brethren, count it all joy when ye fall into divers temptations; knowing this, that the trying of your faith worketh patience. But let patience have her perfect work, that ye may be perfect and entire, wanting nothing. (James 1:2–4)**

Stay in fellowship with God. Then resist the devil by standing on God's promises. When you are acting like Jesus, the devil will run away from you.

> **Submit yourselves therefore to God. Resist the devil and he will flee from you. (James 4:7)**

Apparently there is a special reward for every believer who overcomes temptation.

> **Blessed is the man that endureth temptation: for when he is tried, he shall receive the crown of life, which the Lord hath promised to them that love him. (James 1:12)**

Temptation does not come from God. It comes from your own lusts. When you give in to temptation, you are being led by your own flesh.

> **Let no man say when he is tempted, I am tempted of God: for God cannot be tempted with evil, neither tempteth he any man: but every man is tempted, when he is drawn away of his own lust, and enticed. Then when lust hath conceived, it bringeth forth sin: and sin, when it is finished, bringeth forth death. (James 1:13–15)**

You can depend on the Lord to watch out for you. He will keep you away from situations where you would be tempted.

> **The Lord knoweth how to deliver the godly out of temptations, and to reserve the unjust unto the day of judgment to be punished. (2 Peter 2:9)**

## THORNS

Thorns are things that prevent the word of God from working and things that hinder you from doing the will of God. The devil will do anything to stop you from bearing fruit. He has to keep you down because when people see you bearing fruit, they will know that God is working in you. That sets off a chain reaction that causes even more people to turn to God. Then God will be glorified because of your good works, and the devil will lose control of more and more of his captives.

God told his people to drive out the Canaanites. They let some of them stay. Those Canaanites became "thorns in their sides." We would call them "pains in the neck." If you continue to associate with worldly people, they will be thorns in your side.

> **But if ye will not drive out the inhabitants of the land from before you; then it shall come to pass, that those which ye let remain of them shall be pricks in your eyes, and thorns in your sides, and shall vex you in the land wherein ye dwell. Moreover it shall come to pass, that I shall do unto you, as I thought to do unto them. (Numbers 33:55–56)**

God gave his people the land of Canaan. They had to obey him in order to stay there.

> **Ye shall therefore keep all my statutes, and all my judgments, and do them: that the land, wither I bring you**

> to dwell therein, spew you not out. And ye shall not walk in the manners of the nation, which I cast out before you: for they committed all these things, and therefore I abhorred them. But I have said unto you, Ye shall inherit their land, and I will give it unto you to possess it, a land that floweth with milk and honey: I am the Lord your God, which have separated you from other people. (Leviticus 20:22–24)

Thorns also represent the cares of this world. The crown of thorns was placed on Jesus' head to mock him as being King of the Jews. It symbolizes your cares, and Jesus took them upon himself.

> Then Pilate therefore took Jesus, and scourged him. And the soldiers plaited a crown of thorns, and put it on his head, and they put on him a purple robe, and said, Hail, King of the Jews! and they smote him with their hands.... Then came Jesus forth, wearing the crown of thorns, and the purple robe. And Pilate saith unto them, behold the man! (John 19:2–3, 5)

This is another part of Jesus' "Parable of the Sower." Your heart is like a fertile field. The word of God has to compete with the other things planted there. These thorns crowd it out to keep it from growing to maturity and bearing fruit.

> And these are they which are sown among thorns; such as hear the word, and the cares of this world, and the deceitfulness of riches, and the lusts of other things entering in, choke the word, and it becometh unfruitful. (Mark 4:18–19)

Paul said that his thorn in the flesh was the messenger of Satan. Satan's messenger, the thorn, went ahead of him and incited people against him. Paul had trouble everywhere he went.

**And lest I should be exalted above measure through the abundance of the revelations, there was given to me a thorn in the flesh, the messenger of Satan to buffet me, lest I should be exalted above measure. For this thing I besought the Lord thrice, that it might depart from me. And he said unto me, My grace is sufficient for thee: for my strength is made perfect in weakness. Most gladly therefore will I rather glory in my infirmities, that the power of Christ may rest upon me. (2 Corinthians 12:7–9)**

## TROUBLE

God has promised that if you will call on him, he will deliver you from trouble. This is only for those who believe in him. People in distress will cry out, "Oh, my God," even when they do not know him. He cannot help the ones who worship other gods.

God's people had turned away from him, but they still expected him to deliver them from trouble. He told them to call on the gods they had chosen. Those phony gods could not do anything to help them. He wanted them to realize that he is the only God who was able to deliver them.

**Yet ye have forsaken me, and served other gods: wherefore I will deliver you no more. Go and cry unto the gods which ye have chosen; let them deliver you in the time of your tribulation. (Judges 10:13–14)**

According to this verse, everyone experiences trouble.

**Man that is born of woman is of few days, and full of trouble. (Job 14:1)**

If you are in trouble, do not become obsessed with your situation. Focus your attention on God's word instead. Find out everything that

God says about it. Talk to him about it. Ask him to help you and he will.

> **The Lord also will be refuge for the oppressed, a refuge in times of trouble. (Psalm 9:9)**

When the Lord hears one of his children cry out for help, he will respond.

> **This poor man cried, and the Lord heard him, and saved him out of all his troubles. (Psalm 34:6)**

The Lord will deliver you out of all your troubles. This help is available to you when you do right.

> **The righteous cry, and the Lord heareth, and delivereth them out of all their troubles. (Psalm 34:17)**

God helps those who help others.

> **Blessed is he that considereth the poor: the Lord will deliver him in time of trouble. (Psalm 41:1)**

Thankfulness is the proper attitude to have toward God. It is important that you have this attitude before trouble arrives.

> **Offer unto God thanksgiving; and pay thy vows unto the Most High: and call upon me in the day of trouble; I will deliver thee, and thou shalt glorify me. (Psalm 50:14–15)**

When God delivers you from trouble, be sure and thank him. Tell others what he has done for you.

> **Behold, God is mine helper: the Lord is with them that uphold my soul. He shall reward evil unto mine enemies:**

> cut them off in thy truth. I will freely sacrifice unto thee: I will praise thy name, O Lord; for it is good. For he hath delivered me out of all trouble: and mine eye hath seen his desire upon mine enemies. (Psalm 54:4–7)

This is God's promise to everyone who loves him. Loving God means keeping his commandments.

> Because he hath set his love upon me, therefore will I deliver him: I will set him on high, because he hath known my name. He shall call upon me, and I will answer him: I will be with him in trouble; I will deliver him, and honor him. With long life will I satisfy him, and show him my salvation. (Psalm 91:14–16)

God says you are righteous. You are becoming what he says you are.

> The righteous is delivered out of trouble, and the wicked cometh in his stead. (Proverbs 11:8)

God's blessing gives you riches without sorrow. God's wisdom brings wealth. But the money a wicked man has causes him trouble.

> In the house of the righteous is much treasure: but in the revenues of the wicked is trouble. (Proverbs 15:6)

God-fearing people have a better quality of life than rich people who do not know God.

> Better is little with the fear of the Lord than great treasure and trouble therewith. (Proverbs 15:16)

If you are always thinking about money, you are not thinking about your family.

> **He that is greedy of gain troubleth his own house; but he that hateth gifts shall live. (Proverbs 15:27)**

The difficulties in your life are caused by the things you say.

> **Whoso keepeth his mouth and his tongue keepeth his soul from troubles. (Proverbs 21:23)**

Jesus spoke these words for your benefit, to let you know that he is on your side.

> **These things have I spoken to you, that in me ye might have peace. In the world ye shall have tribulation: but be of good cheer; I have overcome the world. (John 16:33)**

The life of a believer is not an easy life. But the Lord himself watches over you. He will help you and deliver you in times of trouble.

> **But we have this treasure in earthen vessels, that the excellency of the power may be of God, and not of us. We are troubled on every side, yet not distressed; we are perplexed, but not in despair; persecuted, but not forsaken; cast down, but not destroyed; always bearing about in the body the dying of the Lord Jesus, that the life also of Jesus might be made manifest in our body. (2 Corinthians 4:7–10)**

## UNBELIEF

When God led the Children of Israel out of Egypt, he intended to take them directly to the Promised Land. When he ordered them to go into the land, they refused to obey him. Their story represents your spiritual journey through life. Egypt represents the world. They spent forty years wandering in the desert. If they had obeyed God, they could have been living in a place of prosperity. Your spiritual life is just like that. God provides you the things you need to survive, just as he did for them. But it is not God's plan for you that you merely survive. He wants you to be in the place where you will prosper. That is the Promised Land, a land that flows with milk and honey. Unbelief is a lack of faith in God's word. That is what keeps you in the desert. Faith is acting on what God said. You cannot enter the Promised Land without faith in God.

The people had seen miracles, but they still doubted God. He considered destroying the whole nation after they insulted him with their murmuring and complaining.

> And he called the name of the place Massah, and Meribah, because of the chiding of the Children of Israel, and because they tempted the Lord, saying, Is the Lord among us, or not? (Exodus 17:7)

God told Abraham that he would be the father of many nations. Even though his wife was barren and they were both very old, Abraham believed that what God said was true. That is why his faith is legendary. He is the patriarch of the world's three major religions, Christianity, Judaism, and Islam. Christians are not the literal children of Abraham like the others. You are a child of Abraham spiritually, because, like him you believe God's word is true.

> He staggered not at the promise of God through unbelief; but was strong in faith, giving glory to God; and being fully persuaded that, what he had promised, he was able also to perform. And therefore it was imputed to him for righteousness. Now it was not written for his sake alone, that it was imputed to him; but for us also, to whom it shall be imputed, if we believe on him that raised up Jesus our Lord from the dead. (Romans 4:20–24)

The way you are inside colors all your thoughts. An honest man thinks everyone is honest. Wicked people think everyone is wicked. People who don't know God do not trust him.

> Unto the pure all things are pure: but unto them that are defiled and unbelieving is nothing pure; but even their mind and conscience is defiled. They profess that they know God; but in works they deny him, being abominable, and disobedient, and unto every good work reprobate. (Titus 1:15–16)

Do not follow the negative example of the Children of Israel. They were overcome by unbelief. They provoked God to such an extent that he considered destroying them.

> Take heed, brethren, lest there be in any of you an evil heart of unbelief, in departing from the living God. But exhort one another daily, while it is called Today; lest any of you be hardened through the deceitfulness of sin. For we are made partakers of Christ, if we hold the beginning of our confidence steadfast unto the end; while it is said, Today if ye will hear his voice, harden not your hearts, as in the provocation. For some, when they had heard, did provoke: howbeit not all that came out of Egypt by Moses. (Hebrews 3:12–16)

Most Christians never follow the leadership of God. They spend their whole lives in the desert because of unbelief. If you want to succeed where others fail, you will have to put your faith in God's word. You will have to overcome fear by trusting God. You will have to believe that he is faithful and that his word is true. You will have to obey him from the heart.

> But with whom was he grieved forty years? Was it not with them that had sinned, whose carcasses fell in the wilderness? And to whom sware he that they should not enter into his rest, but to them that believed not? So we see that they could not enter in because of unbelief. (Hebrews 3:17–19)

## UNFORGIVENESS

Your flesh tells you if somebody hurts you, hurt him back. God's ways are higher than your ways and they are more effective. He expects you to be like him and not to retaliate against people. God's way of living will cause you to succeed in life. Giving in to your flesh will cause you to fail. God's principle of sowing and reaping ensures that you will get back what you give out. If you forgive, you will be forgiven. If you sow unforgivness, you will reap unforgiveness. You can obey God's word and win, or you can oppose it and lose. If you get caught in the snare of unforgiveness, do not expect to receive anything from God.

Forgiving others is extremely important. It is a part of loving them, as you are commanded by God to do. It is always in your best interest to forgive.

> **Therefore if thou bring thy gift to the altar, and there rememberest that thy brother hath aught against thee; leave there thy gift before the altar, and go thy way; first be reconciled to thy brother, and then come and offer thy gift. (Matthew 5:23–24)**

This portion of The Lord's Prayer says that your forgiveness from God is contingent upon your forgiving others.

> **And forgive us our debts, as we forgive our debtors. (Matthew 6:12)**

This parable illustrates what God expects from you. The man's debt was so large that he could not pay it. You were unable to pay your own sin debt. God has forgiven you for your sins, and he requires that you forgive everyone who sins against you. The point of the story is that you know what forgiveness feels like. Go and give that feeling to others.

> **And when he had begun to reckon, one was brought unto him, which owed him ten thousand talents. But forasmuch**

> as he had not to pay, his lord commanded him to be sold, and his wife, and children, and all that he had, and payment to be made. The servant therefore fell down, and worshipped him, saying, Lord, have patience with me, and I will pay thee all. Then the lord of that servant was moved with compassion, and loosed him and forgave him the debt. But the same servant went out, and found one of his fellowservants, which owed him an hundred pence: and he laid hands on him, and took him by the throat, saying, Pay me that thou owest. And his fellowservant fell down at his feet, and besought him, saying, Have patience with me, and I will pay thee all. And he would not: but went and cast him into prison, till he should pay the debt....And his lord was wroth, and delivered him to the tormentors, till he should pay all that was due unto him. So likewise shall my heavenly Father do also unto you, if ye from your hearts forgive not every one his brother their trespasses. (Matthew 18:25–30,34–35)

The following four passages confirm that forgiveness is not optional. It is mandatory. God is not going to slap you down every time you make a mistake. He expects you to do the same and overlook the shortcomings of others.

> For if ye forgive men their trespasses, your heavenly Father will also forgive you: but if ye forgive not men their trespasses, neither will your Father forgive your trespasses. (Matthew 6:14–15)

> When ye stand praying, forgive, if ye have ought against any: that your Father also which is in heaven may forgive you your trespasses. (Mark 11:25)

> And forgive us our sins; for we also forgive every one that is indebted to us. (Luke 11:4)

**Forbearing one another, and forgiving one another, if any man have a quarrel against any: even as Christ forgave you, so also do ye. (Colossians 3:13)**

## UNJUST GAIN

The Bible says that the love of money is the root of all evil. Unjust gain is taking people's money and giving them nothing in return. Unjust gain comes from taking advantage of people in distress, the poor, and the simple. Just because something is legal, does not make it right. Exorbitant interest on credit card debt is a one example. God calls it "usury," and he is against it. The Bible tells us that God will avenge the victims of financial predators. That is bad news for financial predators.

Riches that you get from a source other than God cause sorrow.

**The blessing of the Lord, it maketh rich, and he addeth no sorrow with it. (Proverbs 10:22)**

Money that is not legitimately earned will disappear quickly. A steady paycheck is better than an occasional windfall.

**Wealth gotten by vanity shall be diminished: but he that gathereth by labor shall increase. (Proverbs 13:11)**

Doing right brings financial rewards. Evil things happen to evil people.

**In the house of the righteous is much treasure: but in the revenues of the wicked is trouble. (Proverbs 15:6)**

Man's wisdom is to pile up money for yourself. God's wisdom is to be a blessing to others. When you are a blessing to others, God will bless you.

> Labor not to be rich: cease from thine own wisdom. (Proverbs 23:4)

The man who gets money by oppressing the poor will leave it for someone else.

> He that by usury and unjust gain increaseth his substance, he shall gather it for him that will pity the poor. (Proverbs 28:8)

People who accumulate riches dishonestly will not have time to enjoy them.

> As the partridge sitteth on eggs, and hatcheth them not; so he that getteth riches, and not by right, shall leave them in the midst of his days, and at his end shall be a fool. (Jeremiah 17:11)

Benefiting from the work of others without paying them is the same as stealing from them.

> Woe unto him that buildeth his house by unrighteousness, and his chambers by wrong; that useth his neighbor's service without wages, and giveth him not for his work. (Jeremiah 22:13)

Every man has to earn his own way in life. It is morally wrong to take other people's money and give them nothing in return.

> Neither did we eat any man's bread for nought; but wrought with labor and travail night and day, that we might not be chargeable to any of you: not because we have not power, but to make ourselves an example unto you to follow us. For even when we were with you, this we commanded you, that if any would not work,

> neither should he eat. For we hear that are some which walk among you disorderly, working not at all, but are busybodies. Now them that are such we command and exhort by our Lord Jesus Christ, that with quietness they work, and eat their own bread. (2 Thessalonians 3:8–12)

God sees everything. If you take advantage of other people financially, it is going to cost you.

> Behold, the hire of the laborers who have reaped down your fields, which is of you kept back by fraud, crieth; and the cries of them which have reaped are entered into the ears of the Lord of Sabaoth. (James 5:4)

## WORKS OF THE FLESH

The "flesh" is your old sinful nature. Non-believers do what their flesh tells them. They don't have any other option. You get to choose. Are you going to be controlled by your flesh? Or, are you going to obey the Spirit of God within you? You cannot trust your own flesh. It thinks only of itself and it is never satisfied. It will do anything to get what it wants. It wants the things that God says you cannot have. You have to crucify your flesh by obeying the Spirit of God. Figuratively speaking, you are putting your flesh to death.

Following Jesus mainly consists of denying yourself. "Losing your life" means giving up the sins you used to love.

> And when he had called the people unto him with his disciples also, he said unto them, Whosoever will come after me, let him deny himself, and take up his cross and follow me. For whosoever will save his life shall lose it; but whosoever shall lose his life for my sake and the gospels, the same shall save it. For what shall it profit a man, if he shall gain the whole world, and lose his own soul? Or what shall a man give in exchange for his soul? (Mark 8:34–37)

"Make no provision for the flesh" means do not do what your flesh tells you.

> **The night is far spent, the day is at hand: let us therefore cast off the works of darkness, and let us put on the armor of light. Let us walk honestly, as in the day; not in rioting and drunkenness, not in chambering and wantonness, not in strife and envying. But put ye on the Lord Jesus Christ, and make not provision for the flesh, to fulfill the lusts thereof. (Romans 13:12–14)**

These are groups of people who are dominated by their flesh. Paul said to the Corinthians, "and such were some of you." True followers of Jesus do not allow their flesh to control them.

> **Know ye not that the unrighteous shall not inherit the kingdom of God? Be not deceived: neither fornicators, nor idolaters, nor adulterers, nor effeminate, nor abusers of themselves with mankind, nor thieves, nor covetous, nor drunkards, nor revilers, nor extortioners, shall inherit the kingdom of God. And such were some of you: but ye are washed, but ye are sanctified, but ye are justified in the name of the Lord Jesus, and by the Spirit of our God. (1 Corinthians 6:9–11)**

You overcome the lust of the flesh by following the promptings of the Holy Spirit. This is what it means to walk in the Spirit.

> **This I say then, Walk in the Spirit, and ye shall not fulfill the lust of the flesh. (Galatians 5:16)**

This is a list of works of the flesh. If you continue in these sins, you will lose what God has provided for you.

> Now the works of the flesh are manifest, which are these; adultery, fornication, uncleanness, lasciviousness, idolatry, witchcraft, hatred, variance, emulations, wrath, strife, seditions, heresies, envyings, murders, drunkenness, revellings, and such like: of the which I tell you before, as I have also told you in time past, that they which do such things shall not inherit the kingdom of God. (Galatians 5:19–21)

Satan is "the prince of the power of the air." He manipulates and controls everyone who is driven by his own lusts.

> Wherein in time past ye walked according to the course of this world, according to the prince of the power of the air, the spirit that now worketh in the children of disobedience: among whom also we all had our conversation in times past in the lusts of our flesh, fulfilling the desires of the flesh and of the mind; and were by nature the children of wrath, even as others. (Ephesians 2:2–3)

The works of the flesh were a big part of your old life, but you have a new life now. You have new desires and new priorities.

> For the time past of our life may suffice us to have wrought the will of the Gentiles, when we walked in lasciviousness, lusts, excess of wine, revellings, banquetings, and abominable idolatries; wherein they think it strange that ye run not with them to the same excess of riot, speaking evil of you: who shall give account to him that is ready to judge the quick and the dead. (1 Peter 4:3–5)

God will never tempt you. He helps you to overcome temptation. Obey God instead of your flesh.

> The Lord knoweth how to deliver the godly out of temptations, and to reserve the unjust unto the day of judgment to be punished: but chiefly them that walk after the flesh in the lust of uncleanness, and despise government. Presumptuous are they, self-willed, they are not afraid to speak evil of dignities. (2 Peter 2:9–10)

## WORRY

The devil uses worry to control your mind. While you are worrying, you are squandering your most valuable resources, your time and your attention. Worrying is the opposite of trusting in God. People think that if they knew the future, they would do the right thing today. If you will do God's will today, he will take care of your future. You determine your own destiny. If you are expecting bad things to happen, that is what you will get. Worry is just another form of fear. Fear works like faith in reverse, to bring about the things you fear. Faith is much better. It brings about the good things you desire. As you develop your skills in loving other people, fear will disappear. And God will protect you from harm and deliver you from trouble.

Always remember that Jesus is God. There is nothing that is too hard for him. And, at the same time, he is your friend.

> Be still, and know that I am God. (Psalms 46:10)

Do not be affected by the actions of others.

> Rest in the Lord, and wait patiently for him: fret not thyself because of him who prospereth in his way, because of the man who brings evil devices to pass. Cease from anger, and forsake wrath: fret not thyself in any wise to do evil. For evildoers shall be cut off: but those who wait upon the Lord, they shall inherit the earth. (Psalms 37:7–9)

Tell the Lord about everything that concerns you. Ask him to intervene in your situation and he will.

> Cast thy burden upon the Lord, and he shall sustain thee: he shall never suffer the righteous to be moved. (Psalm 55:22)

"Take no thought," means to take no anxious thought. Focus your attention on meeting the needs of others. Do not be obsessed with the things you need. God will provide them for you.

> Therefore I say unto you, Take no thought for your life, what ye shall eat, or what ye shall drink; nor yet for your body, what ye shall put on. Is not the life more than meat, and the body than raiment? Behold the fowls of the air: for they sow not, neither do they reap, nor gather into barns; yet your heavenly Father feedeth them. Are ye not much better than they? Which of you by taking thought can add one cubit unto his stature? And why take ye thought for raiment? Consider the lilies of the field, how they grow; they toil not, neither do they spin: and yet I say unto you, that even Solomon in all his glory was not arrayed like one of these. Wherefore, if God so clothe the grass of the field, which today is, and tomorrow is cast into the oven, shall he not much more clothe you, O ye of little faith? (Matthew 6:25–30)

Do not heap up things for yourself. Obey God in everything. When you are busy doing his will, he will provide the things you need.

> Therefore take no thought, saying, What shall we eat? or, What shall we drink? or, Wherewithal shall we be clothed? (For after all these things do the Gentiles seek:) For your heavenly Father knoweth that ye have need of all these

> things. But seek ye first the kingdom of God, and his righteousness; and all these things shall be added unto you. Take therefore no thought for the morrow: for the morrow shall take thought for the things of itself. Sufficient unto the day is the evil thereof. (Matthew 6:31–34)

This is from Jesus' "Parable of the Sower." The seed is the word of God. It is planted in a heart that is filled with cares. Cares in the heart are like weeds in the garden that suck up all the resources. They choke the word and keep that believer from bearing fruit.

> He also that received seed among the thorns is he that heareth the word; and the care of this world, and the deceitfulness of riches, choke the word, and he becometh unfruitful. (Matthew 13:22)

God gave you a gift of inestimable value. Why would he be stingy with things that are worth much less? "All things" would certainly include your material needs.

> He that spared not his own Son, but delivered him up for us all, how shall he not with him also freely give us all things? (Romans 8:32)

God says not to be anxious about anything. Ask him for what you need and he will give you peace.

> Be careful for nothing; but in every thing by prayer and supplication with thanksgiving let your requests be made known unto God. And the peace of God, which passeth all understanding, shall keep your hearts and minds through Christ Jesus. (Philippians 4:6–7)

God has promised that he will provide you everything you need.

> **But my God shall supply all your need according to his riches in glory by Christ Jesus. (Philippians 4:19)**

Exercise will benefit you physically. Being like Jesus will get you everything.

> **For bodily exercise profiteth little: but godliness is profitable unto all things, having promise of the life that now is, and of that which is to come. (1 Timothy 4:8)**

God said that he will never leave you nor forsake you. He will provide the things you need. Be happy with what God gives you.

> **Let your conversation be without covetousness; and be content with such things as ye have: for he hath said, I will never leave thee, nor forsake thee. (Hebrews 13:5)**

If you ask God for something and are not motivated by love, he will deny your request.

> **Ye ask, and receive not, because ye ask amiss, that ye may consume it upon your lusts. (James 4:3)**

God will lift you up, but he requires you to humble yourself first. Humbling yourself before God means honoring him by doing what his word says.

> **Humble yourselves therefore under the mighty hand of God, that he may exalt you in due time: casting all your care upon him; for he careth for you. (1 Peter 5:6–7)**

PART FIVE

# Life's Losers

**For what shall it profit a man, if he shall gain the whole world, and lose his own soul? (Mark 8:36)**

The people in the following groups have some things in common. They despise being governed. They refuse to follow rules. They will not do what God or anyone else tells them to do. They have an eagerness to do whatever they please. They have traded their souls for the things they enjoy, such as alcohol, drugs, and adultery. They have lost the gifts and rewards God had for them. They are destroying their own lives and the lives of the people they love. They do not realize that these addictions are merely symptoms of their real problem, which is sin. Sin is in their hearts. They cannot save themselves with their own will power. Only the Holy Spirit has the power to change their hearts.

If you find yourself in one of the following categories, get in touch with Jesus. He will bring you out of your captivity. You can see that you are on the road to destruction. All you have to do is to turn around and go the other way. Repentance is nothing more than changing your mind and changing your direction. It is making the choice to go God's way. The Holy Spirit will empower you to overcome all your addictions. You supply the willingness to get rid of them. You can control the things in your life, instead of being controlled by them. You can take back the control of your soul, your mind, your emotions, and your will.

## ADULTERERS

Adultery is the general term for all sexual activity outside of marriage. Most people have some experience with it in their youth, but adulterers are those who make it a way of life. Adultery destroys marriages and families. It is devastating to everyone connected to the adulterers, especially their children. The Lord will forgive adultery just like he forgives any other sins. But his forgiveness does not eliminate the destruction that it causes.

Sarah was a beautiful woman. Abraham was afraid that King Abimelech would kill him to obtain her if he knew that he was her husband. So he told the king that she was his sister. God revealed this deception to Abimelech in a dream. God also told him that if he had sexual relations with a married woman, it would have cost him his life.

> And Abraham journeyed from thence toward the south country, and dwelled between Kadesh and Shur, and sojourned in Gerar. And Abraham said of Sarah his wife, She is my sister: and Abimelech king of Gerar sent, and took Sarah. But God came to Abimelech in a dream by night, and said to him, Behold, thou art but a dead man, for the woman which thou hast taken; for she is a man's wife. But Abimelech had not come near her: and he said, Lord, wilt thou slay also a righteous nation? Said he not unto me, She is my sister? and she, even she herself said, He is my brother: in the integrity of my heart and innocency of my hands have I done this. And God said unto him in a dream, Yea, I know that thou didst this in the integrity of thy heart; for I also withheld thee from sinning against me: therefore suffered I thee not to touch her. Now therefore restore the man his wife; for he is a prophet, and he shall pray for thee, and thou shalt live: and if thou restore her not, know thou that thou shalt surely die, thou, and all that are thine. (Genesis 20:1–7)

There is a connection between adultery and death. Adulterers are setting themselves up for death.

> And the man that committeth adultery with another man's wife, even he that committeth adultery with his neighbor's wife, the adulterer and the adulteress shall surely be put to death. (Leviticus 20:10)

This is God's word to men. Stay away from the promiscuous woman. She will separate you from everything you have, your money and your soul.

> For the lips of a strange woman drop as an honeycomb, and her mouth is smoother than oil: but her end is bitter as wormwood, sharp as a two-edged sword. Her feet go down to death; her steps take hold on hell. Lest thou shouldest ponder the path of life, her ways are moveable, that thou canst not know them. Hear me now therefore, O ye children, and depart not from the words of my mouth. Remove thy way far from her, and come not nigh the door of her house: lest thou give thine honor unto others, and thy years unto the cruel: lest strangers be filled with thy wealth; and thy labors be in the house of a stranger; and thou mourn at the last, when thy flesh and thy body are consumed, and say, How have I hated instruction, and my heart despised reproof; and have not obeyed the voice of my teachers, nor inclined mine ear to them that instructed me! (Proverbs 5:6–13)

This is God's warning that adultery never goes unpunished.

> Lust not after her beauty in thine heart; neither let her take thee with her eyelids. For by means of a whorish woman a man is brought to a piece of bread: and the adulteress

> will hunt for the precious life. Can a man take fire in his bosom, and his clothes not be burned? Can one go upon hot coals, and his feet not be burned? So he that goeth in to his neighbor's wife; whosoever toucheth her shall not be innocent. (Proverbs 6:25–29)

An understanding of God's word will keep you from adultery.

> But whoso committeth adultery with a woman lacketh understanding: he that doeth it destroyeth his own soul. (Proverbs 6:32)

God said that his people perish for lack of knowledge. The man who understands the destructiveness of adultery will avoid it.

> He goeth after her straightway, as an ox goeth to the slaughter, or as a fool to the correction of the stocks; till a dart strike through his liver; as a bird hasteth to the snare, and knoweth not that it is for his life. (Proverbs 7:22–23)

This is a picture of a foolish woman. She is selling the fantasy that sneaking around with her is an exciting adventure. It is a very costly adventure. "Simple" means naive. "Her guests are in the depths of hell" is unforgettably haunting. Once a man starts committing adultery, he usually doesn't stop.

> A foolish woman is clamorous: she is simple, and knoweth nothing. For she sitteth at the door of her house, on a seat in the high places of the city, to call passengers who go right on their ways: whoso is simple, let him turn in hither: and as for him that wanteth understanding, she saith to him, Stolen waters are sweet, and bread eaten in secret is pleasant. But he knoweth not that the dead are there; and that her guests are in the depths of hell. (Proverbs 9:13–18)

In this passage Paul instructs believers in how to conduct themselves in church. Treat older men and women as you would your parents. Treat the younger men and women as your brothers and your sisters.

> **Rebuke not an elder, but entreat him as a father; and the younger men as brethren; the older women as mothers; the younger as sisters, with all purity. (1 Timothy 5:1–2)**

Men who are controlled by their flesh are always thinking about sex.

> **Spots they are and blemishes, sporting themselves with their own deceivings while they feast with you; having eyes full of adultery, and that cannot cease from sin; beguiling unstable souls: an heart they have exercised with covetous practices; cursed children. (2 Peter 2:13–14)**

## CHILDREN OF THE DEVIL

Your behavior always reveals who you really are. You will act like your spiritual father, whether it is God or the devil. Satan's only intentions are to steal, to kill, and to destroy. His children are motivated by selfishness, and they grab everything they can for themselves. Satan is known as the Slanderer and the Accuser of the Brethren. His children falsely accuse others of the things that they actually do. They are compulsive liars and speak evil of everyone. God's children are motivated by love, just like their Father.

Jesus called the religious leaders of his day children of the devil. They said that they were children of God. If this were true, they would have recognized Jesus as the Messiah. They did not understand the truth. They only spoke their native language, which is lying. They were all liars and murderers like their spiritual father.

> **Jesus said unto them, If God were your Father, ye would love me: for I proceeded forth and came from God;**

> neither came I of myself, but he sent me. Why do ye not understand my speech? Even because ye cannot hear my word. Ye are of your father the devil, and the lusts of your father ye will do. He was a murderer from the beginning, and abode not in the truth, because there is no truth in him. When he speaketh a lie, he speaketh of his own: for he is a liar, and the father of it. And because I tell you the truth, ye believe me not. Which of you convinceth me of sin? And if I say the truth, why do ye not believe me? He that is of God heareth God's words: ye therefore hear them not, because ye are not of God. (John 8:42–47)

Satan is "the thief." Jesus said that Satan's only objectives are to steal, kill, and destroy. The devil's children do not care about anyone but themselves.

> The thief cometh not, but for to steal, and to kill, and to destroy: I am come that they might have life, and that they might have it more abundantly. (John 10:10)

Satan tries to prevent people from hearing the word of God. This passage tells what happened when a sorcerer named Bar-jesus tried to prevent Paul from teaching the word of God. Paul called Bar-jesus what he was, a child of the devil.

> And when they had gone through the isle unto Paphos, they found a certain sorcerer, a false prophet, a Jew, whose name was Bar-jesus: which was with the deputy of the country, Sergius Paulus, a prudent man; who called for Barnabas and Saul, and desired to hear the word of God. But Elymus the sorcerer (for so is his name by interpretation) withstood them, seeking to turn away the deputy from the faith. Then Saul, (who is also called Paul,) filled with the Holy Ghost, set his eyes on him, and said, O full of all subtilty and all mischief, thou child of the devil,

> thou enemy of all righteousness, wilt thou not cease to pervert the right ways of the Lord? And now, behold, the hand of the Lord is upon thee, and thou shalt be blind, not seeing the sun for a season. And immediately there fell on him a mist and a darkness; and he went about seeking some to lead him by the hand. Then the deputy, when he saw what was done, believed, being astonished at the doctrine of the Lord. (Acts 13:6–12)

When you are a child of God, you will have a desire to do right. God's word is righteousness. When you do what the Bible says, you are doing righteousness.

> Little children, let no man deceive you: he that doeth righteousness is righteous, even as he is righteous. He that committeth sin is of the devil: for the devil sinneth from the beginning. For this purpose the Son of God was manifested, that he might destroy the works of the devil. Whosoever is born of God doth not commit sin; for his seed remaineth in him: and he cannot sin, because he is born of God. In this the children of God are manifest, and the children of the devil: whosoever doeth not righteousness is not of God, neither he that loveth not his brother. (1 John 3:7–10)

## DECEIVERS

Sometimes people will take advantage of you because you are a giver. After they have worn out their welcome, they will move on to greener pastures. The people who deceive you are also deceiving themselves. They think that they are smarter than you, but they do not know about God's way of doing things. They do not know that loving their neighbor is the most productive thing they can do. God is just. He will repay them for the evil things they have done. And he will repay you for your losses.

This passage describes a confidence man. First, he gets your confidence. Then, he gets your money. You might suspect that he is lying, but you cannot be sure. Everywhere he goes, he causes problems. Then, he profits from those problems. He will eventually reap what he has sown.

> A naughty person, a wicked man, walketh with a froward mouth. He winketh with his eyes, he speaketh with his feet, he teacheth with his fingers; frowardness is in his heart, he deviseth mischief continually; he soweth discord. Therefore shall his calamity come suddenly; suddenly shall he be broken without remedy. (Proverbs 6:12–15)

"Dissembling" is concealing the truth, and "deceit" is trickery. The man who dissembles and deceives has a heart that is filled with hatred. Eventually his treachery will be revealed.

> He that hateth dissembleth with his lips, and layeth up deceit within him; when he speaketh fair, believe him not: for there are seven abominations in his heart. Whose hatred is covered by deceit, his wickedness shall be showed before the whole congregation. (Proverbs 26:24–26)

Never depend on people. They will always frustrate you and disappoint you. The Lord will never let you down. Rely on him, and on yourself.

> Take ye heed every one of his neighbor, and trust ye not in any brother: for every brother will utterly supplant, and every neighbor will walk with slanders. And they will deceive every one his neighbor, and will not speak the truth: they have taught their tongue to speak lies, and weary themselves to commit iniquity. (Jeremiah 9:4–5)

God rewards everyone who helps his children. He will judge those who take advantage of them.

> For whosoever shall give you a cup of water to drink in my name, because ye belong to Christ, verily I say unto you, he shall not lose his reward. And whosoever shall offend one of these little ones that believe in me, it is better for him that a millstone were hanged about his neck, and he were cast into the sea. (Mark 9:41–42)

There are preachers and teachers who present ideas and doctrines that do not come from the Bible.

> Now I beseech you, brethren, mark them which cause divisions and offenses contrary to the doctrine which ye have learned; and avoid them. For they that are such serve not our Lord Jesus Christ, but their own belly; and by good words and fair speeches deceive the hearts of the simple. (Romans 16:17–18)

Do not retaliate against anyone who has cheated you. God will deal with them. Hating your neighbor is the equivalent of hating God.

> For this is the will of God, . . .that no man go beyond and defraud his brother in any matter: because that the Lord is the avenger of all such, as we also have forewarned you and testified. For God hath not called us unto uncleanness, but unto holiness. He therefore that despiseth, despiseth not man, but God, who hath also given unto us his Holy Spirit. (1 Thessalonians 4: 3, 6–8)

Many teachers offer an alternative to the Gospel of Christ. They deceive people and lead them into death and hell.

> For many deceivers are entered into the world, who confess not that Jesus Christ is come in the flesh. This is a deceiver and an antichrist. (2 John 7)

## DESPISERS OF GOD'S WORD

God has given you a way to show him that you love him, by loving others. The Lord gives you the desire to love your neighbor. Then he empowers you to fulfill that desire. Worldly people only do what they want to do. They hate God, and they despise his word because it speaks against their favorite things. They love themselves and nobody else.

God rewards everyone who obeys him and destroys those who despise him and his word.

> Know therefore that the Lord thy God, he is God, the faithful God, which keepeth covenant and mercy with them that love him and keep his commandments to a thousand generations; and repayeth them that hate him to their face, to destroy them: he will not be slack to him that hateth him, he will repay him to his face. Thou shalt therefore keep the commandments, and the statutes, and the judgments, which I command thee this day, to do them. (Deuteronomy 7:9–11)

Here God is lamenting the fact that his people, Israel, did not obey him. Their hatred for God's word kept them from the life he intended them to have.

> But my people would not hearken to my voice; and Israel would none of me. So I gave them up unto their own hearts' lust: and they walked in their own counsels. Oh that my people had hearkened unto me, and Israel had walked in my ways! I should soon have subdued their enemies and turned my hand against their adversaries. The haters of the Lord should have submitted themselves unto him: but their

> time should have endured for ever. He should have fed them also with the finest of the wheat: and with honey out of the rock should I have satisfied thee. (Psalm 81:11–16)

If you despise the word of God, you will be destroyed. But if you obey it, you will be rewarded.

> Whoso despiseth the word shall be destroyed: but he that feareth the commandment shall be rewarded. (Proverbs 13:13)

God said that his people did not want to hear what he had to say because they did not want to change their lives.

> Now go, write it before them in a table, and note it in a book, that it may be for the time to come for ever and ever: that this is a rebellious people, lying children, children that will not hear the law of the Lord: which say to the seers, See not; and to the prophets, Prophesy not unto us right things, speak unto us smooth things, prophesy deceits: get you out of the way, turn aside out of the path, cause the Holy One of Israel to cease from before us. (Isaiah 30:8–11)

## THE DRUNKEN

Alcoholics are people who love alcohol more than anything or anyone else. They have surrendered their will to it. It is a cruel master. It causes them to destroy everything they have, and everyone who loves them. It usually turns out that somebody has hurt them terribly. And now they are soothing themselves with chemicals, and using them to escape. Alcohol is only one of the drugs people use to destroy themselves. In our day, there are many more of them, such as crack, cocaine, and methamphetamine.

The Holy Spirit is the greatest power in the universe. He will deliver you from drugs. He will heal you and take away your pain. He will empower you to stay clean and sober. He will give you the self-control you need. He will give you the desire to be free from your addiction. Then he will give you the power to defeat it. You have to supply the willingness to cooperate with God and contribute to your own salvation.

Drunkards think they can stop drinking anytime they want. They are just not ready yet. That is how the deception works.

> Wine is a mocker, strong drink is raging: and whosoever is deceived thereby is not wise. (Proverbs 20:1)

The Bible says not to associate with drinkers. It also says that drunkenness causes poverty.

> Be not among winebibbers; among riotous eater of flesh: for the drunkard and the glutton shall come to poverty: and drowsiness shall clothe a man with rags. (Proverbs 23:20–21)

Drunkenness causes many difficulties. It causes financial, marital, family and health problems. It is a gateway sin that leads to other destructive sins like adultery. It destroys life. It causes frustration, disappointment, anger and strife.

> Who hath woe? Who hath sorrow? Who hath contentions? Who hath babbling? Who hath wounds without cause? Who hath redness of eyes? They that tarry long at the wine; they that go to seek mixed wine. Look not thou upon the wine when it is red, when it giveth his colour in the cup, when it moveth itself aright. At the last it biteth like a serpent, and stingeth like an adder. Thine eyes shall behold strange women, and thine heart shall utter perverse things. (Proverbs 23:29–33)

People drink to forget their problems. They forget that drinking is their biggest problem. It kills them and it anesthetizes them until they die.

> **Give strong drink unto him that is ready to perish, and wine unto those that be of heavy hearts. Let him drink, and forget his poverty, and remember his misery no more. (Proverbs 31:6–7)**

Drunkards never think about God, they only think about themselves.

> **Woe unto them that rise up early in the morning, that they may follow strong drink; that continue unto night, till wine inflame them! And the harp, and the viol, the tabret, and pipe, are in their feasts: but they regard not the work of the Lord, neither consider the operation of his hands. (Isaiah 5:11–12)**

"Surfeiting" is over-eating. Jesus said not to be distracted by the things of the world. "That day" is the day he comes to take you home.

> **And take heed to yourselves, lest at any time your hearts be overcharged with surfeiting, and drunkenness, and cares of this life, and so that day come upon you unawares. (Luke 21:34)**

Jesus said to seek first the kingdom of God and all these (material) things shall be added to you. The kingdom of God is a place of fellowship with the Lord. It's where you submit yourself to his authority. It's where you're willing to do everything he tells you. It's where you're a doer of the word of God. Drunkards do not inherit the kingdom of God.

> **Know ye not that the unrighteous shall not inherit the kingdom of God? Be not deceived: neither fornicators, nor**

> **idolaters, nor adulterers, nor effeminate, nor abusers of themselves with mankind, nor thieves, nor covetous, nor drunkards, nor revilers, nor extortioners, shall inherit the kingdom of God. (1 Corinthians 6:9–10)**

## ENEMIES OF GOD

The Children of Israel became enemies of God when they rebelled against him and rejected his leadership. Isaiah 63:10 says, "But they rebelled, and vexed his holy spirit: therefore he was turned to be their enemy, and he fought against them." There seems to be a principle of God at work here. The way that you treat God determines the way that he treats you. He is a friend to his friends, and an enemy to his enemies. Jesus said to his disciples, "You are my friends, if you do whatsoever I have command you." (John 15:14) This is your opportunity to be the friend of God. If you rebel against the Lord, then you have made yourself the enemy of God.

God says that we may ask him for the things that we desire. In this Psalm, David made his prayer request to God.

> **Let God arise, let his enemies be scattered: let them also that hate him flee before him. (Psalm 68:1)**

God always repays his enemies according to their works.

> **According to their deeds, accordingly he will repay, fury to his adversaries, recompense to his enemies. (Isaiah 59:18)**

God sent his prophet Jeremiah to tell his people to do God's will. They insisted on doing things their own way. Their attitude made them enemies of God.

> **Now therefore go to, speak to the men of Judah, and to the inhabitants of Jerusalem, saying, Thus saith the Lord; Behold, I frame evil against you, and devise a device**

> against you: return ye now every one from his evil way, and make your ways and your doings good. And they said, There is no hope: but we will walk after our own devices, and we will every one do the imagination of his evil heart. (Jeremiah 18:11–12)

God pours out his wrath upon his enemies, but not upon his own children.

> God is jealous, and the Lord revengeth; and is furious; the Lord will take vengeance on his adversaries, and he reserveth wrath for his enemies. The Lord is slow to anger, and great in power, and will not at all acquit the wicked: the Lord hath his way in the whirlwind and in the storm, and the clouds are the dust of his feet. (Nahum 1:2–3)

The world opposes everything that God holds dear. You have to live in this hostile environment without becoming part of it.

> Ye adulterers and adulteresses, know ye not that the friendship of the world is enmity with God? Whosoever therefore will be a friend of the world is the enemy of God. (James 4:4)

## EVILDOERS

Serial killers, suicide bombers, and terrorists are some examples of evildoers. The Secularists believe that people are basically good, that lack of education, poverty and racism cause them to do evil things. When affluent white children started shooting their classmates at their schools in the suburbs, this did not affect their theory. Jesus said that all evil originates within the hearts of men. Only the Holy Spirit can change the human heart.

The Bible says that you will reap what you sow. Everyone who does evil will be repaid with evil.

**The Lord shall reward the doer of evil according to his wickedness. (2 Samuel 3:39)**

The Lord opposes everyone who does evil.

**The face of the Lord is against them that do evil, to cut off the remembrance of them from the earth. (Psalm 34:16)**

Evildoers usually do not live for very long.

**Fret not thyself because of evildoers, neither be thou envious against the workers of iniquity. For they shall soon be cut down like the grass, and wither as the green herb. (Psalm 37:1–2)**

Stop being angry with people, and stop retaliating against them. Wait for the Lord to correct them.

**Cease from anger; and forsake wrath: fret not thyself in any wise to do evil. For evildoers shall be cut off: but those that wait upon the Lord, they shall inherit the earth. (Psalm 37:8–9)**

People do not know that there is a direct relationship between the things they do and the things that happen to them.

**Because sentence against an evil work is not executed speedily, therefore the heart of the sons of men is fully set in them to do evil. (Ecclesiastes 8:11)**

It does not matter how bad you have been. If you will come to Jesus, he will make you part of his family, and he will give you a new kind of life.

> And when ye spread forth your hands, I will hide mine eyes from you: yea, when ye make many prayers, I will not hear: your hands are full of blood. Wash ye, make you clean, put away the evil of your doings from before mine eyes; cease to do evil; Learn to do well; seek judgment, relieve the oppressed, judge the fatherless, plead for the widow. Come now, and let us reason together, saith the Lord: though your sins be as scarlet, they shall be as white as snow; though they be red like crimson, they shall be as wool. If ye be willing and obedient, ye shall eat the good of the land: but if ye refuse and rebel, ye shall be devoured with the sword: for the mouth of the Lord hath spoken it. (Isaiah 1:15–20)

People are not basically good at heart. They are a combination of good and evil. Their hearts are deceitful and wicked before they are changed by the Holy Spirit. Everything you receive in life is based on what is in your heart.

> The heart is deceitful above all things, and desperately wicked: who can know it? I the Lord search the heart, I try the reins, even to give every man according to his ways, and according to the fruit of his doings. (Jeremiah 17:9–10)

These are Jesus' words. He says that all evil originates within the human heart.

> For from within, out of the heart of men, proceed evil thoughts, adulteries, fornications, murders, thefts, covetousness, wickedness, deceit, lasciviousness, an evil eye, blasphemy, pride, foolishness: all these evil things come from within, and defile the man. (Mark 7:20–23)

There was a barrier between you and God, but Jesus removed it. He will accept you just as you are. It is not necessary to clean yourself up before coming to Jesus.

> For God sent not his Son into the world to condemn the world; but that the world through him might be saved. He that believeth on him is not condemned: but he that believeth not is condemned already, because he hath not believed in the name of the only begotten Son of God. And this is the condemnation, that light is come into the world, and men loved darkness rather than light, because their deeds were evil. For every one that doeth evil hateth the light, neither cometh to the light, lest his deeds should be reproved. (John 3:17–20)

God's law of sowing and reaping is just as certain as the physical law of gravity.

> Be not deceived; God is not mocked: for whatsoever a man soweth, that shall he also reap. (Galatians 6:7)

Believing in Jesus does not give you a license to sin.

> But he that doeth wrong shall receive for the wrong which he hath done; and there is no respect of persons. (Colossians 3:25)

The Lord watches over you and hears your prayers.

> For the eyes of the Lord are over the righteous, and his ears are open unto their prayers: but the face of the Lord is against them that do evil. (1 Peter 3:12)

## FALSE PROPHETS

People who make predictions of the future are thought of as prophets. God's prophets did foretell future events, but their main job was to deliver specific messages from God. Pastors and teachers fulfill this role in the New Testament churches of today. John the Baptist was the last of the Old Testament prophets. Jesus is the greatest prophet of all. Everything that he said is a message from God. False prophets rely on familiar spirits instead of the Holy Spirit. These familiar spirits reveal secret things about you. False prophet uses these secrets to establish their credibility. They want to convince you that they have the power to predict the future or talk to the dead. Of course they do not call themselves false prophets. They prefer to be known as psychics or mediums.

God tells his people not to engage in things such as fortune telling and talking to the dead. Because God talks about familiar spirits, you can be sure that they are real.

> There shall not be found among you any one that maketh his son or his daughter to pass through the fire, or that useth divination, or an observer of times, or an enchanter, or a witch. Or a charmer, or a consulter with familiar spirits, or a wizard, or a necromancer. For all who do these things are an abomination unto the Lord. (Deuteronomy 18:11–12)

If a prophet claims that he has a word from the Lord, and it does not come to pass, he is a false prophet. That could not be the word of God, because God never lies.

> But the prophet, which shall presume to speak a word in my name, which I have not commanded him to speak, or that shall speak in the name of other gods, even that prophet shall die. And if thou say in thine heart, How shall we know the word which the Lord hath not spoken? When a prophet speaketh in the name of the Lord, if the thing follow not, nor come to pass, that is the thing which the Lord hath not spoken, but the prophet hath spoken it presumptuously: thou shalt not be afraid of him. (Deuteronomy 18:20–22)

A prophet sent by God will speak God's word. And he will tell God's people to turn away from evil.

> I have not sent these prophets, yet they ran: I have not spoken to them, yet they prophesied. But if they had stood in my counsel, and had caused my people to hear my words, then they should have turned them from their evil way, and from the evil of their doings. (Jeremiah 23:21–22)

A false prophet will say, "Thus saith the Lord," when the Lord has not said anything.

> Behold, I am against the prophets, saith the Lord, that use their tongues, and say, He saith. (Jeremiah 23:31)

Jesus said that you can recognize false prophets. He called them wolves in sheep's clothing, and said, "You shall know them by their fruits." The fruits of the Spirit are love, joy, peace, patience, gentleness, goodness, faith, meekness, and self-control. If a prophet does not have any of this fruit in his life, then God did not send him.

> Beware of false prophets, which come to you in sheep's clothing, but inwardly they are ravening wolves. Ye shall know them by their fruits. Do men gather grapes of thorns, or figs of thistles? Even so every good tree bringeth forth good fruit; but a corrupt tree bringeth forth evil fruit. A good tree cannot bring forth evil fruit, neither can a corrupt tree bring forth good fruit. (Matthew 7:15–18)

There are spirits in this world that have nothing to do with God. False prophets give voice to these lying spirits. This is how you can tell they are not of God. They deny that Jesus is God. They deny that he was actually born in the flesh. They deny that he actually died and that he is alive today. We know all of these things from the Bible. They also deny that the Bible is the word of God.

> Beloved, believe not every spirit, but try the spirits whether they are of God: because many false prophets are gone

> out into the world. Hereby know ye the Spirit of God: every spirit that confesseth that Jesus Christ is come in the flesh is of God: and every spirit that confesseth not that Jesus Christ is come in the flesh is not of God. (1 John 4:1–3)

## FALSE TEACHERS

False teachers present ideas that did not come from God. Their teachings are based on speculation. They use sensational and controversial topics to draw an audience. It is usually their private interpretation of the Bible. Sometimes they claim that the Bible does not say what it says. Instead of promoting the cause of Christ, they are promoting themselves. Instead of serving people, they have people serving them. They take money from God's people and give them nothing in return.

God sent Isaiah to some false teachers to ask them, "What are you doing to my people?" He judged them for taking advantage of his people.

> The Lord will enter into judgment with the ancients of his people, and the princes thereof: for ye have eaten up the vineyard; the spoil of the poor is in your houses. What mean ye that ye beat my people to pieces, and grind the faces of the poor? saith the Lord God of hosts. (Isaiah 3:14–15)

God said that he will judge pastors who have no compassion for God's flock.

> Therefore thus saith the Lord God of Israel against the pastors that feed my people; Ye have scattered my flock, and driven them away, and have not visited them: behold, I will visit upon you the evil of your doings, saith the Lord. And I will gather the remnant of my flock out of all countries whither I have driven them, and will bring them

> again to their folds; and they shall be fruitful and increase. And I will set up shepherds over them which shall feed them: and they shall fear no more, nor be dismayed, neither shall they be lacking, saith the Lord. (Jeremiah 23:2–4)

God sent his prophet to prophesy against pastors who were grasping for financial gain.

> Son of man, prophesy against the shepherds of Israel, prophesy, and say unto them, Thus saith the Lord God unto the shepherds; Woe be to the shepherds of Israel that do feed themselves! Should not the shepherds feed the flocks? Ye eat the fat, and ye clothe you with the wool, ye kill them that are fed: but ye feed not the flock. (Ezekiel 34:2–3)

In this passage, God explains that these priests had not done their jobs. They were supposed to teach the knowledge of God.

> For I desired mercy, and not sacrifice; and the knowledge of God more than burnt offerings....And as troops of robbers wait for a man, so the company of priests murder in the way by consent: for they commit lewdness. (Hosea 6:6, 9)

God said that he rewards everyone who obeys him. False teachers say that God is a liar.

> Your words have been stout against me, saith the Lord. Yet ye say, What have we spoken so much against thee? Ye have said, It is vain to serve God: and what profit is it that we have kept his ordinance, and that we have walked mournfully before the Lord of Hosts? (Malachi 3:13–14)

God's doctrine is the Bible. Most people only want to hear what is pleasing to their ears. They do not want to hear the truth.

> **Preach the word; be instant in season, out of season; reprove, rebuke, exhort with all longsuffering and doctrine. For the time will come when they will not endure sound doctrine; but after their own lusts shall they heap to themselves teachers, having itching ears; and they shall turn away their ears from the truth, and shall be turned unto fables. (2 Timothy 4:2–4)**

## FOOLS

Fools are people who rebel against God and his word. They think that they can defy God and get away with it. They make bad decisions because of their limited knowledge. The Book of Proverbs is a summary of God's wisdom. It also gives a detailed description of fools. They refuse to do what is right.

A fool thinks to himself, "Since God does not exist, I will do whatever I please."

> **The fool hath said in his heart, There is no God. Corrupt are they, and have done abominable iniquity: there is none that doeth good. (Psalm 53:1)**

Fools think they already know everything. They have no interest in learning God's ways. The expression "you can't tell them anything" was inspired by fools.

> **The fear of the Lord is the beginning of knowledge: but fools despise wisdom and instruction. (Proverbs 1:7)**

Fools reject all of God's instruction. If they manage to strike it rich, they are destroyed by their riches.

> They would none of my counsel: they despised all my reproof. Therefore shall they eat of the fruit of their own way, and be filled with their own devices. For the turning away of the simple shall slay them, and the prosperity of fools shall destroy them. (Proverbs 1:30–32)

Wise men apply God's word to their lives and teach others to do the same. Fools die because of their ignorance of God's word.

> The lips of the righteous feed many: but fools die for want of wisdom. (Proverbs 10:21)

Fools spend their lives working for people who are wise. The man who causes trouble for his family will receive nothing from God.

> He that troubleth his own house shall inherit the wind: and the fool shall be servant to the wise of heart. (Proverbs 11:29)

A fool thinks that he is always right. He demonstrates his anger to everyone around him.

> The way of a fool is right in his own eyes: but he that hearkeneth unto counsel is wise. A fool's wrath is presently known: but a prudent man covereth shame. (Proverbs 12:15–16)

Fools constantly do evil things. Associating with them will cause you to be destroyed.

> It is abomination to fools to depart from evil. He that walketh with wise men shall be wise: but a companion of fools shall be destroyed. (Proverbs 13:19–20)

A fool spends his life trying to "find himself." But he is not willing to change his ways.

> **A fool hath no delight in understanding, but that his heart may discover itself. (Proverbs 18:2)**

Fools hate to hear the truth. They do not like being reminded that they are in the wrong.

> **Speak not in the ears of a fool: for he will despise the wisdom of thy words. (Proverbs 23:9)**

Fools never stop talking. And they tell everything they know.

> **A fool uttereth all his mind: but a wise man keepeth it in till afterward. (Proverbs 29:11)**

When a man is a fool everyone around him knows it.

> **Yea also, when he that is a fool walketh by the way, his wisdom faileth him, and he saith to every one that he is a fool. (Ecclesiastes 10:3)**

## HYPOCRITES

Hypocrites say that they believe in Jesus, but they do not know him. They have no relationship with him. They think they are believers, but they are mistaken. They are like Judas. He was present with Jesus in the flesh, but he did not love him. Judas did not accept Jesus as his master. He had his own agenda. Hypocrites know that Jesus is real, but they have missed something. They have not experienced the new birth. The Spirit of Christ is not alive in them.

Hypocrites do not receive the things God promised in the Bible. These things are only for true believers in Jesus. God shows favor to those who please him.

> Hypocrites don't receive anything from the Lord.. . . and the hypocrite's hope shall perish. (Job 8:14)

Hypocrites damage the cause of Christ because new people assume that all believers are like them.

> A hypocrite with his mouth destroyeth his neighbor: but through knowledge shall the just be delivered. (Proverbs 11:9)

This is what Jesus told the super-religious people of his day. External displays of worship are not enough. God requires that you worship him inwardly from your heart.

> Woe unto you, scribes and Pharisees, hypocrites! For ye make clean the outside of the cup and of the platter, but within they are full of extortion and excess. Thou blind Pharisee, cleanse first that which is within the cup and platter, that the outside of them may be clean also. Woe unto you, scribes and Pharisees, hypocrites! for ye are like unto white sepulchres, which indeed appear beautiful outward, but are within full of dead men's bones, and of all uncleanness. Even so ye also outwardly appear righteous unto men, but within ye are full of hypocrisy and iniquity. (Matthew 23:25–28)

These religious leaders had no personal relationship with God. They were following the religious traditions of their fathers.

> He answered and said unto them, Well that Esaias prophesied of you hypocrites, as is written, This people honoreth me with their lips, but their heart is far from me. Howbeit in vain do they worship me, teaching for doctrines the commandments of men. For laying aside the commandment of God, ye hold the tradition of men,

> as the washing of pots and cups: and many other such things ye do. And he said unto them, Full well ye reject the commandment of God, that ye may keep your own tradition. (Mark 7:6–9)

This passage refers to hypocritical Bible teachers. They know what God expects them to do, yet they refuse to do it. Their selfishness causes the destruction of God's people.

> An instructor of the foolish, a teacher of babes, which hast the form of knowledge and of the truth in the law. Thou therefore which teachest another, teachest thou not thyself? Thou that preachest a man should not steal, dost thou steal? Thou that sayest a man should not commit adultery, dost thou commit adultery? Thou that abhorrest idols, dost thou commit sacrilege? Thou that makest thy boast of the law, through breaking the law dishonorest thou God? For the name of God is blasphemed among the Gentiles through you, as it is written. (Romans 2:20–24)

In this passage, Paul listed some of the perils he had faced. One of these was perils among false brethren.

> In journeyings often, in perils of waters, in perils of robbers, in perils by mine own countrymen, in perils by the heathen, in perils in the city, in perils in the wilderness, in perils in the sea, in perils among false brethren. (2 Corinthians 11:26)

There will always be people who abandon God's truth to follow some other spirit. They find a new idea. They like it and they accept it. They ignore the warning of their conscience, and it stops talking to them. Then, they have no inner guidance system.

> **Now the Spirit speaketh expressly, that in the latter times some shall depart from the faith, giving heed to seducing spirits, and doctrines of devils; speaking lies in hypocrisy; having their conscience seared with a hot iron. (1 Timothy 4:1–2)**

## IDOLATERS

Everybody worships something. If not God, then it is some kind of idol. God says that he is a jealous God. He refuses to share you. You cannot allow anything to take God's place in your heart. When Israel turned away from God to worship idols, they went into captivity. If you worship something other than God, you will go into spiritual captivity and be separated from God. That is the equivalent of death.

This is the first of the Ten Commandments that God gave to Moses. God refuses to play second fiddle to any idol. He has to be more valuable to you than anything else.

> **I am the Lord thy God, which brought thee out of the land of Egypt, from the house of bondage. Thou shalt have none other Gods before me. (Deuteronomy 5:6–7)**

If you consistently disobey God, he will withhold his blessing from you. You are not going to succeed without it.

> **Take heed to yourselves, that your heart be not deceived, and ye turn aside, and serve other gods, and worship them; and then the Lord's wrath be kindled against you, and he shut up the heaven, that there be no rain, and that the land yield not her fruit; and lest ye perish quickly from off the good land which the Lord giveth you. (Deuteronomy 11:16–17)**

Idols have no power to help you. If you turn away from God you are on your own.

> Yet ye have forsaken me, and served other gods: wherefore I will deliver you no mammon. (Matthew 6:24)

A whoremonger is a man who has sex with prostitutes. He is fascinated with sex instead of being fascinated with the Lord. He is like the man who is fascinated with money. Both of them are idolaters. They will experience the wrath of God.

> For this more. Go and cry unto the gods which ye have chosen; let them deliver you in the time of your tribulation. (Judges 10:13–14)

This was written about Israel, but it accurately describes life in America. Many have forsaken God to embrace eastern religions and sexual depravity. They have riches and multiple automobiles. They worship arts and technology, and everything else but God.

> Therefore thou hast forsaken thy people the house of Jacob, because they be replenished from the east, and are soothsayers like the Philistines, and they please themselves in the children of strangers. Their land also is full of silver and gold, neither is there any end of their treasures; their land is also full of horses, neither is there any end of their chariots: their land also is full of idols; they worship the work of their own hands, that which their own fingers have made. (Isaiah 2:6–8)

"Mammon" is money. God says we cannot serve him and money. We have to choose one or the other.

> No man can serve two masters: for either he will hate the one, and love the other; or else he will hold to the one, and despise the other: ye cannot serve God and ye know, that no whoremonger, nor unclean person, nor covetous man, who is an idolater, hath any inheritance in the kingdom

> of Christ and of God. Let no man deceive you with vain words: for because of these things cometh the wrath of God upon the children of disobedience. Be not ye therefore partakers with them. (Ephesians 5:5–7)

## LIARS

Most people will lie to stay out of trouble, but these verses are about compulsive liars. Lying is a way of life for them. Satan is called the Father of Lies because he invented the lie. He contradicted God when he told Adam and Eve that they would not die. Lying comes easy for the children of the devil. It is their native language, and it is all they know. They don't see any reason for not lying. They don't care if their lies destroy other people

This is what God says about liars.

> But the mouth of them that speak lies shall be stopped. (Psalm 63:11)

Liars will even lie to God. They say what they think he wants to hear. But they do not mean what they say. They have withheld their hearts from God.

> And they remembered that God was their rock, and the high God their redeemer. Nevertheless they did flatter him with their mouth, and they lied unto him with their tongues. For their heart was not right with him, neither were they steadfast in his covenant. (Psalm 78:35–37)

The Lord cannot stand to be around a liar. That is understandable, since he is Truth. The Truth cannot agree with a lie.

> He that worketh deceit shall not dwell within my house: he that telleth lies shall not tarry in my sight. (Psalm 101:7)

Do not go beyond what God has said in his word.

> **Add thou not unto his words, lest he reprove thee, and thou be found a liar. (Proverbs 30:6)**

The Scribes and Pharisees tried to catch Jesus contradicting the scriptures. They wanted to use his own words against him, to put him to death. He told them that they were incapable of understanding the truth, because they were children of the devil. The truth was like a foreign language to them.

> **Why do ye not understand my speech? Even because ye cannot hear my word. Ye are of your father the devil, and the lusts of your father ye will do: he was a murderer from the beginning, and abode not in the truth, because there is no truth in him. When he speaketh a lie, he speaketh of his own: for he is a liar, and the father of it. And because I tell you the truth, ye believe me not. (John 8:43–45)**

Even though you're trying to keep yourself from sin, you're not going to be without sin.

> **If we say that we have no sin, we deceive ourselves, and the truth is not in us. (1 John 1:8)**

God defines "knowing him," as keeping his commandments.

> **He that saith, I know him, and keepeth not his commandments, is a liar, and the truth is not in him. (1 John 2:4)**

There are many little antichrists in the world. There is a spirit of antichrist that seizes every opportunity to oppose God's people and the Bible.

> Who is a liar but he that denieth that Jesus is the Christ? He is antichrist, that denieth the Father and the Son. (1 John 2:22)

Many people think that they are Christians because they believe that Jesus exists, but that, in itself, is not enough. The Bible says that the devils believe that, and tremble. You must be born again. After you have been born spiritually, you will be different than you were. God will change you on the inside. He will give you new desires including the desire to love others.

> If a man say, I love God, and hateth his brother, he is a liar: for he that loveth not his brother whom he hath seen, how can he love God whom he hath not seen? And this commandment have we from him, that he who loveth God love his brother also. (1 John 4:20–21)

Liars deny that Jesus is the Christ. Liars are on the list of people who will be thrown into the lake of fire.

> But the fearful, and unbelieving, and the abominable, and murderers, and whoremongers, and sorcerers, and idolaters, and all liars, shall have their part in the lake which burneth with fire and brimstone: which is the second death. (Revelation 21:8)

This is what Jesus said about his physical return to Earth.

> And, behold, I come quickly; and my reward is with me, to give every man according as his work shall be. I am Alpha and Omega, the beginning and the end, the first and the last. Blessed are they that do his commandments, that they may have right to the tree of life, and may enter in through the gates of the city. For without are dogs, and sorcerers, and whoremongers, and murderers, and

> idolaters, and whoever loveth and maketh a lie. (Revelation 22:12–15)

## LOVERS OF MONEY

These are people who are fascinated with money. They make all their decisions in terms of how it affects their finances. Their highest priority is the accumulation of money. Everything and everyone else is subordinate to that objective. That includes husbands and wives, children, and the things of God. They save as much money as they can. They invest it and manage it. They love it so much they can't bear to spend it. They desire to possess it, but they do not realize that it possesses them. Money has taken them captive. It has taken God's place in their hearts. God cannot bless them because they are idolaters.

Money makes a very poor god. There are so many things it cannot do. People who worship money do not consider its limitations. They are not thinking about anything else but money.

> They that trust in their wealth, and boast themselves in the multitude of their riches; none of them can by any means redeem his brother, nor give to God a ransom for him: (For the redemption of their soul is precious, and it ceaseth for ever:) that he should still live for ever, and not see corruption. For he seeth that wise men die, likewise the fool and the brutish person perish, and leave their wealth to others. Their inward thought is, that their houses shall continue for ever, and their dwelling places to all generations; they call their lands after their own names. (Psalm 49:6–11)

These are some of the things people do to get rich apart from God.

> Trust not in oppression, and become not vain in robbery: if riches increase, set not your heart upon them. (Psalm 62:10)

An obsession with money will take control of a man's whole life.

> So are the ways of every one that is greedy of gain; which taketh away the life of the owners thereof. (Proverbs 1:19)

This is what God says about riches. Be content with the things you have. Do not try to make yourself rich.

> Labor not to be rich: cease from thine own wisdom. Wilt thou set thine eyes upon that which is not? For riches certainly make themselves wings; they fly away as an eagle toward heaven. (Proverbs 23:4–5)

This is a description of a miser. He is dedicating his whole life to piling up money.

> There is one alone, and there is not a second; yea, he hath neither child nor brother: yet is there no end of all his labor; neither is his eye satisfied with riches; neither saith he, For whom do I labor, and bereave my soul of good? This is also vanity yea, it is a sore travail. (Ecclesiastes 4:8)

To the man who loves money, no amount of it will ever be enough.

> He that loveth silver shall not be satisfied with silver; nor he that loveth abundance with increase: this is also vanity. (Ecclesiastes 5:10)

People who are always grasping for money ensnare themselves. They are willing to do anything for money. But the evil that they do comes back on them.

> But they that will be rich fall into temptation and a snare, and into many foolish and hurtful lusts, which drown men

**in destruction and perdition. For the love of money is the root of all evil: which while some coveted after, they have erred from the faith, and pierced themselves through with many sorrows. (1 Timothy 6:9–10)**

Lovers of Pleasure

These are the people who dedicate their lives to pleasure. They delight in the pleasures of the flesh, everything that involves the five senses—sight and sound, smell and taste, and touch. They seek all the physical pleasures of life—food and drink, art and music, entertainment, and sexual activity. They over-indulge in all of these things. They love pleasure more than they love God. They, too, are idolaters, and the idols that they worship are themselves.

A pleasure-loving person spends everything he makes.

**He that loveth pleasure shall be a poor man: he that loveth wine and oil shall not be rich. (Proverbs 21:17)**

Wise people do not consume all their resources. They hold something in reserve.

**There is treasure to be desired and oil in the dwelling of the wise; but a foolish man spendeth it up. (Proverbs 21:20)**

God passed judgment on the Babylonians. They were lovers of pleasure. They worshipped a mother-goddess. They originated every form of magic and every occult practice. They pioneered the taking of drugs, which was associated with sorcery. All these things were part of the Babylonian religion. They exported it to Egypt, and India and all around the world. People are still buying these same ideas. To a lover of pleasure, they are an attractive alternative to God and the Bible.

> Therefore hear now this, thou that art given to pleasures, that dwellest carelessly, that sayest in thine heart, I am, and none else beside me; I shall not sit as a widow, neither shall I know the loss of children: but these two things shall come to thee in a moment in one day, the loss of children, and widowhood: they shall come upon thee in their perfection for the multitude of thy sorceries, and for the great abundance of thine enchantments. For thou hast trusted in thy wickedness: thou hast said, None seeth me. Thy wisdom and thy knowledge, it hath perverted thee; and thou hast said in thine heart, I am, and none else beside me. (Isaiah 47:8–10)

Being a lover of pleasure is evidence of being spiritually dead.

> But she that liveth in pleasure is dead while she liveth. (1 Timothy 5:6 )

This is a description of what people will be like just before the end of the world. This could easily be that time. People are more like this today than they have ever been before.

> This know also, that in the last days perilous times shall come. For men shall be lovers of their own selves, covetous, boasters, proud, blasphemers, disobedient to parents, unthankful, unholy, without natural affection, trucebreakers, false accusers, incontinent, fierce, despisers of those that are good, traitors, heady, high-minded, lovers of pleasures more than lovers of God; having a form of godliness, but denying the power thereof: from such turn away. (2 Timothy 3:1–5)

Moses could have enjoyed a lifetime of pleasure, but he chose to be one of God's people instead. The kingdom of God is the greatest kingdom of all time. Moses chose rewards and pleasures that last forever. You face the same decision. You can be a part of the cause of Christ, or, you can enjoy the pleasures of sin for a season.

> **By faith Moses, when he was come to years, refused to be called the son of Pharaoh's daughter; choosing rather to suffer affliction with the people of God, than to enjoy the pleasures of sin for a season; esteeming the reproach of Christ greater riches than the treasures in Egypt: for he had respect unto the recompence of the reward. By faith he forsook Egypt, not fearing the wrath of the king: for he endured, as seeing him who is invisible. (Hebrews 11:24–27)**

## MINISTERS OF SATAN

The name "Satan" literally means the adversary. Anyone is capable of being an adversary of God. Unlike God, Satan cannot be everywhere at the same time. He has to use surrogates to accomplish his evil works. These people are not monsters. They are just the ordinary people you meet every day. They are merely serving their own self-interest. They don't realize that they are serving the devil. There are very few people who serve him on purpose. He uses false religions to deceive people into following him. Those who practice these religions sincerely believe their cause is right, but their god is not the one true God. Satan regularly dupes Christians into doing things for him. Do not let Satan use you as a weapon to hurt somebody else.

Never participate in a sacrifice to any other "god."

> **He that sacrificeth unto any god, save unto the Lord only, he shall be utterly destroyed. (Exodus 22:20)**

This is a part of Jesus' "Parable of the Sower." It compares God's word in a man's heart to a seed growing in soil. In this case, Satan steals the man's attention away from the word of God.

> The sower soweth the word. And these are they by the wayside, where the word is sown; but when they have heard, Satan cometh immediately, and taketh away the word that was sown in their hearts. (Mark 4:14–15)

You cannot serve God and Satan at the same time. You have to make the decision once and for all. Whom are you going to serve?

> But I say, that the things which the Gentiles sacrifice, they sacrifice to devils, and not to God: and I would not that ye have fellowship with devils. Ye cannot drink the cup of the Lord, and the cup of devils: ye cannot be partakers of the Lord's table, and of the table of devils. (1 Corinthians 10:20–21)

Paul warned the Corinthians about teachers who were ministers of Satan.

> For such are false apostles, deceitful workers, transforming themselves into the apostles of Christ. And no marvel for Satan himself is transformed into an angel of light. Therefore it is no great thing if his ministers also be transformed as the ministers of righteousness; whose end shall be according to their works. (2 Corinthians 11:13–15)

Moses' brother Aaron was given a sign to show Pharaoh that God had sent them. Aaron's staff turned into a snake, and then back into a staff. Jannes and Jambres were magicians in Pharaoh's court. They could turn their staffs into serpents, but Aaron's serpent swallowed their serpents. Satan's ministers can deceive people temporarily, but their power cannot stand against the power of God.

> Having a form of godliness, but denying the power thereof: from such turn away. For of this sort are they which creep into houses, and lead captive silly women laden with sins,

> led away with divers lusts, ever learning, and never able to come to the knowledge of the truth. Now as Jannes and Jambres withstood Moses, so do these also resist the truth: men of corrupt minds, reprobate concerning the faith. But they shall proceed no further: for their folly shall be manifest unto all men, as theirs also was. (2 Timothy 3:5–9)

## MOCKERS

It is good to have a sense of humor, but mockers make fun of other people. They are never serious. Everything is a joke to them. They are not interested in God and his word. They are only interested in their own little world. They think that they are smarter than everyone else. They think that people who believe the Bible are idiots. But God is not mocked. Mockers reap what they sow just like everyone else.

Fools make jokes about their sins. God shows favor to everyone who does what is right.

> Fools make a mock at sin: but among the righteous there is favor. (Proverbs 14:9)

Don't make fun of poor people. God loves them. You will be punished if you laugh at the misery of others.

> Whoso mocketh the poor reproacheth his Maker: and he that is glad at calamities shall not be unpunished. (Proverbs 17:5)

Drunks mock other people, but getting drunk is, in itself, an act of stupidity.

> Wine is a mocker, strong drink is raging: and whosoever is deceived thereby is not wise. (Proverbs 20:1)

Jesus was tortured and mocked. He suffered great mental and emotional distress in addition to extreme physical pain.

> And the men that held Jesus mocked him, and smote him. And when they had blindfolded him, they struck him on the face, and asked him, saying, Prophesy, who is it that smote thee? And many other things blasphemously spake they against him. (Luke 22:63–65)

While Jesus was dying on the cross, the religious rulers mocked him.

> And the people stood beholding. And the rulers also with them derided him, saying, He saved others; let him save himself, if he be Christ, the chosen of God. And the soldiers also mocked him, coming to him, and offering him vinegar, and saying, If thou be the king of the Jews, save thyself. (Luke 23:35–37)

The Bible says that what you give out is what you get back, whether it is good or bad. You can sow forgiveness and love, or hatred and anger. You will be repaid in kind.

> Be not deceived; God is not mocked: for whatever a man soweth, that shall he also reap. For he that soweth to his flesh shall of the flesh reap corruption; but he that soweth to the Spirit shall of the Spirit reap life everlasting. And let us not be weary in well doing: for in due season we shall reap, if we faint not. (Galatians 6:7–9)

God really hates it when you complain. It is like you are blaming him for the mess you have made. He has told you how to have a good life. You can only reap what you have sown.

> These are murmurers, complainers, walking after their own lusts; and their mouth speaketh great swelling words, having men's persons in admiration because of advantage. But, beloved, remember ye the words which were spoken before of the apostles of our Lord Jesus Christ; how that they told you there should be mockers in the last time, who should walk after their own ungodly lusts. These be they who separate themselves, sensual, having not the Spirit. (Jude 17–19)

## MURDERERS

God's commandment, "Thou shalt not kill" (Exodus 20:13) is translated more clearly as "Thou shalt do no murder." There is a big difference between killing an enemy soldier in a war and in murdering an innocent victim. A murderer who is executed is not being murdered by the state. Capital punishment laws are based on the Law of God. "…The murderer shall surely be put to death." (Numbers 35:16)

God warned Cain that if he did not control his anger, it would take control of him. Cain did not listen to God. He became a murderer because of his anger.

> And Cain talked with Abel his brother: and it came to pass, when they were in the field, that Cain rose up against Abel his brother, and slew him. And the Lord said unto Cain, Where is Abel thy brother? And he said, I know not: am I my brother's keeper? And he said, What hast thou done? The voice of thy brother's blood crieth unto me from the ground. And now art thou cursed from the earth, which hath opened her mouth to receive thy brother's blood from thy hand; when thou tillest the ground, it shall not henceforth yield unto thee her strength; a fugitive and a vagabond shalt thou be in the earth. (Genesis 4:6–12)

In his written word, God authorized the death penalty for murderers.

> **Whoso sheddeth man's blood, by man shall his blood be shed: for in the image of God made he man. (Genesis 9:6)**

God repeats himself again in this verse. He says that murderers should be executed.

> **And he that killeth any man shall surely be put to death. (Leviticus 24:17)**

Israel departed from God's ways. They offered human sacrifices to their horrible, worthless pagan gods. They sacrificed their own children to idols. This passage was written about them, but it also could be said about the people of America.

> **But were mingled among the heathen, and learned their works. And they served their idols: which were a snare unto them. Yea, they sacrificed their sons and their daughters unto devils, and shed innocent blood, even the blood of their sons and of their daughters, whom they sacrificed unto the idols of Canaan: and the land was polluted with blood. Thus were they defiled with their own works, and went a whoring with their own inventions. (Psalm 106:35–38)**

When a man takes the life of another, he unknowingly destroys his own life too.

> **For their feet run to evil, and make haste to shed blood. Surely the net is spread in the sight of any bird. And they lay wait for their own blood; they lurk privily for their own lives. (Proverbs 1:16–18)**

There is a direct connection between hatred and murder. If you are so angry that you feel like killing somebody, you are being controlled by these emotions. Jesus said these things defile you. God makes it mandatory that you forgive the people who have hurt you. If you do, he will take away the anger and hatred. The pattern is always the same. When you do your part, he'll do his part.

> **Whosoever hateth his brother is a murderer: and ye know that no murderer hath eternal life abiding in him. (1 John 3:15)**

## RELIGIOUS OPPORTUNISTS

God's truth is always available, but there is also a lot of worthless junk in the spiritual marketplace. There is a lot of money to be made in the fleecing of the flock. People are drawn to anything related to the supernatural. Millions of people make their living by making a business of religion. Many are sincere and others are not. They do not see anything wrong with selling a false religion or a false gospel.

In this verse, God is speaking to religious opportunists. They think that everyone is like them, even God. "To reprove" means to correct.

> **These things hast thou done, and I kept silence; thou thoughtest that I was altogether such a one as thyself: but I will reprove thee, and set them in order before thine eyes. (Psalm 50:21)**

The men in this passage are predators. They make a good living from promoting their own ideas, but God's people receive nothing in return for their money.

> **For among my people are found wicked men: they lay wait, as he that setteth snares; they set a trap, they catch men. As a cage is full of birds, so are their houses full of**

> deceit: therefore they are become great, and waxed rich. They are waxen fat, they shine: yea, they overpass the deeds of the wicked: they judge not the cause, the cause of the fatherless, yet they prosper; and the right of the needy do they not judge....The prophets prophesy falsely, and the priests bear rule by their means; and my people love to have it so: and what will ye do in the end thereof? (Jeremiah 5:26–28, 31)

These ministers are not interested in God's word or his people. They only care about what they can get for themselves.

> For the priest's lips should keep knowledge, and they should seek the law at his mouth: for he is the messenger of the Lord of hosts. But ye are departed out of the way; ye have caused many to stumble at the law; ye have corrupted the covenant of Levi, saith the Lord of hosts. Therefore have I also made you contemptible and base before all the people, according as ye have not kept my ways, but have been partial in the law. (Malachi 2:9)

Jesus drove religious opportunists out of the temple. They were not ministering to God's people. They were taking advantage of them instead. They were enriching themselves in God's house.

> And the Jews' Passover was at hand, and Jesus went up to Jerusalem, And found in the temple those that sold oxen and sheep, and doves, and the changers of money sitting: and when he had made a scourge of small cords, he drove them all out of the temple, and the sheep, and the oxen; and poured out the changers' money, and overthrew the tables; and said unto them that sold doves, Take these things hence; make not my Father's house an house of merchandise. (John 2:13–16)

These people are selling their own ideas. They expand what the Bible says so they can set up little kingdoms of their own.

> **For I know this, that after my departing shall grievous wolves enter in among you, not sparing the flock. And of your own selves shall men arise, speaking perverse things, to draw away disciples after them. (Acts 20:29–30)**

## ROBBERS

A robber takes things that do not belong to him. He steals more than just material goods. He also steals your peace and your joy. Satan is a thief and a robber. He steals the word of God from you so you will not benefit from it. He gets you to focus your attention onto other things. He convinces you that the word of God will not work for you. He robs you of the true riches that God has for you. He is stealing your eternal possessions. He invented robbery and he's the father of everyone who steals. Don't be like the devil. Don't take things that are not yours. Don't enrich yourself at someone else's expense. You do not have to take things from others. Jesus will give you your own things.

These are the Lord's commands. Never steal. Treat people right, and never lie.

> **Ye shall not steal, neither deal falsely, neither lie one to another. (Leviticus 19:11)**

God sets high standards of honesty for you to follow.

> **Thou shalt not defraud thy neighbor, neither rob him: the wages of him that is hired shall not abide with thee all night until the morning. (Leviticus 19:13)**

Do not take advantage of the poor. God will avenge them. "To spoil" someone is to take away their possessions.

> Rob not the poor, because he is poor: neither oppress the afflicted in the gate: for the Lord will plead their cause, and spoil the soul of those that spoiled them. (Proverbs 22:22–23)

Do not be a partner to anyone who is a thief.

> Whoso is partner with a thief hateth his own soul. (Proverbs 29:24)

If you become too poor, you might steal. If you become too rich, you might think you do not need God. The ideal solution lies somewhere between these two extremes.

> Remove far from me vanity and lies: give me neither poverty nor riches; feed me with food convenient for me: lest I be full, and deny thee, and say, Who is the Lord? or lest I be poor, and steal, and take the name of my God in vain. (Proverbs 30:8–9)

Some judges are corrupt. They rule in favor of the party who pays them a bribe.

> Woe unto them that decree unrighteous decrees, and that write grievousness which they have prescribed; to turn aside the needy from judgment, and to take away the right from the poor of my people, that widows may be their prey, and that they may rob the fatherless! (Isaiah 10:1–2)

Jesus quoted this verse when he drove the moneychangers out of the temple. He combined it with a portion of the next passage, from Chapter Seven of the Book of Jeremiah.

> For mine house shall be called an house of prayer for all people. (Isaiah 56:7)

This is God's warning to religious leaders. Don't defraud God's people.

> Behold, ye trust in lying words, that cannot profit. Will ye steal, murder, and commit adultery, and swear falsely, and burn incense unto Baal, and walk after other gods whom ye know not; and come and stand before me in this house, which is called by my name, and say, We are delivered to do all these abominations? Is this house, which is called by my name, become a den of robbers in your eyes? Behold, even I have seen it, saith the Lord. (Jeremiah 7:8–11)

These teachers used their authority to steal the true meaning of God's words.

> Therefore, behold, I am against the prophets, saith the Lord, that steal my words every one from his neighbor. (Jeremiah 23:30)

Always follow the Golden Rule. You do not want anybody to steal from you, so do not steal from anyone else. If you are ever tempted to steal, remember this passage. There is a curse that applies to everyone who is a thief.

> Then said he unto me, This is the curse that goeth forth over the face of the whole earth: for every one that stealeth shall be cut off as on this side according to it; and every one that sweareth shall be cut off as on that side according to it. I will bring it forth, saith the Lord of hosts, and it shall enter into the house of the thief, and into the house of him that sweareth falsely by my name: and it shall remain in the midst of his house, and shall consume it with the timber thereof and the stones thereof. (Zechariah 5:3–4)

When Jesus drove the moneychangers out of the temple, it affected the income of the rulers of the temple. That is when they decided to kill him. God's house was supposed to be a house of prayer, but they had made it into a den of thieves.

> And they came to Jerusalem: and Jesus went into the temple, and began to cast out them that sold and bought in the temple, and overthrew the tables of the moneychangers, and the seats of them that sold doves;... And he taught, saying unto them, Is it not written, My house shall be called of all nations, the house of prayer? but ye have made it a den of thieves. And the scribes and chief priests heard it, and sought how they might destroy him: for they feared him, because all the people was astonished at his doctrine. (Mark 11:15, 17–18)

This is Jesus' explanation of "Parable of the Sower." The word of God is the seed. In this case, Satan steals it out of the heart.

> Now the parable is this: The seed is the word of God. Those by the way side are they that hear; then cometh the devil, and taketh away the word out of their hearts, lest they should believe and be saved. (Luke 8:11–12)

Jesus' desire is to give. Satan's desire is to steal everything the Lord has for you.

> The thief cometh not, but for to steal, and to kill, and to destroy: I am come that they might have life, and they might have it more abundantly. (John 10:10)

## THE SELF-CENTERED

The world is full of self-centered people who constantly think and talk about themselves. They think that the world revolves around them.

They pay no attention to other people. They are oblivious to the needs of others. They do not care that other people have hopes and dreams just like they do.

This is the conclusion of the story of the prodigal son. He had asked his father to give him his inheritance early. Then, he squandered it all. However, the prodigal son's older brother thought only of himself, and cared only about himself. The prodigal son was sorry for his sin. His father was filled with joy when he returned, but his older brother didn't care about either of them. He did not want to celebrate. All he knew was that the fatted calf represented money out of his pocket.

> Now his elder son was in the field: and as he came and drew nigh to the house, he heard music and dancing. And he called one of the servants, and asked what these things meant. And he said unto him, Thy brother is come; and thy father hath killed the fatted calf, because he hath received him safe and sound. And he was angry, and would not go in: therefore came his father out, and entreated him. And he answering said to his father, Lo, these many years do I serve thee, neither transgressed I at any time thy commandment: and yet thou never gavest me a kid, that I might make merry with my friends: but as soon as this thy son was come, which hath devoured thy living with harlots, thou hast killed for him the fatted calf. And he said unto him, Son, thou art ever with me, and all that I have is thine. It was meet that we should make merry, and be glad: for this thy brother was dead, and is alive again; and was lost, and is found. (Luke 15:25–32)

You have to overcome the natural tendency to be selfish.

> For all seek their own, not the things which are Jesus Christ's. (Philippians 2:21)

## THE SELF-RIGHTEOUS

A self-righteous person does not think he needs to change. God showed Job what to do in order to overcome his problems. He had to stop being self-righteous. He had to learn that he could never be righteousness enough on his own to satisfy God and that he needed a Savior, a Redeemer. He said, by faith, "I know that my Redeemer liveth." This was many centuries before Jesus was born in the flesh, but Jesus was still Job's Redeemer, just as he is yours today.

Job had to change his attitude of self-righteousness.

> So these three men ceased to answer Job, because he was righteous in his own eyes. Then was kindled the wrath of Elihu the son of Barachel the Buzite, of the kindred of Ram: against Job was his wrath kindled, because he justified himself rather than God. (Job 32:1–2)

God is pleased with you when you do what is right. It is true that the righteousness that you do will never save you. All your righteousnesses are as filthy rags in God's sight. You also needed Jesus to be your Savior. God counts your faith in him as righteousness.

> Thou meetest him that rejoiceth and worketh righteousness, those that remember thee in thy ways: behold, thou art wroth; for we have sinned: in those is continuance, and we shall be saved. But we are all as an unclean thing, and all our righteousnesses are as filthy rags; and we all do fade as a leaf; and our iniquities, like the wind, have taken us away. (Isaiah 64:5–6)

This is part of Jesus' Sermon on the Mount. The scribes and Pharisees were experts in how to keep the Law of Moses. But their keeping of the law did not make them righteous.

> **For I say unto you, That except your righteousness shall exceed the righteousness of the scribes and Pharisees, ye shall in no case enter into the kingdom of heaven. (Matthew 5:20)**

The Pharisees hated Jesus because he told them the truth about themselves. They loved money more than they loved God.

> **No servant can serve two masters: for either he will hate the one, and love the other; or else he will hold to the one, and despise the other. Ye cannot serve God and mammon. And the Pharisees also, who were covetous, heard all these things: and they derided him. And he said unto them, Ye are they which justify yourselves before men; but God knoweth your hearts: for that which is highly esteemed among men is abomination in the sight of God. (Luke 16:15)**

In this passage, Paul said that it was not necessary for Jewish Christians to follow the Jewish law.

> **Brethren, my heart's desire and prayer to God for Israel is, that they might be saved. For I bear them record that they have a zeal of God, but not according to knowledge. For they being ignorant of God's righteousness, and going about to establish their own righteousness, have not submitted themselves unto the righteousness of God. For Christ is the end of the law for righteousness to every one that believeth. (Romans 10:1–3)**

## SPIRITS AGAINST CHRIST

Many people think that the Bible is just another book, and they will laugh at you for taking it seriously. They think that it is an insult to be called a fundamentalist. Sometimes people will be hostile to you for no apparent reason. There is a spirit behind all of this hostility, a spirit that hates you because you belong to Jesus. The spirit of antichrist denies the Father-Son relationship between God and Jesus. It says that Jesus was just a man, and that God did not raise him from the dead. This is an attack against God and the integrity of his word.

The Holy Spirit reveals the truth about Jesus.

> Wherefore I give you to understand, that no man speaking by the Spirit of God calleth Jesus accursed: and that no man can say that Jesus is the Lord, but by the Holy Ghost. (1 Corinthians 12:3)

This passage refers to hypocrites, who do not have the Holy Spirit.

> They profess that they know God; but in works they deny him, being abominable, and disobedient, and unto every good work reprobate. (Titus 1:16)

The spirit of antichrist has been on the Earth since the time of the Apostles.

> Little children, it is the last time: and as ye have heard that antichrist shall come, even now are there many antichrists; whereby we know that it is the last time. (1 John 2:18)

The spirit of antichrist expresses itself through those who deny that Jesus is the Son of God.

> Who is a liar but he that denieth that Jesus is the Christ? He is antichrist, that denieth the Father and the Son. Whosoever denieth the Son, the same hath not the Father. (1 John 2:22–23)

Spirits communicate through words. If an idea is inconsistent with the word of God, it is not of God.

> Beloved, believe not every spirit, but try the spirits whether they are of God: because many false prophets are gone out into the world. Hereby know ye the Spirit of God: every spirit that confesseth that Jesus Christ is come in the flesh is of God. (1 John 4:1–2)

The spirit of anti-christ is the attitude that denies that Jesus is God.

> And every spirit that confesseth not that Jesus Christ is come in the flesh is not of God: and this is that spirit of anti-christ, whereof ye have heard that it should come; and even now already is in the world. (1 John 4:3)

Deceivers promote ideas that contradict the Word of God.

> For many deceivers are entered into the world, who confess not that Jesus Christ is come in the flesh. This is a deceiver and an antichrist. (2 John 7)

## THE SPIRITUALLY BLIND

When you are born again, the Holy Spirit will show you how to apply God's wisdom to your life. He will inspire you and give you insights from a variety of sources. All of these ideas will be consistent with the Bible. People who have not been born again do not know about these things. They cannot see God's truths at all and cannot understand the Bible.

Ask God to do for you the same thing for you that he did for David.

> Open thou mine eyes, that I may behold wondrous things out of thy law. (Psalm 119:18)

Idolaters are spiritually blind. They cannot see that their "gods" are worthless.

> They shall be turned back, they shall be greatly ashamed, that trust in graven images, that say to the molten images, Ye are our gods. Hear, ye deaf; and look, ye blind, that ye may see. Who is blind, but my servant? Or deaf, as my messenger that I sent? Who is blind as he that is perfect, and blind as the Lord's servant? Seeing many things, but thou observest not; opening the ears, but he heareth not. (Isaiah 42:17–20)

Jesus read these words aloud to a local congregation. He told them that he was the fulfillment of this prophecy. They could not see that this was the truth. They became so angry at Jesus that they tried to kill him.

> And there was delivered unto him the book of the prophet Esaias. And when he had opened the book, he found the place where it was written, The Spirit of the Lord is upon me, because he hath anointed me to preach the gospel to the poor; he hath sent me to heal the brokenhearted, to preach deliverance to the captives, and recovering of sight to the blind, to set at liberty them that are bruised, to preach the acceptable year of the Lord.. . . And he began to say unto them, This day is this scripture fulfilled in your ears. (Luke 4:17–19,21)

Saul had been persecuting believers in Jesus. This is the story of his conversion. He was on the road to Damascus, and Jesus appeared to him. He was stricken blind due to the brilliance of God's glory. Jesus healed him, changed his name to Paul, and sent him to open the eyes of the spiritually blind. He became the Apostle to the Gentiles.

> And I said, Who art thou, Lord? And he said, I am Jesus whom thou persecutest. But rise, and stand upon thy feet: for I have appeared unto thee for this purpose, to make thee a minister and a witness both of these things

> which thou hast seen, and of those things in the which I will appear unto thee; delivering thee from the people, and from the Gentiles, unto whom now I send thee, to open their eyes, and to turn them from darkness to light, and from the power of Satan unto God, that they may receive forgiveness of sins, and inheritance among them which are sanctified by faith that is in me. (Acts 26:15–18)

## THE SPIRITUALLY DEAD

Satan told Adam and Eve that they would not die if they ate from the forbidden tree. Adam and Eve died, just like God said they would. First they died spiritually, and then they died physically. Going against God's word always leads to death. People who are not born again are spiritually dead and separated from God. The first birth is physical. The new birth is a spiritual reconnection to God. Being born again is like being resurrected from the dead. It will cause you to live forever.

Believing in Jesus is a matter of life and death. There is no life apart from God.

> He that believeth on the Son hath everlasting life: and he who believeth not the Son shall not see life; but the wrath of God abideth on him. (John 3:36)

Jesus' resurrection ended the reign of spiritual death and established a new era of spiritual life. This spiritual life is for everyone who believes in Jesus.

> Verily, verily, I say unto you, He that heareth my word, and believeth on him that sent me, hath everlasting life, and shall not come into condemnation; but is passed from death unto life. Verily, verily, I say unto you, The hour is coming, and now is, when the dead shall hear the voice of the Son of God: and they that hear shall live. (John 5:24–25)

Jesus revealed these facts about himself in a conversation with Martha, the sister of Lazarus.

> Jesus said unto her, I am the resurrection, and the life: he that believeth in me, though he were dead, yet shall he live: and whosoever liveth and believeth in me shall never die. Believest thou this? (John 11:25–26)

You have been raised from the dead. And now you will have to get used to a new way of living.

> And have no fellowship with the unfruitful works of darkness, but rather reprove them. For it is a shame even to speak of those things which are done of them in secret. But all things that are reproved are made manifest by the light: for whatsoever doth make manifest is light. Wherefore he saith Awake thou that sleepest, and arise from the dead, and Christ shall give thee light. See then that ye walk circumspectly, not as fools, but as wise, redeeming the time, because the days are evil. (Ephesians 5:11–16)

This event is known as the Great White Throne Judgment. It is the final judgment for everyone who has rejected Christ. They will be judged according to their works, but their works will not save them from the lake of fire. You will not be present at this judgment because your name is written in the Lamb's Book of Life.

> And I saw the dead, small and great, stand before God; and the books were opened: and another book was opened, which is the book of life: and the dead were judged out of those things which were written in the books, according to their works. (Revelation 20:12)

## THE SPIRITUALLY DEAF

People who do not know Jesus are spiritually deaf. The Bible makes no sense to them because they cannot understand spiritual things. The Holy Spirit has opened your spiritual ears. When you are reading the Bible, it is as if God is speaking directly to you. The Holy Spirit will bring Bible verses to your remembrance, and will tell you how those verses apply to your life. He also speaks to you through your conscience, but if you will not hear God, He will not hear you.

> **He that turneth away his ear from hearing the law, even his prayer shall be abomination. (Proverbs 28:9)**

Salvation begins with hearing the word of God.

> **And in that day shall the deaf hear the words of the book, and the eyes of the blind shall see out of obscurity, and out of darkness. (Isaiah 29:18)**

You have to be born again in order to understand the Bible. God's word does not make sense to people who are spiritually deaf.

> **To whom shall I speak, and give warning, that they may hear? Behold their ear is uncircumcised, and they cannot hearken: behold, the word of the Lord is unto them a reproach; they have no delight in it. (Jeremiah 6:10)**

Jesus explained why his teachings were in parables. They were designed to benefit God's children. Outsiders cannot understand the truths that they contain.

> **Therefore speak I to them in parables: because they seeing see not; and hearing they hear not, neither do they understand. And in them is fulfilled the prophecy of**

> Esaias, which saith, By hearing ye shall hear, and shall not understand: and seeing ye shall see, and shall not perceive. For this people's heart is waxed gross, and their ears are dull of hearing. (Matthew 13:13–15)

You start out by learning a few basic truths. Then, the Holy Spirit will teach you more. If you stop learning about God's word, you will forget the things that you have already learned.

> For there is nothing hid, which shall not be manifested; neither was any thing kept secret, but that it should come abroad. If any man have ears to hear, let him hear. And he said unto them, Take heed what ye hear: with what measure ye mete, it shall be measured to you: and unto you that hear shall more be given. For he that hath, to him shall be given. And he that hath not, from him shall be taken even that which he hath. (Mark 4:22–25)

God's children accept his words and value them highly. Outsiders have no interest in God's ideas.

> He that is of God heareth God's words: ye therefore hear them not, because ye are not of God. (John 8:47)

There is tremendous power in the word of God spoken aloud by a man of God.

> For whosoever shall call upon the name of the Lord shall be saved. How then shall they call on him in whom they have not believed? And how shall they believe in him of whom they have not heard? And how shall they hear without a preacher? (Romans 10:13–14)

God uses his word to create faith in you.

> **So then faith cometh by hearing, and hearing by the word of God. (Romans 10:17)**

You are saved by grace, not by works. Grace is the unmerited favor of God. God makes salvation available by grace so that you can receive it through faith. The Lord opens deaf ears to hear his word.

> **Even so then at this present time also there is a remnant according to the election of grace. And if by grace, then is it no more of works: otherwise grace is no more grace. But if it be of works, then is it no more grace: otherwise work is no more work. What then? Israel hath not obtained that which he seeketh for; but the election hath obtained it, and the rest were blinded (According as it is written, God hath given them the spirit of slumber, eyes that they should not see, and ears that they should not hear;) unto this day. (Romans 11:7–8)**

## THE WICKED

The wicked and the righteous live in two different worlds. The wicked are incapable of understanding God's word. The wicked cannot understand how a God of love can send anyone to hell. The righteous understand that people send themselves to hell. God has already done everything that is necessary to prevent them from going there. The wicked do not go to hell because of their sins. They go to hell because they have rejected Jesus. They will be judged by their own works, which are woefully inadequate. They will eventually be cast into the lake of fire. The wicked are the biggest losers of them all. Because they are separated from God, they are dead already. They just don't know it.

This passage describes the life of the wicked. Their lives are cut short, and then they go into eternal misery.

> **They take the timbrel and harp, and rejoice at the sound of the organ. They spend their days in wealth, and in a**

> moment go down to the grave. Therefore they say unto God, Depart from us; for we desire not the knowledge of thy ways. What is the Almighty, that we should serve him? And what profit should we have, if we pray unto him? Lo, their good is not in their hand: the counsel of the wicked is far from me. How oft is the candle of the wicked put out! And how oft cometh their destruction upon them! God distributeth sorrows in his anger. (Job 21:12–17)

God will keep you from getting killed, but he does not extend this protection to the wicked. They face the wrath of God every day of their lives.

> He preserveth not the life of the wicked. (Job 36:6)

> And God is angry with the wicked every day. (Psalm 7:11)

The wicked do not escape God's judgment in this life. Sorrows are included in the package with wickedness.

> Upon the wicked he shall rain snares, fire and brimstone, and a horrible tempest: this shall be the portion of their cup. (Psalm 11:6)

> Many sorrows shall be to the wicked. (Psalm 32:10)

The wicked die as a result of the evil they have caused.

> Evil shall slay the wicked. (Psalm 34:21)

> The years of the wicked shall be shortened. (Proverbs 10:27)

Wicked people are dishonest about money. Righteous people give it away.

**The wicked borroweth, and payeth not again: but the righteous showeth mercy, and giveth. (Psalm 37:21)**

In the mind of the wicked right and wrong are reversed. Their intentions are wrong. To them, wrong is right and right is wrong.

**The Lord preserveth the strangers; he relieveth the fatherless and widow: but the way of the wicked he turneth upside down. (Psalms 146:9)**

The righteous man gets what he wants. The wicked man gets what he fears.

**The fear of the wicked, it shall come upon him: but the desire of the righteous shall be granted. (Proverbs 10:24)**

The circumstances of your life are the results of your own actions.

**Behold, the righteous shall be recompensed in the earth: much more the wicked and the sinner. (Proverbs 11:31)**

The wicked love their way of life so much that they do not want to change it.

**The way of the wicked seduceth them. (Proverbs 12:26)**

The wicked may have many things, but peace is not one of them.

**But the wicked are like the troubled sea, when it cannot rest, whose waters cast up mire and dirt. There is no peace, saith my God, to the wicked. (Isaiah 57:20–21)**

## WORKERS OF INIQUITY

Workers of iniquity may appear to be religious, but their religion is worthless. They might know about the Lord, but they do not have a personal relationship with him, and he does not know them. When a man sincerely believes that Jesus is God, he will pay attention to him. When the workers of iniquity stand before Jesus, he will say, "I never knew you." He knows those who obey him. He imputes righteousness to everyone who puts their faith in him. When God says a man is righteous, then he is righteous. He will end up doing what is right. Workers of iniquity always do what is wrong.

Workers of iniquity are those who take advantage of God's people.

> Have all the workers of iniquity no knowledge? Who eat up my people as they eat bread, and call not upon the Lord. (Psalm 14:4)

Workers of iniquity think that they can hurt God's children and get away with it. God is full of mercy, but he will eventually punish them.

> Lord, how long shall the wicked, how long shall the wicked triumph? How long shall they utter and speak hard things, and all the workers of iniquity boast themselves? They break in pieces thy people, O Lord, and afflict thine heritage. They slay the widow and the stranger, and murder the fatherless. Yet they say, The Lord shall not see, neither shall the God of Jacob regard it. Understand, ye brutish among the people: and ye fools, when will ye be wise? He that planted the ear, shall he not hear? He that formed the eye, shall he not see? He that chastiseth the heathen, shall not he correct? He that teacheth man knowledge, shall not he know? The Lord knoweth the thoughts of man, that they are vanity. (Psalm 94:3–11)

Workers of iniquity are eating at the devil's communion table. "Eating the bread of wickedness" and "drinking the wine of violence" is a figurative way of saying that they practice wickedness and are violent.

> Enter not into the path of the wicked, and go not in the way of evil men. Avoid it, pass not by it, turn from it, and pass away. For they sleep not, except they have done mischief; and their sleep is taken away, unless they cause some to fall. For they eat the bread of wickedness, and drink the wine of violence. (Proverbs 4:14–17 )

There are things that God cannot tolerate. You cannot be in fellowship with him and continue to do these things.

> Behold, ye trust in lying words, that cannot profit. Will ye steal, murder, and commit adultery, and swear falsely, and burn incense unto Baal, and walk after other gods who ye know not; and come and stand before me in this house, which is called by my name, and say, We are delivered to do all these abominations? (Jeremiah 7:8–10)

Workers of iniquity seem to be religious, but they have no personal relationship with Jesus.

> Not every one that saith unto me, Lord, Lord, shall enter into the kingdom of heaven; but he that doeth the will of my Father which is in heaven. Many will say to me in that day, Lord, Lord, have we not prophesied in thy name? And in thy name have cast out devils? And in thy name done many wonderful works? And then will I profess unto them, I never knew you: depart from me, ye that work iniquity. (Matthew 7:21–23)

In this passage Jesus explains the Parable of the Tares. "Tares" are weeds that look like wheat, and grow together with wheat. Tares are the devil's children who pretend to be children of God. You cannot tell the true believers from the false ones. Only the Lord knows which is which. He will separate them at the time of the end of the world.

> Then Jesus sent the multitude away, and went into the house: and his disciples came unto him, saying, Declare unto us the parable of the tares of the field. He answered and said unto them, He that soweth the good seed is the Son of man; the field is the world; the good seed are the children of the kingdom; but the tares are the children of the wicked one; the enemy that sowed them is the devil; the harvest is the end of the world; and the reapers are angels. As therefore the tares are gathered and burned in the fire; so shall it be in the end of the world. The Son of man shall send forth his angels, and they shall gather out of his kingdom all things that offend, and them which do iniquity; and shall cast them into a furnace of fire: there shall be wailing and gnashing of teeth. (Matthew 13:36–42)

This is what Jesus said to the religious leaders who rejected him as the Messiah.

> Then shall ye begin to say, We have eaten and drunk in thy presence, and thou hast taught in our streets. But he shall say, I tell you, I know you not whence ye are; depart from me, all ye workers of iniquity. There shall be weeping and gnashing of teeth, when ye shall see Abraham, and Isaac, and Jacob, and all the prophets, in the kingdom of God, and you yourselves thrust out. (Luke 13:26–28)

Workers of iniquity claim to know God, but their behavior proves that they are liars.

> Unto the pure all things are pure: but unto them that are defiled and unbelieving is nothing pure; but even their mind and conscience is defiled. They profess that they know God; but in works they deny him, being abominable, and disobedient, and unto every good work reprobate. (Titus 1:15–16)

## CONCLUSION

# CHOOSE YOUR OWN FUTURE

The ideas that are acceptable to you will determine your future. For example, if you refuse to participate in adultery, you will have an excellent life. If you make it a part of your life, you will have to experience the heartache and the misery that comes with it. When you find yourself saying, "I know I'm not supposed to do this, but I'm going to do it anyway," you are setting yourself up for disaster. Cain knew what God required of him, but he substituted something else. He usurped God's authority by overruling him. Cain thought "this ought to be good enough for him." Cain's sacrifice was unacceptable to God. Instead of correcting this mistake, Cain became so angry that he murdered his brother over it. The Children of Israel knew that God was leading them to the Promised Land, yet they refused to go into it. They overruled God's decision and changed their destiny from prosperity to poverty. They refused to live the way God intended them to live. They could have lived in a place of richness. They opted to remain in a barren desert for the rest of their lives. Why did they sabotage themselves? Because they preferred their own ideas over God's ideas. They rejected God's leadership and followed their own thinking. They had a religion, but they had no faith in God. They did not believe in the integrity of his word. Religion consists of external things. Faith is an attitude of the heart. God is a discerner of the thoughts and intents of your heart. You must have faith in God before you can be a success in life.

Your life is like the journey taken by the Children of Israel. Jesus took you out of Egypt, and led you into the desert. The desert is his proving ground. He expects that you will learn to trust him while you are there. God will take care of you while you are in the desert. When you have learned to obey him, then you are ready to enter the Promised Land.

Most Christians never go into the Promised Land. They spend their whole lives wandering around the desert. They never live the abundant life God prepared for them. They are still God's people. They have not lost their salvation, but the good news of salvation is the only thing they know. They cannot understand why the promises of God were never fulfilled in them. The Bible says that pleasing God is the prerequisite to receiving things from him. "And whatsoever we ask, we receive of him because we keep his commandments, and do those things that are pleasing in his sight" (1 John 3:22).

The Promised Land is a land of milk and honey. Milk represents your basic needs and honey stands for the things that make life sweet. God said in Isaiah 61:19, "If ye be willing and obedient, ye shall eat the good of the land." Whether you enter the Promised Land or not is up to you. In order to go there you will have to renew your mind. You accomplish this by learning the Bible and making it a part of your life. It will create an attitude of faith in God. God is pleased with you when your faith is in him. The Children of Israel murmured and complained because all they thought about was how uncomfortable they were in the desert. They did not talk about the new life of prosperity awaiting them in the Promised Land.

They sent ten spies to check out the Promised Land. They saw that it was a very fruitful land, but it was inhabited by giants. Only Joshua and Caleb believed that God would give them the land. They urged the others to agree with them, that they go in and take the land. Their faith filled words are recorded in Numbers 14:9–10. "If the Lord delight in us, then he will bring us into this land, and give it us; a land which floweth with milk and honey. Only rebel not ye against the Lord, neither fear ye the people of the land; for they are bread for us: their defense is departed from them, and the Lord is with us: fear them not."

But the people believed the negative report of the other spies, and accepted their ideas instead of God's. They decided they would not enter the land. They gave in to the spirit of fear. Instead of believing in God and in his word, they provoked him. He judged them and their punishment was to spend the rest of their lives in the desert. Joshua and Caleb were the only survivors of that original group. They led the children of the others into the Promised Land.

When your faith in God is stronger than your fear, you are ready to go into the Promised Land. It's the spiritual place where you fellowship with God. It's where you walk with God and talk with him. It's where you prefer his will instead of yours. You know that you can trust him, and that he is not withholding any good thing from you.

The Promised Land is where you are filled with joy and peace and love and self-control. It's where you can do all things through Christ and where he supplies all your needs. It's where you are content with what you have. It's where God hears and answers all your prayers. It's where all the promises of God apply to you and to your children. And it's where you have Jesus as your mentor, your confidant and your best friend.

It pleases God when you spend time with him. You can be the friend of God. He is the most powerful, the most influential and the most creative being in the universe. He created the universe and he created you. If you want your life to change, get rid of your old thoughts and learn to think like Jesus. The more you resemble him, the happier you will be.

Jesus is the firstborn of many brethren. He said, "my mother and my brethren are these who hear the word of God, and do it"(Luke 8:21). It is God's will for you to be like Jesus. Jesus was led by the Spirit of God. It is your destiny to become one of these sons of God. "For as many as are led by the Spirit of God, they are the sons of God." (Romans 8:14)

You are free to choose your own future. You can remain in the desert and barely get along, or you can live a life that others only dream about. Are you going to settle for a lifetime of mediocrity? Or, are you going to exert yourself to live a life of faith in God? The Bible says that the people who know their God shall be strong and do exploits. Are you ready for the challenge and the adventure that God has designed for you?

Are you ready to enter the Promised Land? All you have to do is to make up your mind once and for all, "I will do everything that God commands. I will love God with all my heart, all my soul, all my mind, and all my strength. And I will love my neighbor as myself. I will overlook their shortcomings and forgive them when they offend me. I will forget about the past and stop complaining about the present. I will focus my attention on Jesus and follow his leadership."

You believe in God, and you know that he keeps his word. Show him the respect he deserves. Act like you believe him by doing what he says in his word. If it seems difficult, do it anyway. If it seems to be costing you a lot, do it anyway. That is how you separate yourself from the world, and crucify your flesh. That is how you overcome the devil. That is how you present yourself a living sacrifice to God. That is how you glorify God.

When you do what is right, you are showing God that you love him, and he will be pleased with you. You can know in advance what your future will be. The promises of God will be fulfilled in you, and he will cause all things to work together for your good. You will receive the blessing of the Lord. It includes health, and wealth, and long life. "The blessing of the Lord, it maketh rich and he addeth no sorrow to it" (Proverbs 10:22). The following verse will apply to you. "Surely goodness and mercy shall follow me all the days of my life: and I will dwell in the house of the Lord for ever." (Psalm 23:6)

Thank you for taking the time to read this book. I hope that it has helped you. I will close with one last passage and it is my prayer for you, in the mighty name of Jesus.

*The Lord bless thee, and keep thee:*
*the Lord make his face shine upon thee, and be gracious unto thee:*
*The Lord lift up his countenance upon thee, and give thee peace.*
*Amen.*